RUSSIAN RESURRECTION

Strength in Suffering – A History of Russia's Evangelical Church

MICHAEL ROWE

Marshall Pickering
An Imprint of HarperCollins*Publishers*

Marshall Pickering is an Imprint of
HarperCollins*Religious*
77-85 Fulham Palace Road, London W6 8JB

First published in Great Britain
in 1994 by Marshall Pickering

1 3 5 7 9 10 8 6 4 2

A catalogue record for this book is
available from the British Library

ISBN 0 551 02702 9

Typeset by Harper Phototypesetters Limited,
Northampton, England
Printed and bound in Great Britain by
HarperCollinsManufacturing Glasgow

Contents

Introduction

'THE DIRECTOR OF this school is begging us to come and teach the Bible to the children,' a Christian teacher told me in Odessa this year. 'The staff can see that the pupils are hard and selfish because they have no moral framework. The parents tell us: "We are a lost generation, it's too late to help us to believe in anything, but please help our children to find values in life." ' The teachers were all educated to be atheists and they just don't know what to teach to fill the moral vacuum. Christians have an important contribution to make in regenerating society, even if it will take a whole generation to make a real impact. A pastor from Kiev commented: 'If ten per cent of the people of our country were real committed Christians I believe it would make all the difference between success and failure for the new society we want to build.'

The Christian Churches in the countries that used to form the Soviet Union have an unprecedented opportunity to put their faith into practice in word and deed. People are open to the Gospel and willing to take the Christian faith seriously. Many of those in authority have a positive attitude to Christianity and expect the churches to play an important role in society. But, whatever the hopes and aspirations, the future will inevitably be moulded by the past: communism has left a dreadful legacy of environmental disasters, stifled initiative, ethnic hostility and moral vacuum. The churches have also been scarred by decades of persecution: places of worship and other property expropriated and destroyed, leaders trapped into collaboration with the KGB, all but the lucky few deprived of any Christian education, charity and social outreach suppressed. Although the decades of Communism have been rejected as an abberration in the history of Russia and the other nations that made up the Soviet empire, the stability of the Communist order still has a strong appeal to many and the future remains far from clear.

The challenge of making good use of freedom may be a new one for Russian Christians, but their experience of lack of freedom could prove to be a good grounding in a new era of religious liberty as well as a preparation for times of trouble that may still lie ahead. They have learned to trust God daily, to take every opportunity to serve Him offered by whatever freedom they had and to carry on serving Him in the face of opposition and persecution.

Russia's road to religious freedom has been long and tortuous. For nine centuries Eastern Orthodox Christianity was the state religion and the rights of other branches of Christianity were limited. In particular, it was forbidden to convert anybody from Orthodoxy to some other denomination or religion. Religious dissenters who rejected the Orthodox Church for whatever reason were subjected to persecutions, imprisonment and banishment to remote corners of the empire. Yet their faithfulness to their beliefs finally brought religious toleration for a few short years at the beginning of this century, before the Bolshevik Revolution unleashed an assault on all kinds of religion.

For evangelical Christians and other Nonconformist religious minorities persecution was an almost constant feature of their life under both Tsarist and Communist rule. There have not been many periods of Russian history when there was religious tolerance. Only in the last ten years before the 1917 revolution, when Russia embarked on constitutional reform, was there any semblance of religious freedom. Before 1905 it was a criminal offence to convert somebody from the Orthodox Church and not only were evangelists imprisoned, exiled or deported but many of their followers were harassed, beaten, driven out of their homes or saw their children taken away to be brought up in a monastery. From the seventeenth century onwards religious dissenters settled deep in the Siberian forests to escape persecution, and whole communities were exiled to remote corners of the empire.

After the Communists seized power in 1917 they hoped for the support of the previously persecuted religious minorities who would not want to see a return to the old order. They concentrated their anti-religious attack first and foremost on the Russian Orthodox Church, which had been one of the most powerful bodies in pre-revolutionary Russian society, and on the Roman Catholic Church, which they saw as the Church most opposed to revolutionary change on the international arena. However, by the 1930s all churches and religions faced an all-out onslaught as Stalin ruthlessly tried to eliminate all real, potential and imagined opposition to his totalitarian rule. No section of society was spared, even the Communist Party was decimated as Stalin in his paranoia removed all those who did not owe their position in the party to himself; many were simply arrested at random in order to terrorize the rest into unquestioning obedience. Active Christians were especially at risk because their faith was the only open expression of views that were fundamentally different from Communism.

Persecution is not something that one would wish on anybody and it has many destructive and damaging consequences both for the Church as a whole and for individual Christians. It will be many years before some of the wounds inflicted over the past seventy years will be fully healed. And yet the Russian Church is living testimony to a miracle – the miracle of the survival of faith, of the sustaining power of God, of the grace of the Holy Spirit which takes away bitterness and hatred for the persecutors. Driven almost completely underground, daring to meet only in twos and threes, Christians nurtured their faith, treasured their tattered Bibles and when the pressure eased once more stepped out boldly to share the Good News with their neighbours. In prisons, concentration camps and remote places of exile Christians sought one another out and risked punishment cells, extended sentences and death to pray together. Many thousands did not survive the harsh conditions and died far from home, their final resting place remaining anonymous and unknown to their families. Those who did return to their families and churches often found that their arrest had not deterred their fellow Christians and that new leaders and preachers had stepped forward to take their places.

The damage done by persecution was immense. Physically almost all the institutions of the Churches were destroyed: seminaries and Bible schools, publishing houses and magazines were closed down and their staff scattered and arrested. Tens of thousands of church buildings and places of worship of all faiths were expropriated, converted for secular use, demolished or simply left to rot and collapse. The most active believers were arrested. Spiritually whole nations were cut off from their religious roots and deprived of even the most basic knowledge of faith; many

Christian leaders were cowed into submission, afraid for themselves and for their churches, accepting interference out of fear that resistance would merely provoke total repression.

Persecution came in waves, and between each wave there came a lull. Though physically weakened the churches came out into the open to preach the Gospel again and out of each wave of persecution came a wave of renewal, different for each church and at each period. People reacted to persecution in two opposite ways. Some were overcome by a spirit of timidity, believing that future persecution should be avoided at all cost. Others were emboldened by the conviction that 'the gates of hell will not prevail'; they had experienced for themselves that their strength was in the Lord, and had learned to rely on Him. That experience was liberating and gave them the power to achieve much that in human terms seemed impossible: clandestine printing presses, relief programmes, Sunday schools, children's camps. They got a vision from God and relied on Him for the strength and the resources to implement it.

Looking on from the outside, we can be encouraged in our faith by their experience. We would be wrong to idealize them and regard them as heroes. They would encourage us to wonder with them at what God has done for them and through them and to remember when we see those who chose a different path that 'there but for the grace of God go I'.

Today the Churches in Russia and the other nations that have emerged from the ruins of the Soviet Union are facing a totally new situation. They have a degree of liberty that is beyond the living memory of most Christians. They have unprecedented opportunities, but seemingly little or no experience of how to make use of them. There may be a temptation to rely on the resources and expertise of the churches in the West. How can they apply the experience and the lessons of the last seventy years?

PART I

Holy Russia

ONE

Christian Beginnings

'THEY DID NOT know whether they were in heaven or on earth. They only knew that God dwells there among men. They could never forget that beauty.' This is how the ancient Russian chronicle records the visit of emissaries of Prince Vladimir of Rus, as the first Russian state was known, to the Cathedral of St Sophia in Constantinople. As a result of their glowing report Christianity became the official religion of Kievan Rus in 988. By order of the prince, the population of Kiev was baptized en masse in the river Dnieper that flows through the city. Soldiers, merchants and slaves gathered on the bank of the river and filed into the water to be baptized by bearded Greek priests in the ancient symbol of washing away the past and rising from the waters to begin a new life. The priests must have been reminded of the Gospel narrative of the crowds flocking to be baptized in the river Jordan by John the Baptist. Would a dove flutter down from heaven as a sign that God would bless this people?

According to the chronicle, Vladimir's decision was quite pragmatic. Paganism, which he at first actively promoted, failed to unite the nation. In order to reconcile the feuding cities and become a civilized state, he felt, Rus needed to adopt one of the world's great religions. He therefore sent out emissaries to examine Judaism, Islam and Western and Eastern Christianity. Vladimir rejected Judaism on the grounds that, although there were communities of Jews all over the known world, they were everywhere minorities and without political power. Islam, with its ban on alcohol, was ruled out as being impracticable, for how could one last through the long winter without being warmed by vodka? Vladimir could not accept the submission to the Pope that adoption of Roman Catholicism would mean. The emissaries from Constantinople, however, came back with glowing reports of Orthodox Christianity.

The Russians, or more accurately their Eastern Slav ancestors, were one of the last European nations to be evangelized and become Christian. The Christian faith barely touched any of the Slav peoples until the ninth century. Archaeologists tell us that there were Christians among the Greek settlers along the northern coast of the Black Sea early in the history of the Church. The apostle Andrew, brother of Peter, is said by early church historians to have preached to the Scythians, the nomadic people who lived on the steppes north of the Black Sea, and to have softened their hearts. St Paul, writing to the Colossians of the universality of the Gospel, refers to the Scythians (Colossians 3:11 – some modern translations replace Scythians with 'savages'), implying that there were Christians even among this nation on the fringe of the 'civilized' world. According to the Russian chronicler Nestor, St Andrew travelled up the river Dnieper, reaching the hills on which Kiev was later founded, and prophesied that God's grace would shine on those hills, that a great city would be built there and that God would raise up many churches. Sadly, there is no historical evidence that Andrew was in Kiev: the story remains a legend. Peter's disciple, Clement, Bishop of Rome, was exiled to Khersones in the Crimea at the end of the first century, where he found a Christian congregation already in existence, and by the fourth century the Christian faith was reported to have taken firm root among the Scythians.

Further east, the Armenians became the first Christian nation in 301, several years before Constantine became the first Christian Roman Emperor. Armenian tradition traces the Church there back to the first century through the work of the apostles St Thaddaeus (Jude) and especially St Bartholomew, who is believed to have been martyred in Armenia. In neighbouring Georgia the apostle Andrew is said to be the founder of the Church, though it was thanks to Georgia's patron saint St Nino in the early fourth century that Christianity became widespread. It became the national religion in 326 when Nino converted King Mirian. Further north on the Black Sea coast in Abkhazia, according to local tradition, the apostle St Simon the Canaanite (also known as Simon the Zealot), who often travelled with St Thaddeus (Jude), was martyred in

AD 55 by the local pagans who dragged him from his hermit's cave and beheaded him on a rock by the river Psyrdskha. In the ninth century a church dedicated to the apostle was built on the site and later a monastery was established there. However, all this was long before the Slavs reached any of these lands.

The first Slav nations to be converted to Christianity were the Czechs, the Bulgarians and the Poles. The first missionaries were the 'apostles of the Slavs', Saints Cyril and Methodius, Macedonian monks fluent both in Greek and the local Slav dialect. In the ninth century, they worked in the Czech kingdom of Moravia and from there sent out preachers to the other Slav peoples. The Polish and Czech Churches later fell under the sphere of influence of the Western, Roman Church, while the Bulgarians remained part of Eastern Christianity centred on Byzantium (Constantinople).

At this time the Russian nation did not yet exist, but Eastern Slav tribes already spread from close to the Baltic Sea in the north to the shores of the Black Sea in the south. In the ninth century Viking chieftains explored and conquered the waterways in this vast territory known as Rus and became its rulers, quickly assimilating to their Slav subjects. The princes of Kiev gradually gained ascendancy and became the chief of the rulers of Rus. During the tenth century contact increased with Byzantium and its Eastern Christianity. Among the high-placed inhabitants of Kiev who were baptized into the Christian faith was Princess Olga, who was regent from 946 to 960. It was her grandson Prince Vladimir who decreed that Christianity become the official religion of Rus.

Adoption of Orthodox Christianity brought with it a political benefit in the form of a closer relationship with Kiev's powerful southern neighbour – the Byzantine Empire. The rapprochement was sealed by the marriage of Vladimir to the Emperor's sister. However, the pragmatic advantages may not have been the only factor and it seems that Vladimir embraced the Christian faith with sincerity and enthusiasm. Pagan idols and temples to the Slav god Perun were destroyed and paganism outlawed. Vladimir took steps to ensure that the conversion of the people was not merely nominal, by inviting priests from Byzantium to come and teach and by sponsoring the building of churches. The understanding of the faith was helped by the Orthodox approach to missionary work, which encouraged worship in the local language. Saints Cyril and Methodius had devised an alphabet suitable for the Slavonic languages and had already translated the New Testament, the liturgy and other church texts into Old Bulgarian, which was readily understood by the East Slav tribes ruled from Kiev. During the eleventh century a strong Church took root, bishops were appointed and monastic communities were established. The language of the services and of the translations of the Gospel texts were gradually adapted to Eastern Slav speech and the Church began to mould the development of a national culture. The monasteries became centres of both spirituality and learning and church art flourished.

Thus Rus became part of Christian Europe. However, it was not long before it began to be isolated again. In 1053 the growing rift between Western and Eastern Christianity became a formal split, and the east became a backwater, not sharing the more dynamic development of Western Europe. Less than two centuries later Rus was cut off altogether from the Christian world by the Mongol invasion. In 1240 Kiev fell, and only the city of Novgorod in the northwest remained beyond the Mongol empire. For all their cruelty, from which the Church did not escape, the pagan Mongols preferred to rule indirectly through subject princes and so did not interfere in religious life. The Church survived and enshrined the very idea of the nation, keeping alive not just faith but the nation itself under foreign domination. The bond between Church and nation was forged in this period of oppression far more strongly than by princely decree or even the missionary endeavours of the Church.

As Mongol rule weakened it was Moscow that emerged as the dominant principality. It was Prince Dmitri Donskoi of Moscow who first rebelled against the Mongols by fortifying the city. When the Mongols launched an expedition to crush Moscow, Dmitri decided to resist and was backed by the monk Sergius of the nearby Trinity monastery, who assured the prince of God's blessing. The Muscovites went out and defeated the enemy in the legendary Battle of Kulikovo Field in 1380. Sergius came to be regarded as much as Prince Dmitri as the founder of the new state of Muscovy, and after his canonization became its patron saint. Thus began a new period of identification of the Church with both the nation and the state, a relationship that was very much within the tradition of Byzantine Christianity.

As Muscovy grew stronger and began to unite the territories that became Russia, Byzantium, the centre of Eastern Orthodox Christianity, itself came under threat from the Muslim Ottomans, finally falling in 1453. A century later Russia had become the greatest Orthodox nation, and the head of the Russian Church was recognized as a Patriarch by the other Orthodox Churches. The Russian Tsar, like the Byzantine Emperor before him, was regarded as a divinely appointed ruler. The authority of the Church was backed by the power of the state and 'heresy', or religious dissent, was a crime against the Tsar. In sixteenth-century Muscovy there were some in the monasteries who believed that the state should have no authority in spiritual matters and that the Church should not call on the power of the state to combat heresy. Instead the Church should respond to heretics with pastoral care and prayer. Monasteries should be examples of poverty and humility, maintaining themselves through their own labour, and not acquiring riches and land. However, they were persecuted by their opponents, who deployed the power of the state against them, subjecting them to arrest, imprisonment and exile.

The first great movement of dissent in the Church came in the seventeenth century, when Patriarch Nikon revised the Church's liturgical practice in accordance with the best in Greek scholarship. Many of the details seem insignificant to an outsider, but Nikon's blunt attack on Russian tradition, and his ruthless use of the apparatus of state to crush those who protested, alienated many who might otherwise have supported his reforms and sparked fierce resistance. One of Nikon's leading opponents was Archpriest Avvakum, whose autobiography reveals tremendous spiritual depth and amazing fortitude in the face of bitter persecution. The irreconcilable conflict led to a schism in the Church, with the protesters being excommunicated and in turn pronouncing an anathema on Nikon and his followers. Thus was born the movement usually known in English as the Old Believers, but more accurately translated as the Old Ritualists, who preserved the rituals that had become part of the Russian heritage. It was only under the onslaught of Communist persecution of all religion that the two sides finally lifted their excommunication of each other four hundred years later.

Families and whole communities were exiled to distant corners of the Russian Empire, others fled from persecution, founding settlements deep in the forests, where they remained cut off from the outside world, in some cases for centuries. Even within the last few decades survey teams have stumbled upon remote communities who had no knowledge of electricity and other modern inventions and who were totally unaware of the 1917 Bolshevik Revolution.

The split greatly weakened the Church and at the same time made it more dependent on the state, on which it relied to punish the 'heretics'. This laid the ground for the total submission of Church to state at the beginning of the eighteenth century under Tsar Peter the Great. He made an enormous impact on many areas of Russian life, opening the country up to the West and building a new capital, St Petersburg, as a 'window to the West'. Peter saw the Russian church as a conservative force that might hinder change, and he further weakened it by preventing the election of a patriarch, and finally abolished the post of patriarch altogether, replacing it with a 'Holy Synod' headed by a layman appointed by the Tsar. Thus the Church was totally subject to the authority of the Tsar and was in effect turned into a government department.

A greater religious pluralism arose, as foreign traders and craftsmen established their own religious communities: in major cities new Lutheran, Catholic and Anglican parishes were founded. Up to 1917 the population of St Petersburg was about ten per cent Protestant. As early as the sixteenth century there had been a small Lutheran congregation in Moscow made up of Germans, Latvians and Estonians taken prisoner during Ivan the Terrible's attempt to conquer the Baltic lands. In the seventeenth century a second Lutheran church, and a Reformed church, opened in Moscow.

While the Old Ritualists clinging to ancient tradition were open in their opposition to the Orthodox Church, there was at about the same time another dissenting movement within the Church which was completely clandestine. Some of its distinctive beliefs were heretical, yet its members were among the most active participants in Orthodox parish life. Some writers trace its roots back to Russian paganism, but the movement's own oral history goes back no further than the seventeenth century. In popular parlance the movement's adherents were called *Khlysty*, which means Flagellants. They did indeed practise mortification of the flesh and at their secret meetings often got into a frenzy, but there is no evidence that they whipped themselves or each other. Their name is a corruption of *Khristy* (Christs), for their central belief was that Christ was reincarnated in their leaders. They called themselves 'God's people'. If discovered, they too faced persecution, imprisonment and exile.

Other religious movements arose at this time. Two of them grew quite large. The *Dukhobors* (Spirit wrestlers), who emerged from among the Old Ritualists, are well known for their pacifism and passive resistance to state authority. They had a reputation similar to the early Quakers in England, and also sought an inner light and guidance from the Holy Spirit. Most of their communities were exiled to the Caucasus mountains, from where many emigrated to Canada in the nineteenth century. The *Molokans* (Milk drinkers), who emerged from the Dukhobors in the eighteenth century, rejected all of the ritualism of the Orthodox Church as external, seeking instead an internal spirituality. They did not keep the Orthodox rules of fasting, which during Lent included abstinence from all animal products, including milk; hence they became known to their Orthodox neighbours as the people who drank milk. Their own name for their movement was 'Spiritual Christians', though they accepted the nickname, saying: 'We desire "the sincere milk of the Word, that we may grow thereby" (I Peter 2:2). We must have it unadulterated – uncontaminated by the fingers of priests, and undiluted by any mixture of man's devices; and we will have as much as we can get of it, for we love our Bibles!' In this respect they might be regarded as a form of Russian Protestantism, though they had no knowledge of the Reformation. Like the other dissenters, they too were persecuted and exiled.

The first widespread Protestant movements were German. As well as the Lutheran and Reformed congregations, consisting mostly of traders and craftsmen, there were also Mennonites. During the Reformation in Germany the Mennonites fought for separation of the Church from the state authorities. They were thus precursors of the Baptists and the other Nonconformist Churches. In Germany, where Lutheranism became the official Church in many states, Mennonites were persecuted for their pacifism and other views. In the 1780s they answered the call of the Russian Empress Catherine II for farmers to come to settle the under-populated steppes along the Volga and in Ukraine, and later in the Urals and Siberia. They were granted not only land, but also the privileges of religious freedom within their own communities and of not serving in the Russian army. These special conditions attracted many thousands of Mennonites. Other Germans were also drawn by the offer of virgin land for settlement, and were also free to set up their own Lutheran or Catholic parishes.

Catherine boasted of the religious tolerance in the Russian Empire, on one occasion commenting that even the Jesuits were permitted, though she banned them a few years later! The German settlements were quite self-contained, and few of their inhabitants ever needed to learn Russian or Ukrainian. Their religious life was also completely isolated from that of the people around them, and for this reason posed no threat to the Orthodox Church. The Bible and other Christian literature was available to them, and they were able to keep in touch with religious life in Germany through correspondence and visitors.

TWO

The Birth of the
Evangelical Movement

I N THE FIRST part of the the nineteenth century in other German villages scattered across the Ukraine and along the river Volga an awakening took place. Mennonites and other German settlers experienced an evangelical renewal under the influence of Pietist preachers from Germany. One of the key features of Pietism was the holding of group meetings for Bible study and prayer, called in German *Bibelstunden* (Bible hours) or simply *Stunden* (hours). The Mennonites split into two sections, the Church Mennonites following their traditions more closely and the Mennonite Brethren being strongly influenced by the Baptists. Although both baptized adults, the Church Mennonites did so by sprinkling, while the Brethren adopted the Baptist practice of total immersion.

In the German settlements missionaries of the Basel Mission in Switzerland had considerable influence. The Basel Mission secured permission from Tsar Alexander I to work among the German settlers in the Caucasus and Ukraine. In the Caucasus they also preached the Gospel to Muslims and worked to bring an evangelical awakening to the Armenians, though after Nicholas I succeeded Alexander in 1825 this side of their work was banned. They continued to send evangelists to the German settlements though.

Johannes Bonekemper, a Reformed pastor, who arrived in the German village of Rohrbach near Odessa, in 1824, was one of the most influential Basel missionaries. Beginning work among Reformed families in two villages he organized a parish which soon covered five neighbouring Lutheran villages as well. He supported and encouraged the Bible hours which some of his parishioners already held. He conducted Bible studies for those preparing for confirmation and adult members of the parish also began to attend these.

'Over the last three months, the attendance at our normal Sunday and festival services has been unusually observant and numerous,' wrote Pastor Johannes Bonekemper in his diary in 1829.

> and also the weekly catechismal sermons . . . have been listened to with reverence beyond our expectations. But even more in demand are the private gatherings . . . Over the last fortnight I have been visited by various people either by day or by night (or rather, in the evening, like Nicodemus for fear of the Jews). During these visits, people tell me of their fear, their need and the danger in which their souls stand and beg me to tell them what they must do to be saved.

Five years of patient prayer and pastoral service in Rohrbach were at last beginning to bear fruit. In another five years hundreds of people in Johannes' parish had experienced a quickening through the Holy Spirit and were attending weekly Bible and fellowship meetings in addition to regular church services. As the spiritual life of the parish deepened a revival began in surrounding parishes. Soon all of the Lutheran settlements were influenced and *Stunden* were being held in many places.

Johannes Bonekemper moved to a new work in Romania in 1848, but in 1865 his son Karl returned to the parish as its pastor. The *Stunden* were still being held and he described what he found. The attenders at the *Stunden* are those in the local parish

> who like to bring their spiritual life into their daily living. Our 'Stundists' were always fervent in prayer at congregational worship, but in addition they meet for *Stunden* in the parish house or more often in two private homes when this is more convenient. I keep an eye on them and when I am free visit their meetings. During the meetings the house becomes an improvised chapel. I don't preach a sermon, but give a short homily and explain passages from the Holy Scriptures, taking into acount the level of the hearers and applying the Word of God to daily life. Then the brothers sing

hymns glorifying the Saviour and quietly go home. They usually meet on Sundays after lunch and in the evening.

Another early Protestant influence came through a Scottish Presbyterian missionary named William Melville. In the 1820s he came to Russia and travelled in the Caucasus and Ukraine distributing the Bible among both Orthodox and Molokans, some of whom accepted the sacrament of baptism under his influence. From 1848 he continued his work under the auspices of the British and Foreign Bible Society, based in Odessa, where he lived until the 1880s.

One of the great hindrances to the emergence of Russian Protestant Churches and of an evangelical movement was the absence of a translation of the Bible in Russian. The Orthodox Church continued to use the Old Slavonic translations of the liturgy done by Cyril and Methodius, though somewhat Russified over the centuries, and the Old Slavonic Bible. However, as the Russian language developed these texts became less and less understandable for the ordinary person. In any case the vast majority of the population were illiterate. Therefore, for most people knowledge of the Bible was limited to what they could follow of the Gospel readings in church. In the nineteenth century this began to change. Tsar Alexander I was greatly troubled by the Napoleonic Wars and his spiritual search led him to a Christian faith that was at once evangelical and mystical. He is said to have read the Bible every day. In January 1813, with the encouragement and blessing of Alexander, a Russian Bible Society was established – modelled on the British and Foreign Bible Society, with its aim of making the Scriptures available to Christians of all denominations without interpretations or commentary. The president of the new Bible Society was a close friend and adviser of Alexander, Prince A. N. Golitsyn. In the first year six branches were formed, large donations were received from the Tsar and from the Orthodox Church and distribution of the Slavonic Bible began.

As the Society's annual report for 1814 indicates, even the Slavonic Bible, with all its difficulties, was warmly received:

> Simple and poor people, soldiers and Cossacks, impoverished widows, middle-class people, peasants and settlers, craftsmen and clergy all were seized with a desire to receive the Word of salvation, recognizing that in it they could have eternal life. People who had never seen a Bible, old people in their seventies and eighties who

admitted that they had never read this book, were fired with the desire to read it. Who told them all that such exceptional benefit could be received from reading the Bible? Who else, if not our Heavenly Father.

From 1816 to 1823 there were 15 printings of the whole Slavonic Bible; altogether 184,000 Bibles in Slavonic and in forty other languages were printed up to 1823, as well as over 300,000 New Testaments.

The Tsar was keen that the Bible should be translated into modern Russian, and asked Golitsyn to make a proposal. The Holy Synod of the Russian Orthodox Church agreed in 1816 and a commission was promptly established and began work. The new translation of the four gospels was published in 20,000 copies in 1818 and by 1822 the whole New Testament had been completed. In 1820 work began on the Old Testament: the Psalms were completed in 1821 and published in 1822, and by 1825 the Pentateuch and the Books of Joshua, Judges and Ruth had been translated and printed.

At the same time, the Russian capital, St Petersburg, became host to a variety of Western preachers. Although called to the city's foreign churches, they had a wider influence: the atmosphere of religious tolerance and seeking after truth encouraged by the Tsar himself brought many into their churches to hear them and they were able to direct their preaching as much to their Russian listeners as to their own congregations. At the royal court, among the German nobility from the Baltic provinces, there were also sincere Christians. There were the beginnings of a religious awakening.

However, there was opposition from within the Orthodox Church, led by Metropolitan Serafim. The critics objected to cooperation between the Orthodox and those whom they regarded as heretics and to the publishing of the Bible being taken out of the control of the Church. Under pressure Golitsyn resigned in 1824, and was replaced as Bible Society President by Serafim, who promptly compiled a report for the Tsar on the harmful nature of the Society, concluding with a request to be allowed to close down the Society and all its branches and local committees throughout the Empire, which by this time numbered 289. Alexander did not agree to this request, but in 1826 his successor Nicholas I suspended all work of the Society and it was not resumed until after his death in 1855. The most influential Western priests and pastors were expelled from St Petersburg.

Despite the ban on Bible translation work, the professor of Hebrew at the St Petersburg Theological Academy, Father Gerasim Pavsky, secretly translated the Old Testament. His translations were duplicated in 500 copies without his knowledge by some of his students in 1839-41 and distributed mainly to priests who were interested. When the authorities found out, they made life very difficult for Fr Pavsky and tracked down and destroyed almost all the copies of his work. However, another priest, Father Makari Glukharev, a missionary in the Altai region of Siberia, shared the vision, and produced his own translation, based in part on Father Pavsky's work. His efforts were condemned by the Holy Synod as 'profane and harmful to Orthodoxy'. Although there was no Bible publishing in Russia, the British and Foreign Bible Society published Russian New Testaments in London and Leipzig and distributed them in Russia.

A powerful proponent of the need for Bible translation was Metropolitan Filaret of Moscow. After the coronation in 1856 of the more liberal Alexander II - known as the great reformer - Filaret put a proposal to the Holy Synod to resume translation work. The Synod accepted his proposal, but opponents managed to delay its implementation for another two years. Finally in 1858 the Synod resolved to retranslate the New Testament first and then work on the Old Testament, making it clear, to satisfy the conservatives, that the translation was not to be for use in worship, but only for private study to aid understanding. The four gospels were published in 1860 and the revised New Testament appeared in 1862. The Old Testament translation was completed in 1876 and the whole Bible published. Under the influence of the conservatives in the Church the translation still contained many archaisms, some of which were an obstacle to full understanding, when words had acquired a different meaning in modern Russian.

The new edition of the New Testament stimulated new interest in Bible distribution work. In 1863 a group of friends from various nationalities and denominations began collecting money to organize distribution of the new translations. As their work grew it was formalized in 1866 as the Society for the Distribution of the Holy Scriptures in Russia. The Society was recognized by the government in 1869, and in the following thirty years distributed over one and a half million copies of the Scriptures - Bibles, New Testaments, the book of Psalms and other individual books. About 150,000 were donated or sold at a subsidy in hospitals, schools and almshouses and to poor people.

Everywhere the Society's workers found a hunger for the word of God.

One of the founders, Otto Forchhammer, by birth a Dane, who in 1863 was already sixty, personally distributed 58,000 copies of the Scriptures. Of his visit to a remote village on the edge of the Kirgiz steppes, he wrote:

> I never met such a thirst for the Word of God as in Alexandrov Gai . . . People came to my house from all directions for the holy books; when I walked along the street people constantly stopped me and asked for a New Testament.

Another distributor was known as 'the old lady with the books'. Sinklitiliya Filippova was over seventy when she began Bible distribution in 1865. In St Petersburg and surrounding towns, she personally distributed 17,000 copies of the Scriptures on the street, in markets, churches, factories, cemeteries and taverns in fourteen years. In one tavern she was chatting to about twenty cobblers from a nearby workshop. She had sold all her books, when one of their friends, a man aged about thirty, came in and also asked for a New Testament. When he heard that she had none left he wept saying: 'You know, I am a great sinner, and I will not inherit the Kingdom of God if I cannot get hold of a New Testament.' She was so moved that she took her personal copy that she always had with her and gave it to him. In gratitude he went down on his knees at her feet. 'What are you doing?' she said. 'Bow down to God.'

The availability of the new translation and gradual growth in literacy for the first time enabled people to study the Bible for themselves. Communities such as the Molokans were eager to read the Bible more widely. One of the key influences in helping people to understand the New Testament were the evangelical German farmers holding their *Stunden* for Bible reading and prayer with their families and labourers. Despite the ban on converting the Orthodox to other Christian denominations, some of these German farmers were bold enough to permit their Ukrainian labourers to attend these meetings.

The first Ukrainian to be converted through the German farmers is believed to be a peasant called Fyodor Onishchenko. In the 1850s he was an itinerant labourer, working for German farmers in the area of Nikolayev, from whom he learnt of their faith. He tells of his own conversion:

> Before I was like a pig, like the cattle, even worse, because the cattle do what is right for them. I was despicable . . . One day I was praying in the field, weeping, and I cried out: 'Lord, bring me to

my senses, change me for the better!' It was as though someone, I didn't see who, took my coat off me, and I felt a burden lifted, I became free and I knew God.

This was in about 1857 or 1858. He returned to his village of Osnova, in Odessa district, where he began to sow the seed.

At the end of the 1850s Mykhailo Ratushny, a neighbour of Fyodor Onishchenko in Osnova, worked as a casual labourer at harvest-time for several seasons for a Christian German farmer in Rohrbach, Johannes Bonekemper's former parish. A friendship developed and Mykhailo was invited to a prayer meeting, where he experienced a religion that was very different from the Orthodoxy that he had been brought up in: prayers by those present, reading from the Bible, a short reflection on the reading and a few hymns. And no ikons, which hung not only in church but in every Orthodox home, and no priest to say the service and give his blessing. Mykhailo thought deeply about these things, discussed them with his employer and, returning to his village after the harvest, spoke to his neighbours about them. They already knew of Fyodor's conversion experience.

Puzzled by religious practices so different from their own, the villagers decided to ask the village priest about them. He, however, had no answers to their questions and could not explain the meaning of Orthodox ritual to their satisfaction. Instead, the villagers continued to discuss among themselves the meaning of life and of God and the Christian faith of the German farmers. Through the winter they met in each other's homes and by spring they were a little church with Mykhailo Ratushny as their preacher. Their German neighbours gave them advice and encouragement, tried to answer their questions and gave them Bible teaching. Mykhailo dated his own evangelical conversion as 1860, and Orthodox Church sources indicate that a small fellowship came into being in the winter of 1860-61. By 1865 there were twenty members, and seven people from nearby villages had been converted. By 1867 they were meeting in three villages.

Elsewhere in southern Ukraine there were similar experiences, with Orthodox peasants being converted through the witness of German and Mennonite settlers. As the word spread, prayer meetings were started in village after village. Throughout the 1860s peasants spent the long winter evenings teaching themselves to read so that they could study the Bible for themselves. From the word *Stunde*, the German name for the Bible study hours, these Christians received the nickname of Stundists. The

Stundists in some instances found a ready response among the Old Ritualists; even though their religious practice was very conservative, they had already rejected the official Church and were prepared to place the search for truth before all else. By 1867 it was recognized as a widespread movement with over 300 adherents.

At first the Stundists continued to attend the Orthodox Church as well as studying the Bible in their homes, and went to the priest for baptisms, marriages and funerals. However, the village priests, often themselves the sons of priests who learnt their duties by watching their fathers, were mostly poorly educated and held in low regard by the peasantry. The priests made their living by charging fees for their services. A religion that was understandable, gave answers to the deep questions of life and did not require a priest had an enormous attraction for the Ukrainian peasants. Through the abolition of serfdom in 1861, one of the great reforms of Tsar Alexander II, the serfs were being freed from the bondage of their feudal masters and granted small parcels of land, enabling them to be independent farmers, even if many of them were at a basic subsistence level because of the retention of much of the land by the big estates. Freed from their feudal masters, the peasants now saw the opportunity of freeing themselves from the priests as well. Many of the priests had so little training that they knew no other response to this religious awakening than to call the police. Thus persecution soon came on this young movement.

However, it was not until 1870 that the Stundists concluded sadly that the Orthodox Church was too inflexible to accommodate them. They were accused by the priests of lacking respect for the ikons, for they now used the Bible instead as a focus for their prayers, and became victims of increasing harassment from both the Church and the secular authorities at the instigation of local priests. In May 1870 the Osnova Stundists brought their ikons to the priest, in order not to be accused any longer of showing them disrespect and as a sign of their break with the Church. They ceased to come to the priest for baptisms, marriages and funerals.

Another of the Stundist pioneers was a blacksmith from the village of Lyubomirka, near Yelizavetgrad, north of Odessa, named Ivan Ryaboshapka. He too worked for a German Christian farmer and as a result of their discussions found new faith. He bought a New Testament and his neighbours began to gather to hear him read it. By this time he owned a mill, and the mill house was a good place for people to gather. In 1864 a revival had touched almost all of the inhabitants in the nearby German settlement of Alt-Danzig and under the influence of Mennonite Brethren preachers they had accepted the need for believers' baptism as adults. Ivan Ryaboshapka discussed this issue with them and after his conversion himself desired to make public profession of forgiveness of sins and new life in Christ through believers' baptism. His German friends hesitated because of the persecution that they knew he would face. However, in June 1869 another new Christian, Yefim Tsymbal, from the village of Karlovka, was baptized with thirty Germans by Abram Unger in Alt-Danzig. The Germans had not intended to baptize Yefim, but when he stepped into the water and declared that if Abram would not baptize him the Lord would show him who would, Abram went ahead and baptized him. Yefim in turn baptized Ivan Ryaboshapka in April 1870, who then baptized Mykhailo Ratushny in June 1871. Through these three men the Stundist movement began to grow closer to the Baptist Church.

In the same years there was an evangelical renewal among the Molokans. According to one eye witness from this period they had

> a more intimate acquaintance with the Word of God than may be found in almost any Protestant church. Every one of them knows many of the most beautiful psalms, and the most important chapters from the New Testament and prophets, by heart. Their service principally consists in reading the Word of God with a few explanations. Their hymn book, too, is the Bible. To a monotonous tune they sing for hours a chapter, then pray a chapter kneeling, then again sing a chapter. Thus they usually sing nine chapters standing and pray nine chapters kneeling, all in chorus and by memory . . . Our rhythmical singing, and extempore praying, they call 'adding to, and taking from, the Word of God'.

They rejected all ritual and understood the sacraments of the Lord's supper and baptism as spiritual allegories.

In Tauria province (southern Ukraine, including the Crimea) the revival among the Molokans was a result of the preaching of Yakub Kasha (Jacob the priest). He was an Assyrian Presbyterian, who had attended Bible School in Persia. Moving to Ukraine in search of his elder brother, he acquired a working knowledge of Russian and soon felt a calling to preach the Gospel to Russians and Ukrainians. He took a Russian name, Yakov Delyakov, and in the 1860s became a colporteur for the Odessa branch of the British and Foreign Bible Society and travelled the towns and villages of southern Ukraine selling household goods and offering his customers a Bible or New Testament. He would talk to them about repentance, salvation and assurance of the forgiveness of sins and baptism, explaining that baptism in itself does not give new life or salvation. He especially loved to share the Gospel with the Molokans and after his visits to the Molokan villages of Novo-Vasilevka and Astrakhanka in 1865-6 his followers began to be called the New Molokans. In 1867 a congregation formed under the leadership of Zinovi Zakharov, from which grew a movement of Evangelical Molokans.

Many of the Molokans had been exiled to the Caucasus and here too they came under evangelical influence. Many of them had a personal faith in Christ - their knowledge of the Scriptures providing an excellent foundation for evangelical preaching. Some, from their reading of the New Testament, had begun to practise baptism, but had not linked it to repentance and conversion. One of these was a talented young man, Nikita Voronin, who lived in Tiflis - modern-day Tbilisi, the capital of Georgia. As he reflected on salvation he became conscious of his own sinfulness, repented and experienced new birth. He soon met Yakov Delyakov, who was visiting Tiflis, and discovered that he had the same understanding of repentance, conversion and new birth. Voronin had a strong desire to be baptized as a public confession of his new-found faith, and Delyakov intoduced him to the leader of a small German Baptist congregation in the city, Martin Kahlweit, who had been converted and baptized in a Baptist church in Kaunas province (modern Lithuania), and later moved to Tiflis.

Martin Kahlweit takes up the story:

> We held firmly to what we had been taught, that is we read the Word of God, prayed and did not neglect fellowship. Although there were only four of us - I, my wife and two sisters - we met regularly. The Lord blessed us, and to our great joy our group began to grow and soon there were fifteen of us in Tiflis, all Germans. Among the Russians our name [i.e. Baptists] was still unknown. Several years later contact with Russians began through brother Yakov Delyakov. He brought to us the first Molokan who was sincerely seeking truth in the Scripture and wished to be baptized. This was Nikita Voronin, and after I baptized him he began preaching the Word of God at the Molokan meeting.

Nikita was baptized secretly at night in the river Kura in Tiflis in August 1867, and this event is considered to be the beginning of the Russian

Baptist Church. Voronin was a very able person with a passionate love for God's work. He constantly spoke of the love of Jesus; he was a very sociable and hospitable person and his home became a place of constant lively discussions and prayers. Within six months a small Russian Baptist congregation formed as a result of Voronin's preaching and conversations. In 1871 two young men from the Molokans were baptized in the Tiflis congregation. Vasili Pavlov and Vasili Ivanov were to become great leaders of the Russian Baptist Church working closely together for almost half a century. Vasili Ivanov soon formed a Baptist church in his home village and in 1873 began preaching in other villages. Often the Orthodox were more willing to listen than the Molokans. Vasili Pavlov later wrote that many Molokans at first could not accept the Baptist teaching on adult baptism, as they regarded baptism as a 'departure from the pure spiritual teaching of Christ and a return to external ritual'; they were afraid that baptism might be a 'transition back to the Orthodox Church, for the rejection of which they and their forefathers had borne so much suffering'.

In 1875, on Martin Kahlweit's advice, the Tiflis congregation decided to send Vasili Pavlov to study in Hamburg, where the German Baptists were just establishing a theological seminary. Vasili was picked because he had received a good education in school and was gifted for languages, having learnt German as a child and later ancient Hebrew in a Jewish *heder.* Subsequently he also learnt Latin and Greek in order to understand the Bible better, and many other languages in order to broaden his theological reading. In 1876 he was ordained as a Baptist minister and commissioned as a missionary by the famous German Baptist missionary J. G. Oncken. Developments in the Caucasus and Ukraine had been quite separate, but, having read some newspaper reports of Stundist activity, Vasili visited Ukraine on his return journey from Hamburg and met Mykhailo Ratushny, Ivan Ryaboshapka and other leaders.

After his return to Tiflis Vasili Pavlov and another preacher named Rodionov set out on a long missionary tour through the Transcaucasian province – what is today Georgia, Armenia and Azerbaijan – reaching as far as Mount Ararat in the south and the Caspian Sea in the east. They began in Vasili's home village and visited the small groups of Christians that had formed in the Molokan villages where Vasili Ivanov had preached, as well as other villages populated by Molokans. Their programme ended abruptly when they were arrested on charges of spreading the Lutheran faith and sent back to Tiflis. They were not held under arrest for long, however, and this was the only occasion in the first ten years of evangelical work in the Caucasus that anybody was arrested, perhaps because they were preaching primarily to Molokans. To convert Orthodox believers to another denomination was a criminal offence, but to preach to non-Orthodox was not illegal.

In 1879 Vasili Pavlov visited Vladikavkaz on the northern slopes of the Caucasus mountains. One of the Tiflis members, E. M. Bogdanov, had moved there a few years earlier and had gathered a small group of believers. Vasili baptized seven new converts, bringing into being the first Baptist church in the North Caucasus. Bogdanov preached in the villages of the region. In April 1879, Vasili Ivanov was sent to preach in the Baku area. Several Molokan families were converted, and with time churches grew up around them. Thus the movement spread throughout the Caucasus region. In 1880 the Tiflis congregation officially became Baptist: they invited the German Baptist pastor from Odessa, August Liebing, and the preacher from St Petersburg, Ivan Kargel, to ordain Vasili Pavlov as their pastor. During their visit they organized officially as a Baptist church and adopted the Hamburg Baptist confession of faith. In the same year the local authorities registered the church, recognizing Vasili Pavlov as its pastor.

While these two evangelical movements were developing in the south among Ukrainian villagers and Molokan exiles, a third revival was beginning in the capital St Petersburg. While in the south the converts were largely of humble origin – peasants, farmers and traders – the St Petersburg revival took place in a totally different, even unlikely, milieu: the drawing rooms of the aristocracy. This high-society Christian awakening owed its birth to the preaching of an English aristocrat, Lord Radstock, a member of the Waldegrave family whose roots go back beyond William the Conqueror. Educated at Harrow and Balliol College, Oxford, as a young officer Radstock was sent to the battlefields of the Crimean War. Although hostilities had ceased by the time he arrived in the Crimea, he nevertheless fell victim to the appalling insanitary conditions (those same conditions which led Florence Nightingale to lay the foundations of modern nursing) and was struck down by a fever, from which he nearly died. On recovery, nurtured by the Christian upbringing given by his mother and encouraged by a Christian friend, he committed himself to Christ and, returning to England, joined the Brethren church and devoted himself to Christian work. A few years later Radstock gave up his military career, no small sacrifice as he had recruited and trained his own battalion of the West Middlesex Volunteers, in order to be able to respond to the many invitations to preach which he was receiving. Not an eloquent speaker,

Radstock's simple sincerity touched the hearts of his listeners. In 1867 he was invited to Holland, in 1868 to Paris and in 1872 to Switzerland.

Ever since becoming a Christian in the Crimea, Radstock had longed to return to Russia and the opportunity finally came. In Switzerland he met Yelizaveta Chertkova, wife of the Tsar's Adjutant General, who was mourning the death of her youngest son; she was travelling through Western Europe in search of religious comfort, but found no relief in either Catholic or Protestant churches until she heard Lord Radstock's simple preaching of salvation in Christ. She thought to herself: 'Here's a man that Russia needs', and invited him to come to St Petersburg. Returning to Russia, she devoted herself to charity, not only giving generously of her wealth but also sharing the good news of Christ.

At Easter 1874, taking up Madame Chertkova's invitation, Lord Radstock arrived in St Petersburg. During Holy Week he preached in English and French at a small Anglo-American Congregational church, and was then invited to hold meetings in the homes of members of the capital's high society. As well as Madame Chertkova, Princess Natalia Lieven had become a Christian abroad, on a visit to England, and there were other ladies keen to invite Lord Radstock to their salons. Soon he was engaged in a busy round of meetings. Almost every day he would be invited to speak at the social hour of 5.00 p.m. He would enter the salon where the guests were gathered, briefly kneel in prayer and then invite his audience to pray with him. A Bible reading would be followed by his exposition of the text, the whole meeting lasting for an hour or so. He would then invite those who wished to stay for further discussion and made individual appointments with those who were most interested. He would spend eight to fourteen hours a day in spiritual conversation with seekers. Altogether some forty people opened their homes for Lord Radstock's preaching. Some of them were from families influenced by the religious awakening in St Petersburg in the 1820s. Although he spoke in French, Radstock was readily understood by the aristocracy, most of whom were as fluent in French as in Russian and some of whom, indeed, preferred French to their native tongue. When non-French speakers were present translation into Russian could be provided.

One of Lord Radstock's early St Petersburg converts was Count Modest Korff, Lord Chamberlain at the court. In 1867 at the Paris World Exhibition he had come across the British and Foreign Bible Society's stand, where he was given a Russian New Testament; although he was a purely nominal member of the Orthodox Church, he agreed to receive

Scriptures from the Society for free distribution in Russia. Returning home he was somewhat shocked to discover that 3000 John's gospels had arrived for him. He requested permission to distribute them from the Holy Synod, sure that he would be relieved of his obligation by a refusal! However, to his surprise, permission was granted, and, when he had exhausted the supply of gospels, New Testaments and Bibles were sent from London. At the first Russian national trade fair in 1874 in St Petersburg Count Korff was asked to organize Bible distribution. His Bible kiosk gave away 62,000 copies of the Scriptures during the fair. Thus he became involved in Christian work and was ready to give himself fully to Christ when he heard Lord Radstock. He recalls Radstock's preaching:

> He hardly spoke of dogmatic issues and never touched the fundamental principles of Orthodoxy, but he knew and loved the Bible as a letter from his Friend. His whole being was filled with trust in God.

Another early listener was impressed by the positive nature of Radstock's message:

> He never makes threats of torment in hell, but explains the immeasurable love of God, to which people respond with indifference and cruelty of heart. He forces us to realize how ungrateful we are and thus touches the listeners' most noble feelings.

His meetings were conducted 'in a conversational tone, almost a whisper, without emotion or eloquence, but with a deep conviction'. Among the high-placed ladies who responded to Radstock's straightforward preaching were Princess Yekaterina Golitsyna, granddaughter of Prince Golitsyn, the president of the Russian Bible Society of sixty years earlier, Princess Gagarina and Yekaterina Chertkova's sister Alexandra, wife of a Guards colonel, Vasili Pashkov. Colonel Pashkov himself was unimpressed with Lord Radstock, and was amazed that people should want to listen to him. In order to avoid him Pashkov took a long trip to Moscow, but in vain. When the colonel returned home his wife invited Radstock to dinner and he could not escape from meeting him. As Radstock prayed with him, Pashkov was convinced of his sin. He later wrote:

> The Lord awakened in me a desire to be liberated from sin, which bound me in all kinds of ways. When I found in the Word of God

that the Lord wants to make a covenant with me and that He promises not to recall my sins and crimes any more and to write His law in my heart through the Holy Spirit, I felt a yearning to receive forgiveness from the holy God and to experience personally liberation from the power of sin.

Not only were people accepting Christ personally through Lord Radstock's ministry, but lives were being perceptibly changed. One person who commented cynically on the change in some of his friends was Count Alexei Bobrinsky, a successful man who had become one of the Tsar's ministers at the young age of forty. The second time he met Radstock, Count Bobrinsky admitted to finding many contradictions in the Bible, and for their next meeting prepared a whole list of passages he found contradictory. However, in discussing these passages he had a strange experience:

Every verse of the Bible which I quoted to prove that I was correct turned against me like an arrow. I felt the power of the Holy Spirit and I cannot explain how, but I know that I was born again.

He too was changed and his former cynicism vanished.

Many of these high-society Christians were extremely wealthy, and as well as taking every opportunity to share their faith - Count Bobrinsky, for example, sought out the famous writer Leo Tolstoy - began to use their fortunes for charitable ends. Madame Chertkova joined the Women's Committee for Prison Visiting and with her sister Alexandra and Princess Gagarina set up dressmaking shops and laundries employing poor women, with profits being ploughed back into charity. Colonel Pashkov opened a subsidized canteen for students and poor workers, staffed by Christian volunteers. In the evenings the canteen was used for services and talks held by Pashkov. Madame Julia Zasetskaya, daughter of the well-known poet and hero of the war of 1812 against Napoleon, Denis Davydov, set up the first night refuge in St Petersburg and worked there among the homeless herself. The Princesses Lieven and Gagarina, as well as Madame Chertkova and Colonel Pashkov, made their homes available for regular Christian worship.

When Lord Radstock returned to England, Colonel Pashkov took over the leadership of the young movement, assisted by Count Korff. Services were organized at which all were welcome, from the highest nobility to their housemaids and manservants. The aristocratic Christians preached the Gospel to the peasants who worked on their country estates, establishing little congregations far and wide. In December 1876 Pashkov and Korff, together with Princess Gagarina and Madame Chertkova, received official permission to found the Society for Spiritual and Moral Reading, which was also supported by Princess Lieven's father, who was master of ceremonies at the court. The Society published books, brochures, leaflets and tracts for free distribution. Until it was disbanded in 1884 it published two hundred books and brochures, some of which had as many as twelve editions. Among them were John Bunyan's *Pilgrim's Progress* (translated by Julia Zasetskaya) and sermons by Charles Spurgeon, as well as works by some Orthodox writers and collections of hymns and Christian songs. The literature printed by the society was distributed by colporteurs and also posted out to churches far from the capital. In 1882 Colonel Pashkov paid for the printing of a new edition of the Russian Bible by the British and Foreign Bible Society with a carefully proofread text, which became the standard version.

Lord Radstock visited St Petersburg again in 1875 and 1878, also travelling to Moscow. Already his work and the preaching of his converts had begun to arouse opposition from the Orthodox Church, which accused him of leading people astray. A novel attacking and mocking him was published in 1876, its author also writing an open letter to Radstock accusing him of lack of respect for the Orthodox Church and the perversion of Orthodox Christians and demanding that Radstock should leave Russia. In autumn 1878 Radstock and his family were deported from Russia and banned from returning. However, the movement already had strong leadership and Radstock had also introduced some of his friends to the St Petersburg Christians, including George Muller of Bristol and Dr Frederick Baedecker, a German businessman who had settled in England in 1859 and become a Christian at one of Radstock's meetings in 1866. Through Radstock's high-society contacts Dr Baedecker was later able to secure official permission to travel the length and breadth of Russia visiting prisons and distributing the Scriptures.

THREE

Persecution under the Tsars

'THE NUMBER OF exiles sent over the Caucasus has been greatly increased,' wrote Lord Radstock's friend Dr Frederick Baedeker at the beginning of the twentieth century.

They are mostly Stundists, Molokans and Baptists, men and women who have been taught by the Word of God ... In Transcaucasia they are set at liberty and land is sometimes allotted to them for cultivation. They generally construct for themselves a hut made of earth and covered with turf and branches. Thus Russia treats her best citizens. And these men are real heroes of patient endurance.

Dr Baedeker twice made the long trek to visit thirty evangelical families exiled to the remote settlement of Giryusy for their faithfulness in living and preaching the Gospel. To reach Giryusy you had to travel by a little-used track over the mountains from Shusha, about sixty miles away. The journey was exciting, the way abounding in perilous passes and gloomy ravines in which occasionally outlaws would be lying in wait. The track ended at Giryusy - the savage mountains beyond were left utterly to the wild beasts. For over twenty years this place was home to a succession of persecuted Christians. Undaunted they supported one another and gathered for prayer and communion despite the best efforts of the authorities to stop them.

Persecution of the new evangelical movements did not begin everywhere at the same time. At first the social status of the aristocratic Christian leaders in St Petersburg protected them from the displeasure of the conservative wing of the Orthodox Church and of the establishment. The Tiflis Baptists were also left in peace and even received official registration of their congregation and their pastor. However, the Ukrainian Stundists experienced trials and tribulations from the outset. Mykhailo Ratushny and six others were imprisoned in Odessa in July 1867, but released when two English travellers appealed personally to the Tsar. In Lyubomirka Ivan Ryaboshapka and his co-leader M. Kravchenko were held in detention for two months in 1870. They asked the governor-general for permission to establish a new village in the steppe and build their own school and church there, but their request was refused. Instead the local Orthodox priest began to persecute those he suspected of having become Stundists. At Easter he chased one peasant out of the churchyard and tied another to the fence and told the parishioners to spit at him. However, many people were more in sympathy with the victims than with the priest. By 1873, the new priest in Lyubomirka reported to his archbishop that the Stundists had supporters in three neighbouring villages and that in Lyubomirka itself they had grown to 45 families from 20 in 1870. Indeed, of 150 households the priest considered only three to be truly Orthodox. He noted that the Stundists' 'strict moral life . . . mutual assistance . . . and improved living conditions' made the rest of the villagers favourably disposed towards them. In 1873 the 'Evangelical Brethren', as they called themselves, built a church, but on 11 June the sanctuary was sealed by the authorities and their communion chalice confiscated. The next day all the papers relating to the congregation were confiscated from Ryaboshapka.

The other early congregations had similar experiences. In January 1872 a drunken mob attacked a prayer meeting in Konstantinovka, near Nikolayev, and dragged the worshippers to the prison. Five men and one woman were particularly badly beaten. In Bastanka village some of the believers received as many as 150 strokes. In February 1872, when Mennonite pastor Johann Wieler held a communion service in Russian in Rohrbach at which a number of recently baptized Ukrainian Christians were present he was detained by the local police. From then on Mykhailo Ratushny took on the leadership of the Ukrainian believers. In August 1872 at least 11 Stundists from Chaplinka, Kiev province, were arrested and held in Tarashcha prison. In May 1873 some were released, but eight were transferred to Kiev prison, where they were tortured, put on trial and detained until the end of 1874. Yakim Bely and Iosyf Tyshkevich died in Kiev prison, the first Ukrainian evangelical martyrs. The governor-general of New Russia, as southern Ukraine was known, did, however, carefully study the appeals from the believers and the reports from the authorities. He instructed the Kherson governor that people who left the Orthodox Church could not be prosecuted because the law did not provide for any sanctions against them. For his fairness he was accused of sympathizing with the Stundists or even being one himself. The Odessa prosecutor insisted that as long as he was in the post no cases against Stundists would be brought to court. Nevertheless, the governor of Kherson province proposed in 1873 that the chief 'propagandists' of Stundism should be exiled and a series of trials followed until 1878. However, the trials were public and the liberal press took up the defence of the Stundists, and even the West European press began to take an interest.

In March 1879 the State Council at the request of the Ministry of Internal Affairs drafted a document defining the rights of Baptists. It proposed that they should be allowed to practise their faith and hold public worship in prayer houses approved for the purpose by the provincial governor; that their elected leaders should perform riutals and preach only after they had been confirmed in their positions by the governor; and that registration of births, marriages and deaths should be carried out by the local civil authorities. With the approval of the Ministry of Justice the document was confirmed by the Tsar and signed by the Minister of Internal Affairs on 15 August and came into force on 12 September. This ruling confirmed the rights of the Mennonites and foreign Baptists who were already exempt from the religious restrictions imposed on the Russian Orthodox and raised the hopes of the Russian Baptists. The registration of births, deaths and marriages was an especially important matter as the Baptists and Stundists could not go to the Orthodox priests and their own records were not recognized by the authorities. Their marriages were therefore invalid, their children were consequently illegitimate and denied the right of inheritance, and their dead could not be buried in cemeteries.

The new regulations were not, however, applied equally. In Tiflis the Baptist church was registered with Vasili Pavlov officially confirmed as pastor and worshipped freely until 1886. In the territory of Poland that fell under Russian rule after the partitions of Poland at the end of the eighteenth century and in the Baltic provinces, German Baptists also benefited from the new law. Hitherto they had not enjoyed the special privileges of the German settlers in Ukraine. In St Petersburg, too, the

German Baptist congregation under pastor Ivan Kargel was immediately given official recognition. On the other hand, the Ukrainian Baptists and Stundists in particular met all kinds of obstacles. Some were told their congregations were too small; local officials put off decisions by asking for clarification of the law from the Holy Synod and the Senate. In 1882 the Ministry of Internal Affairs issued a circular stating that the law did not apply to Russian Baptists, but only to foreigners who had Russian citizenship and were Baptists and to Russian citizens who had converted to the Baptists from some other non-Orthodox denomination. On these grounds the churches in Lyubomirka and the other Ukrainian villages were not registered and the way was opened for further persecutions.

This period of persecution was to last for over twenty years and was associated with the tenure of office, from 1880 to 1905, of Konstantin Pobedonostsev as Procurator of the Holy Synod, that is the Tsar's lay appointee to head the administration of the Orthodox Church. Almost immediately after he was appointed, in May 1880, Pobedonostsev proposed measures to limit the influence of Colonel Pashkov and the St Petersburg evangelical congregation. Pobedonostsev was alarmed by the growing links between Pashkov in the capital and the Stundists in Ukraine and proposed that Pashkov's prayer meetings and preaching should be banned, that Pashkov himself should be exiled from Russia, at least for a while, and that 'vigilant measures' should be taken against other evangelical meetings in St Petersburg and throughout the country. Pobedonostsev's authority and influence increased considerably in 1881 when the relatively liberal regime of Tsar Alexander II was abruptly ended by his assassination by revolutionary terrorists. Pobedonostsev had been the tutor of Alexander III, who succeeded his father (and, indeed, of the next and last Tsar, Nicholas II), and exerted an enormous conservative influence over all domestic affairs. In April 1882, in his report to the Minister of Internal Affairs, Pobedonostsev repeated his warnings about the activity of Colonel Pashkov and Count Bobrinsky and insisted that they should be exiled. He was also involved in preparing the 1882 Ministry of Internal Affairs circular excluding the Russian Stundists and Baptists from the regulations defining the rights of Baptists.

Pobedonostsev was concerned at the steady growth and increasing organization of the evangelicals. Throughout the 1870s, as the Stundist congregations had grown and spread, a network of personal contacts had developed. In 1882 Mennonite leaders Johann Wieler and Peter Friesen proposed a joint conference with the Baptists and Stundists, which took place in May. The Mennonite Brethren had been holding annual conferences for ten years, but for the Russians it was a new experience. There were nineteen Russian and Ukrainian representatives from Ukraine and the Caucasus. Colonel Pashkov sent a letter on behalf of the congregation in St Petersburg. Almost everybody noted people's thirst to hear God's Word and therefore evangelism was seen as the major priority. Ivan Ryaboshapka, Mykhailo Ratushny and Vasili Pavlov were elected evangelists. By this time, through contact with Mennonite Brethren and German Baptists, most of the Stundists had accepted Baptist teaching on adult baptism and this was also a unifying factor. The St Petersburg Christians, however, did not require the rebaptism of those baptized as infants; Colonel Pashkov's request to the conference for full felowship, including sharing communion, was discussed, but a decision was shelved in order not to cause a rift between the two movements.

In 1883 a new law was passed granting freedom of worship for non-Orthodox denominations. Congregations were permitted to meet in private homes or in special buildings, provided rules of decency and public order were not violated. Their leaders were not to be prosecuted for conducting worship, except in cases where they were 'guilty of spreading their errors among the Orthodox' or of other criminal offences. This law was in essence a precursor of Soviet legislation governing religion, which on the one hand guaranteed freedom of religious worship, but on the other allowed the authorities to close down churches accused of violations of public order and banned evangelism. As long as the evangelicals worshipped quietly without attracting attention and without preaching to outsiders, they had religious freedom. Colonel Pashkov and his co-workers in St Petersburg immediately felt the pressure. The police placed them under surveillance, followed their movements and eavesdropped on their conversations. Many of their followers were questioned and some were obliged to give an undertaking not to leave the city.

In 1884, despite these ominous signs, Colonel Pashkov decided to invite evangelicals of all the different movements to a conference in St Petersburg, in order to help them to meet each other and to promote cooperation. On 24 March an invitation was sent out to Stundists, Baptists, Mennonite Brethren and Evangelical Molokans to come to an eight-day conference in St Petersburg beginning on 1 April. Pashkov booked an entire hotel to house his guests, offering free acommodation and food to those who could not afford to pay their own way. Over 70 delegates arrived by 1 April and with guests and participants from the host congregation around 100 people were present at the conference sessions, which took place in Princess Lieven's palace and in the residences of Pashkov and Count Korff. The delegates included Vasili Pavlov from Tiflis, Mykhailo Ratushny and Ivan Ryaboshapka from the Ukrainian Stundists, Pastor Johann Wieler from the Mennonite Brethren and the pioneer missionary Yakov Delyakov. Guests from abroad included Ivan Kargel, earlier of the St Petersburg Baptists, but now pastoring a church in Bulgaria, and Lord Radstock's friend Dr Baedeker.

The conference made a lasting impression on the participants, who showed mutual respect despite their differences. One potentially divisive issue was again baptism. Vasili Pavlov noted in his memoirs that he and his fellow Baptists did not take communion at the opening service because most of those taking part had not been baptized as adults on profession of faith. When baptism came up for discussion on the third day Pashkov and Dr Baedeker proposed that it should be removed from the agenda when they saw that it was causing disagreement. However, there was unanimity on the need for evangelism, that preachers could be paid and that women could preach.

However, after five days of discussions and fellowship, the conference was prematurely terminated on 6 April. As they left the evening meeting to return to their hotel all of the visiting delegates were arrested by a large contingent of police and taken to the notorious prison in the Peter and Paul Fortress where revolutionaries were detained. They were interrogated about the conference, who had organized it and who had paid their costs, and at once charged with 'nihilism' and possession of revolutionary documents and printed materials which had allegedly been found in their rooms at the hotel. The next day they appeared in court where the charges were thrown out, but, as they had no legitimate reason to be in the capital, they were ordered to return to their homes forthwith and threatened with arrest and punishment if they were caught in St Petersburg again. They were promptly escorted to the railway stations and forced to buy tickets for home and put on their trains by the police. The first indication that Colonel Pashkov had that something was amiss was when nobody arrived for the next morning's session. There was nobody at the hotel and Pashkov became increasingly anxious. He learnt the full story two days later when one of the participants from the Caucasus made his way back to St Petersburg. He had managed to buy a ticket for Riga instead of his distant home and had risked arrest by returning to Pashkov to tell him what had happened.

The Russian Baptists held a conference on 30 April and 1 May 1884 in Novovasilevka in southern Ukraine attended by 33 delegates representing 12 churches. The Baptists from the Caucasus could not be present, but sent letters of support, and Vasili Pavlov and Vasili Ivanov from Tiflis were both recognized as ministers by the conference, as were Mykhailo Ratushny and Ivan Ryaboshapka and others of Stundist background. At the conference the Union of Russian Baptists of Southern Russia and the Caucasus was formed, with pastor Johann Wieler as president. Once again they decided against passing a resolution on baptism in order not to hinder evangelical unity. The primary aim of the union was the preaching of the Gospel; on issues of doctrine they hoped to achieve unity; non-doctrinal matters were to be decided by each congregation.

The St Petersburg conference sufficiently alarmed the authorities for Pobedonostsev to be able to act against Colonel Pashkov. On 24 May 1884 an imperial decree was issued disbanding Pashkov's Society for Spiritual and Moral Reading and ordering measures to be taken throughout the Empire to prevent the further spread of Pashkov's teaching. In June Colonel Pashkov and Count Korff were exiled from Russia, with two weeks' notice to leave. Both died in exile, though in 1892 Pashkov received permission to return for three months. He arrived unannounced at a service at Princess Lieven's and there was great rejoicing. When the Tsar heard that Pashkov was preaching, he summoned him and ordered him to leave at once and never to return.

After the exile of Pashkov and Korff, Princess Lieven was ordered to stop her Christian work. The Tsar's adjutant-general was sent to convey this message to her, but she replied to him: 'Ask His Imperial Highness whom I should rather obey, God or the Tsar?' She never got a direct reply, but the services continued without hindrance. Later she heard that the Tsar had commented: 'She is a widow, leave her in peace.' There was a plan to exile Princess Lieven and Madame Chertkova, but nothing came of it. Count Bobrinsky went to live on his estate in Tula province and only visited the capital occasionally. Services were held in Princess Lieven's palace and were mostly led by the Princess or Madame Chertkova. Some of the factory workers preached, and despite their lack of education their love for the Lord shone through and their sermons were well received. Dr Baedeker was a regular visitor and when Ivan Kargel moved to Finland, then part of the Russian Empire, he too came to preach from time to time. Before long he was invited to move back to St Petersburg as their pastor. He and his family were accommodated at Princess Lieven's. As he had Turkish citizenship, Kargel was able to work relatively unhindered. The Gospel continued to be preached on the estates belonging to Pashkov and other wealthy Christians, and congregations were founded there. A St Petersburg worker named Kirpichnikov was a particularly ardent witness on Pashkov's estate in the Nizhni Novgorod province. A former inveterate drunkard, he was converted after his wife was miraculously healed. For their Christian work he and his wife were exiled to the Minusinsk district of Siberia in 1887.

Persecution also intensified in Ukraine. Although their exemplary life was widely recognized – some Stundists were even elected as village elders – the evangelicals were fined and sentenced to community labour for holding prayer and Bible-study meetings. From 1884 there was an orchestrated campaign to get village assemblies to demand their exile. Before acting on these resolutions, however, the provincial authorities sought the advice of the Orthodox Bishop of Odessa, who felt that the Stundists should be combated by improving the teaching and pastoral work of the Orthodox Church. In his view only the leaders needed to be exiled. In 1885 Pobedonostsev proposed that Mykhailo Ratushny, Ivan Ryaboshapka and several others should be exiled. Mykhailo and others were placed under police surveillance and banned from leaving their home villages. From 1886 evangelicals were the victims of attacks by mobs encouraged by local officials, who dragged them out of services and stoned them. Between 1889 and 1891 six leaders were sent into exile for five years to Giryusy. The soil there was stony and poor. The local people could barely scrape a living and supplemented their meagre income by taking seasonal work away from the village. The exiles, however, could not even do this, as they were restricted to the village. Such was the cruelty of the police posted to Giryusy to guard the exiles that there were cases where they trampled down the produce the exiles succeeded in cultivating in their garden plots.

Persecution came a little later in the Caucasus. In Tiflis there were for a while two congregations, led by Vasili Pavlov and Nikita Voronin. In 1883-4 Vasili Pavlov travelled throughout the Caucasus region and also preached in the Molokan communities in Samara province, while Vasili Ivanov preached among the Molokans in the Caucasus and in Tambov province. Several new congregations were formed as a result. Two Molokan brothers who were later to become leaders of the Baptist Union, Dei and Gavriil Mazaev, were baptized in 1884. In 1886 the pioneer missionary Yakov Delyakov joined the Baptists.

However, a new head of the Orthodox Church in Georgia, Bishop Pavel, who arrived in Tiflis in 1885, began to work against them. He claimed that the Baptist Church was in violation of the law. Although it was properly registered under the 1879 regulations, he insisted that the congregation was breaking the 1883 law by actively evangelizing among the Orthodox and also by supporting the Ukrainian Stundists. He recommended that Nikita Voronin should be exiled to a part of the Caucasus with Muslim or Armenian population, as he was the most dangerous, having spread the Baptist faith in the Caucasus, maintained active contacts with the Stundists and published a hymn book and the Baptist statement of faith. In exile he should be prevented from having contact with Baptists or Stundists. Bishop Pavel proposed that Vasili Pavlov should be informed that he was no longer recognized as a Baptist pastor and be ordered to stop preaching. If he failed to comply he too should be punished. In March 1887 Pavlov, Voronin and the Armenian preacher Abraham Amirkhanyants were arrested and detained in Tiflis prison. Amirkhanyants believed in the practice of infant baptism, and had often debated the issue with Pavlov. These discussions had not brought the two men any closer together in their views and had created a degree of personal animosity between them. However, when they met in prison after their arrest they embraced and wept and knelt in prayer together. Putting the divisive issue behind them, they combined their efforts in preaching to their fellow prisoners.

In April they were exiled for four years with their families to Orenburg in the Urals. Pavlov and Voronin made contact with local Molokans and held small services. Amirkhanyants continued the work he had already begun of translating the Bible into the Azerbaijani language. He was a gifted linguist who also translated the Bible into the Ararat dialect of Armenian and parts of the Bible into Kurdish. He knew the Koran so well that he could discuss it with the most learned mullahs and was regarded by Muslims as an authority on the Koran in his own right.

A further wave of persecution followed in 1891. In Tiflis the church building was closed. Baptists met in homes in different parts of the city or outside the city in the open air. Vasili Pavlov, having completed his four years' exile, returned to Tiflis, but was soon arrested and sent back to Orenburg. He commented: 'This evidently was of the Lord, for on my return to Orenburg I had a great reaping time, baptizing more than 150 persons.' From Orenburg the evangelical message spread to the neighbouring Ufa province, where three churches were established.

However, Orenburg was also a place of great personal tragedy for Vasili. When his wife and children joined him there in 1892 one of his daughters died in a drowning accident and two more daughters, his younger son and his wife all died of cholera, leaving him alone with his nine-year-old son. He remained there till 1895. Martin Kalweit and others from Tiflis and the congregations in the North Caucasus were also exiled, some to Giryusy and the rest to other remote Caucasian villages.

In Balashov, a small town in Saratov province on the Volga, a young Orthodox man named Andrei Yevstratenko was zealous in his persecution of 'heretics'. When four Baptists arrived in the town, he organized his friends and broke up their meeting by throwing stones and breaking the windows of the house in which they were preaching. In the spring of 1890 Vasili Ivanov visited the town and received similar treatment. However, Vasili made an impression on Andrei and after several conversations the former persecutor began attending Baptist worship, and the following year was baptized into church membership. Soon after, six of the eleven families in the church were exiled to Siberia and Andrei became the leader of the diminished congregation. Soon he and the others were imprisoned by administrative order, and on release were arrested every time they met for worship and fined until they were penniless. With nothing more to lose they began to meet openly and suffered many beatings. Finally, Andrei was arrested in 1893 and exiled to Siberia; he was freed from his sentence only in 1905.

Despite the many difficulties and official repression, the evangelical movement grew and spread steadily. According to official records there were about 1000 Baptists in Kherson, Yekaterinslav and Kiev provinces of Ukraine in 1881, while in Kherson province alone in May 1882 Baptists and Stundists combined were over 3000. In 1884 Ukrainian Baptist churches had over 2000 members and by 1893 over 4500. Through the witness of exiles and the work of missionaries little evangelical churches were formed in many of the Russian provinces too. In St Petersburg, as well as the main services at Princess Lieven's, smaller meetings took place in various parts of the city. The meeting places had to be constantly changed. About 25 Christians would gather, two or three would give short sermons and then those gathered would pray and read the Bible together. More often than not, in order not to give the meeting place away, the group would have to forgo singing hymns. One of those who grew in the faith in these little groups was Ivan Prokhanov, a student who had become a Christian at the Baptist church in Vladikavkaz, North Caucasus, in 1887.

Pursuing his studies at the Technological Institute in St Petersburg from 1888 to 1893 Ivan became actively involved in the life of the church. In 1889 he began publishing a Christian journal named *Beseda* (*Heart-to-heart*) which was secretly produced on a duplicator and mailed by registered post to evangelical churches and groups and also to the exiles in Siberia and the Caucasus. In 1891 his own father was exiled to Giryusy.

While the Russian and Ukrainian believers faced many restrictions, Lord Radstock's friend Dr Frederick Baedeker enjoyed an extraordinary freedom to preach in the prisons of the Russian Empire. With the help of Count Korff, who was a member of the Petersburg Prisons Committee, and Madame Chertkova, a member of the Women's Prison Visitors Committee, Dr Baedeker was able to accompany some of the Petersburg Christians on their visits to the city's prisons to distribute New Testaments. His heart was greatly moved and he felt a strong desire to tell the prisoners of God's love. Baedeker shared his vision with a countess, who secured a permit for him from the Director of the Prisons Department. The permit stated that he was 'under special command to visit the prisons of Russia and to supply the convicts with copies of the Holy Scriptures'. This official document opened the door of every prison and almost everywhere gave Dr Baedeker the freedom to address the prisoners. Although already in his sixties when he received this permit, and furthermore in weak health as he had only one lung, for eighteen years Frederick Baedeker made frequent visits to Russia, travelling throughout the Empire. A year or two after receiving the permit he met the Director of Prisons, and found him a man full of ideas for reform. The director encouraged him to visit the prisons of eastern Siberia and on the island of Sakhalin in the Sea of Japan. He promised to give him full information about the prisons and to have boxes of Scriptures delivered to the various prisons to await his arrival.

In 1889, in the company of Ivan Kargel, Dr Baedeker undertook a trip the whole length of Siberia, ending with a steamer trip down the Amur and across the sea to Sakhalin. The journey was very hard, with much of it in a tarantass – a four-wheeled horse-drawn carriage without springs – over bumpy, unmade roads. They filled the bottom of the tarantass with their Bibles and New Testaments as a kind of ballast, then loaded their luggage, laid as flat as possible; then everything was covered with rugs and mattresses on which they slept as they journeyed through the night. From Kranoyarsk, while Dr Baedeker visited the prisons, Ivan Kargel sailed over 300 miles by steamer up the river Yenisei to Minusinsk to visit the Kirpichnikovs in their place of exile. Through their witness, and that of later exiles who joined them, the first evangelical churches in Siberia were founded in the Minusinsk area. On that trip Dr Baedeker addressed 40,000 prisoners and distributed 12,000 New Testaments. He wondered whether he would have the strength to complete the journey, and regarded it as a once-in-a-lifetime venture, making the most of every opportunity and reaching the heart of the Siberian prison system – the mines on the Manchurian border. Yet five years later, now aged 70, he made the trip again, this time accompanied by an Armenian Christian from Baku named Patvakan Taranyants.

On his many visits Dr Baedeker learnt a lot of Russian, but was not sufficiently confident of his knowledge of the language to preach. He would speak in English, German or French and was generally able to find Christian interpreters to help translate his addresses into Russian and many of the minority languages of the Empire. Sometimes he would have as many as five interpreters all translating at once into different languages, each surrounded by a crowd eager to hear the Gospel in their native tongue, while a small group who understood whichever language he was speaking in would gather round Dr Baedeker himself. Sometimes he was translated first into Russian, and then from Russian into some other language. On one occasion he remarked drily: 'I like to preach by interpreter – it gives me a rest!' Of course, he relied on good translators. Visiting a prison in Helsinki he was once translated by an eminent professor; the convicts stood respectfully listening, but totally unmoved. On the next visit he was accompanied by Baroness Mathilda von Wreda, an ardent young Christian who dedicated her life to prison ministry. Her translation quickly provoked a response, as prisoners openly wept. Dr Baedeker asked one of the prison officers why on the previous visit the men had listened with indifference and even resentment, whereas on this occasion the Word of God had touched their hearts. The officer explained that, although Dr Baedeker had addressed the convicts as 'my beloved friends' and 'my brothers', the professor had translated these expressions as 'men' and 'prisoners'. On the other hand the Baroness had translated literally. The secret of Dr Baedeker's preaching was that he came not as someone moralizing about their crimes but filled with obvious love and compassion for the prisoners in their miserable circumstances, sharing with them the love of God. In many instances his visit to a prison was the first time that anybody had showed any care for the prisoners as human beings.

In 1892 George Muller blessed Dr Baedeker for special ministry 'to the banished brethren'. His access to the prison network also enabled him to

travel to the remote places of exile. In 1895 and 1901 he visted the thirty
or so exiled Christian families in Giryusy. 'One could not help thinking,'
he wrote, 'how differently we should have felt if we had been sent as
banished ones along these wild and dangerous mountain tracks. The joy
of the brethren in seeing us, and ours in meeting them, was a great feast,
short but sweet. The brethren here meet in each other's rooms and sing
and pray together.'

Throughout these years the Baptist Union held regular conferences,
though at different times many of the leaders were prevented by exile or
police harassment from attending. The founding president, Johann Wieler,
was forced by persecution for baptizing Russian converts to emigrate from
Russia in 1886 – becoming the first of many exiles to be pastor of the
Baptist church in Tulcea in Romania, where he died two years later. The
1886 conference elected Dei Mazayev as president, a position he held until
1911. The conferences aligned the congregations in Ukraine and the
Caucasus very much with the Strict Baptist tradition. Resolutions were
passed prohibiting open communion, at which Christians who had not
been baptized on profession of faith were permitted to participate; turning
down the proposal of the Evangelical Molokans to hold joint congresses
and insisting on reception of new members only by baptism – even if they
had been baptized before – and preferably on condition that they promise
not to share in the Lord's Supper with those who were not members of
the Baptist Union. Nevertheless, the 1891 conference approved the
publication of Prokhanov's *Beseda*, which included material from
contributors of various evangelical churches, hoping that it would
contribute to a clear understanding of the truth. For several years after
1891, however, it was impossible to hold conferences and the Baptist
Union was virtually dormant.

Only a part of the evangelical movement accepted the strict views of
the Baptist Union. Congregations with a less exclusive attitude went
under various names. The St Petersburg Christians, popularly known to
outsiders as 'Radstockites' or 'Pashkovites' after their two founders,
usually simply called themselves 'believers', though from the mid-1890s
they took the title 'Believers of Evangelical Faith'. Around Kiev the
Stundists called their congregations 'evangelical brotherhoods'. In
Sevastopol, Crimea, a gospel preacher named Golubev, who had become
a Christian in Colonel Pashkov's house in St Petersburg, gathered a small
congregation in the early 1890s, and adopted the name 'Evangelical
Christians'. Subsequently others began to use this title, although they

remained independent congregations without any form of union or association.

The accession of the last Tsar, Nicholas II, to the Russian throne in 1894 brought no relief to the persecution. On the contrary, the first years of his reign were marked by an intensification of repressive measures. On 3 September 1894 the Ministry of the Interior issued a new circular following a review of the working of the 1883 law. This circular stated that it was necessary to distinguish between the most harmful non-Orthodox denominations and the less harmful. The Stundists were identified as belonging to the former category by both the civil authorities and the Holy Synod, and with the agreement of the government and Pobedonostsev, as procurator of the Holy Synod, the circular withdrew from them the rights and privileges granted by the 1883 law. As their services not only strengthened the Stundists themselves in their faith but were also the main means of spreading their teaching to the Orthodox, they were to be banned from holding public worship.

In the interpretation of the authorities the term Stundist included all evangelicals, and a new wave of arrests and banishment began. Nikita Voronin from Tiflis was once more exiled, this time for four years to Vologda province in the north of Russia; Ivan Ryaboshapka was banished to Yerevan, Armenia, for five years; the pastor in Kiev, Timoshenko, despite leaving the city, was arrested and exiled to Poland. Vasili Ivanov, travelling as an itinerant evangelist, was arrested several times and in January 1895 held in Yelizavetpol prison before being sent in fetters with a convict gang to Slutsk in western Ukraine to serve five years of exile. Far from gaining freedom through an amnesty to mark the coronation of the new Tsar, as many had expected, those already in exile found their sentences extended from three to five years. Some Christians sought to evade their persecutors by leaving their villages and settling in Siberia and Central Asia or among the Muslim tribes of the North Caucasus.

Vasili Pavlov, completing his second exile term in Orenburg, realized that if he remained in Russia he would almost certainly be arrested again. He accepted an invitation to serve as pastor in the Russian-German Baptist church in Tulcea, Romania. He left Orenburg in June 1895, having planted congregations that now had 140 members, and on his way to Tiflis stopped in villages along the Volga where he had earlier preached. He also visited the churches in Vladikavkaz and Baku and the exiles in Geakchae before leaving for Romania. From there he wrote reports on the persecution of his fellow-believers in Russia which were printed in the magazine

Svobodnaya mysl (*Free Thought*) edited by Vladimir Bonch-Bruyevich and published by Madame Chertkova's two sons in London. Bonch-Bruyevich, who was later to be Lenin's cabinet secretary in the first Soviet government, was influential in persuading the Bolsheviks to take a positive attitude to the religious minorities who were persecuted by the Tsarist regime.

In St Petersburg, young Ivan Prokhanov was also receiving unwelcome attention from the authorities. As well as editing the underground journal *Beseda*, he was writing poetry and hymns and taking an active part in the life of the Church. He was advised by the church elders to leave Russia in order to publish information about the persecution and organize aid and the sending of Christian literature for the churches. Even while he was preparing to leave, the secret police were trying to find him. On one occasion, when he visited the leader of one of the city's small Christian groups, a police agent arrived making enquiries about him just a few minutes after he had left. In February 1895 he went abroad via Finland, eventually settling in England, where he collected information on the persecution, some of which was published in Paris and some printed in *Beseda*, now published first in Sweden and then in Romania by another exile. Ivan studied for a year at Bristol Baptist College and also attended courses in theology in Paris and Berlin.

Even those whose only crime was to maintain a Christian family life were persecuted. In 1895 a new Christian named Tvorozhnikov was arrested. He had become a Christian while on seasonal work in St Petersburg and returning home to his village in Tver province he stopped attending the Orthodox church and instead began to read the New Testament with his family. Soon his wife and mother became Christians too. He was tried and sentenced to prison. He couldn't understand what he was guilty of and asked the court why nobody would explain from the Scriptures in what way he was in error. Children from evangelical families were taken by force under police escort to be baptized by Orthodox missionaries. Some children, especially those whose fathers had been exiled, were taken away from their parents altogether and brought up in monasteries or given to Orthodox families to bring up.

Fyodor Kostromin, an ex-Cossack soldier, who had served in the Russo-Turkish war of 1878 that liberated Bulgaria from Ottoman rule, became a Christian after he had left the army to settle down to farming in a village in the Don Cossack country of eastern Ukraine. He immediately began to share his faith with his Cossack neighbours. For three years Fyodor met no hindrance, but then the authorities noted the success of his preaching.

He was detained without trial for three months, but on release continued his ministry undeterred. For another three years he was in and out of prison until he was arrested in 1890 for repeatedly violating the restrictions on evangelical preaching. He was sentenced to loss of civil rights, including his privileges as an ex-soldier, confiscation of property and exile to Giryusy in the Caucasus. His wife was exiled to the north and their eight children were sent to be brought up in monasteries. Each child was sent to a different monastery, and none knew where any of the others were, and nor did the parents have any information. For nine years Fyodor had no news of his family, but was promised that if he would return to the Orthodox Church he would be reunited with his loved ones. At last his many petitions were answered and he was allowed to be with his wife and three eldest sons, provided they left Russia for ever. His appeals for the return of his other children were in vain, so sadly he agreed to go to Tulcea in Romania, where his wife and three sons joined him. Later they moved to Burgas, in Bulgaria, where Fyodor preached among the Russian exiles. When, at last, on account of his military record, he was allowed to return to Russia and his civil rights were restored, his other children had vanished without trace.

In 1894 the Society for the Distribution of the Scriptures in Russia was banned, and restrictions were placed on the work of the British and Foreign Bible Society. In southern Ukraine the Bible Society's colporteurs were banned from distributing Bibles, and elsewhere known or suspected Baptists were forbidden to work for the Society.

The publicity which the persecution received both in the Russian press and also in Western Europe through the efforts of Vasili Pavlov and Ivan Prokhanov and others living in exile abroad placed increasing pressure on the Tsar and his government. The Orthodox philosopher and theologian Vladimir Solovyov wrote to Pobedonostsev in 1892, pointing out that the use of force against religious dissenters was a sign of official Orthodoxy's spiritual weakness. Solovyov was representative of a section of opinion within the Orthodox Church which saw a need for reform and called for the restoration of the Church's independence from the state. From 1901 until 1903, when the authorities banned its activities, the Religious-Philosophical Society in St Petersburg, of which Solovyov was a leading member, tried to bridge the gap between the Church and intellectuals. Religious freedom was one of its main concerns. The society's discussions inaugurated a wider debate on church reform, especially in the religious press. The society enjoyed the blessing of the Metropolitan of St Petersburg,

Antoni, who had been appointed in 1898, and who did much to strengthen the charitable work of the Church, which he considered to be quite inadequate. In 1900, he inaugurated a new Orthodox prison ministry by personally visiting the prisons of St Petersburg, emphasizing that the Church should go to the outcasts in a spirit of love. Antoni visited the prisons every Easter and even succeeded in getting access to the political prisons in the Peter and Paul Fortress and in Schlusselburg. He did much to encourage within the Church a spirit of service to the people, especially to the needy, in marked contrast to the state-backed coercion that typified much of the Church's work.

Although the Russian evangelicals, many of whom had abandoned Orthodoxy, were a particular target for coercion, they were not the only one. Many Jews succumbed to the pressure to convert to Orthodoxy, as this liberated them from the restrictions of the Jewish 'Pale of Settlement'. Tens of thousands of Lutheran Estonians were bullied or tricked into accepting Orthodoxy, where they were trapped by the laws forbidding conversion away from the Orthodox Church. However, alongside this coercive 'missionary' work there was also much genuine pioneer mission work, especially amongst the native tribes of Siberia. Orthodox missionaries worked in Alaska before the territory was sold to the United States, and also in Japan. Some work was done on translating the Bible into minority languages.

One of those who made an important contribution to the pressure on the government was a Baptist from Kiev, Ivan Kushnerov. In 1894 he began to work in defence of those who were being imprisoned. Many of the evangelicals who were put on trial were poorly educated, and had no idea of their legal rights or of proper legal procedure. The lawyers assigned to them by the court usually had no interest in risking their careers by actively promoting the case for the defence, and as a result there were often irregularities in the conduct of the trials. In many instances the believers did not realize the significance to the authorities of the term 'Stundist' and accepted the designation without protest as synonymous with 'Christian'. In fact, though, most of the laws under which they were prosecuted referred specifically to Stundists, and their acceptance of the name relieved the court from calling expert witnesses to prove that the defendants belonged to a dangerous sect. Ivan Kushnerov began attending court hearings from the local magistrates right up to the State Senate. He spoke out for the defence and exposed the illegalities of the courts. As a result of his efforts in many of the cases that went to the appeals division of the Senate the original guilty verdicts were overturned.

In 1896 the Senate issued a legal ruling to the effect that the 1894 law applied only to Stundists and was not to be used by the authorities against other denominations and that Baptists were not the same as Stundists. After this ruling the appeals division more frequently quashed the verdicts of lower courts, and judges and magistrates were reminded that Baptists should not be categorized as Stundists and that believers should not be punished merely for belonging to a particular denomination, but only for specific violations of the law. Orthodox conservatives tried to counter these court rulings by arguing that the distinction between Baptists and Stundists was a false one, and introducing the term Stundo-Baptists! However, the tide was slowly turning in favour of religious liberty.

In 1898, for the first time since January 1891, the Baptist Union was able to hold a conference, to which representatives from Evangelical Christian congregations were also invited. Further conferences followed in 1902, 1903 and 1904, at which Evangelical Christians were present. Some of the Evangelical Christian congregations applied for membership of the Baptist Union but keeping their distinctive name. In 1903 the conference approved for the first time the title Evangelical Christian-Baptist, which was later universally accepted within the movement.

During the early 1900s one of the St Petersburg aristocratic Christians, Baron Pavel Nikolai, began to develop a Student Christian Movement. He had been converted at the age of 25, and became friendly with Ivan Kargel. He knew several European languages and helped Dr Baedeker as a translator. In 1899 he met the international secretary of SCM, John Mott, and took up Christian work among students, organizing discussions, giving lectures and preaching in St Petersburg, Moscow, Kiev and other university cities. He gave up his job as an official in the State Council in order to dedicate himself full time to this work.

In December 1898 Ivan Prokhanov managed to return to Russia. Having left Russia secretly, he had no passport and it was difficult to return officially. However, by travelling to Constantinople and giving himself up to the Turkish authorities as a Russian subject without a passport, he got himself deported from Turkey to Odessa, from where he made his way home to Vladikavkaz. There he found that his father had been freed from his exile. He was appointed as a lecturer in science at the Technical Institute in Riga, but after two years was dismissed for being a 'leader of the Stundists'. He found work as a mechanical engineer in St Petersburg and resumed his Christian work in the city. In 1901 Vasili Pavlov returned from his voluntary exile in Romania to his home church in Tiflis. His old friend and colleague Vasili Ivanov had already completed his term of exile and settled in the cosmopolitan oil city of Baku, where he preached to Azerbaijanis, Kurds, Turks and Armenians as well as to Russians, building up a church of over 300 members.

FOUR

The Dawn of
Religious Liberty

'IN APRIL 1905 on the joyous morning of Christ's resurrection,' recalled Princess Sofie Lieven, daughter of one of the founding families of the St Petersburg Evangelical Christians,

> at the service in the great hall of our house my mother addressed the crowded congregation and said with a radiant face that she had joyful news to give to the brothers and sisters, which would be read by brother Odintsov. Loudly and clearly he read out a decree of the Tsar outlining the details of the freedom which was being granted to us for each one to believe according to his own conscience. The congregation fell to its knees and each one of us with tears of joy thanked the Lord in our own words for this gift beyond price.

Tsar Nicholas II's decree on religious liberty of April 17 was one of many concessions to public opinion made during the revolutionary unrest that swept through Russia in 1905.

The revolution began with a wave of protest at all levels of society sparked off by the violent suppression of a peaceful workers' demonstration in St Petersburg on what became known as Bloody Sunday in January 1905. The religious procession of workers, led by Father Georgi Gapon, an Orthodox priest and Christian Socialist, organizer of the first

Russian Christian trade union, and, it emerged later, a secret police agent, was mercilessly whipped by Cossack guards on horseback and then fired on by the infantry. Two hundred people were killed. The aim of the demonstration had been to present a petition to the Tsar in the Winter Palace calling for constitutional reform. Father Gapon, it seems, was backed by the secret police in the hope that the workers' movement could be channelled into a moderate form of trade unionism rather than falling under the influence of the more radical Socialist Revolutionaries and Social Democrats – the latter already divided between the Mensheviks and the more extreme Bolsheviks, later to call themselves Communists, led by Lenin. Gapon, while agreeing to cooperate with the secret police, also pursued his own aims of promoting Christian socialism.

The workers' petition was but one of many manifestations of a general dissatisfaction and desire for reform which had been growing stronger for several years and which was intensified by the ignominious defeat of Russia by Japan in 1904. In this short war over spheres of influence in the Far East, especially in Manchuria, the Russian Baltic Fleet sailed halfway round the world only to lose spectacularly to the Japanese navy at the Battle of Tsushima, and the Russian army was forced out of Manchuria. The Russian people became thoroughly disillusioned with the Tsar and his autocratic structure of government. The popular demands included an elected parliament with control over legislation and the state budget, civil and political rights, such as the inviolability of the person and the home and freedom of the press and of association, and religious liberty.

Bloody Sunday further polarized opinion, bringing revolution onto the streets of St Petersburg and the other major cities, and the Tsar was forced to begin to make concessions. By the end of 1905 Russia had a constitution and a parliament elected by popular vote. However, the parliament had little real power, as the initiative for legislative proposals lay with the government, the Tsar reserved the right to issue decrees without parliamentary approval and ministers were still answerable above all to the Tsar. Once the revolutionary unrest had diminished, the Tsar and his ministers slowed and reversed the processes of reform. The first two parliaments were dissolved within months as the majority of deputies were totally opposed to the government, and only at the third attempt were the elections manipulated sufficiently to produce a reasonably compliant parliament which ran its full term of five years. The fourth parliament was suspended at the outbreak of the First World War. Given peace, Russia's halting progress towards democracy and economic reform might eventually have been crowned with success, but the war not only ended Russia's limited democracy but brought the country to the brink of collapse.

Among the earliest concessions were promises of religious liberty. A February 1905 manifesto from the Tsar proclaimed religious tolerance wihout lifting the restrictions on non-Orthodox activity. However, the decree of 17 April followed by a manifesto of 25 June 1905 introduced much wider religious freedoms and granted an amnesty to all those imprisoned or exiled for religious offences. The April decree was the result of the work of a government committee in which Antoni, the Metropolitan of St Petersburg took part. Speaking as the Church's most senior hierarch, he voiced his opposition to forcible conversion or the use of compulsion to bring people back to Orthodoxy and supported the release from the Orthodox Church of all those who were legally bound to it but whose true allegiance lay elsewhere. He rejected the use of the police and administrative methods against non-Orthodox denominations. The committee also examined a report compiled by Ivan Kushnerov outlining the history of the evangelical movement and its current position, to which were appended 22 documents in which court cases, physical violence and discrimination were described. Ivan Prokhanov had submitted the report to the Ministry of the Interior on 8 January; with Antoni's support for a change of policy, the report was well received by the committee, and was even printed in a small quantity by the Ministry of the Interior. Thus, at last it became legally possible for people to leave the Orthodox Church. The Tsar's manifesto of 17 October ending autocracy and granting basic civil and political liberties reinforced freedom of conscience and was followed by the resignation of Pobedonostsev from his post of Procurator of the Holy Synod. Everything that for 25 years he had stood for, in political as well as religious life, had crumbled and his position was untenable.

The April decree was issued at Easter and was greeted with much rejoicing among the evangelicals. At a special celebratory service Ivan Prokhanov noted that freedom was 'a result of the sufferings of those who languished in prison and exile and of many years of prayer. We have joyfully reaped what for long years we sowed with our tears.' However, it was not until October 1906 that a decree was passed giving the procedures for the legal recognition of Old Ritualist and other dissenting Christian congregations. The regulations required that the elected pastor of the congregation should be confirmed in office by the provincial governor. For a congregation to be registered an application signed by 50 members had to be submitted to the provincial authorities. A registered congregation could own property to a maximum value of 5000 roubles, only members aged 25 and over were entitled to vote at church business meetings and the pastor was obliged to keep a register of births, deaths and marriages.

Despite these continuing legal restrictions many evangelical congregations decided to register. One of the first was in Kiev, in 1907; the two St Petersburg Evangelical Christian congregations, led by Ivan Prokhanov and Ivan Kargel, followed in 1908, as did the Russian Baptist church in the capital formed by William Fetler. Both Evangelical Christian and Baptist leaders recommended congregations to register, but many refused because they suspected that the purpose of the law was to subordinate the pastors to the authorities and they feared that they would be deprived of the right to remove pastors who had been confirmed in office by the governor.

Hostile local authorities ignored the law or delayed its implementation. Sometimes the authorities arbitrarily refused to register congregations that fulfilled all the conditions. There were many instances in which congregational records of births and marriages were not recognized, and newborn children were listed still as illegitimate. Evangelicals were prevented from burying the dead in cemeteries. Children were barred from school. People were still beaten up for holding services and prayer meetings. Things got so bad that some families and even whole congregations decided to emigrate from Russia.

Nevertheless, despite the attitude of many in authority, the evangelicals now had the law on their side and there were many opportunities to consolidate existing work and to engage in new activities. Released from the earlier strict regulations the evangelical movement grew in numbers and geographical spread. Between 1905 and 1911, according to the statistics kept by the government's Department of Spiritual Affairs, membership more than doubled to 50,000. Of these over 11,000 belonged to the Baptist Union, which grew by 20 per cent in 1909 alone. Of the Baptist Union's 149 congregations in 1910, 58 (44 per cent) had been founded since 1900. Twenty per cent of evangelicals were in Siberia and another five per cent in the Far East – both regions where twenty years earlier there had been no evangelical churches. A Baptist missionary society was organized in June 1907 as part of the Baptist Union, with Vasili Pavlov as its president. The Baptist Union continued its annual conferences, with the 1907 conference approving the holding of regional conferences. The Union also agreed to establish regional sections in the

Caucasus, Siberia and the Far East. Each of these sections set up their own missionary societies. From 41 delegates in 1907 the attendance at the Baptist Union congresses grew to 81 in 1911.

Following in the steps of Dr Baedeker, a Baptist pastor named Adam Podin began an extensive prison ministry. A Russian born in Latvia and fluent in seven languages, Podin had already travelled with Dr Baedeker and translated for him. In 1906 he was approached by an official with a request that he should visit prisons and exile settlements. The necessary papers were issued giving him permission to hold Gospel services in prisons and for exiles and prisoners in transit. He was also provided with thousands of copies of the New Testament for free distribution. At Perm in the Urals, from where convicts were sent on to Siberia, he spoke to 6000 prisoners in groups of up to 800, many of them unlikely ever to see their homes again, as the harsh conditions meant that the majority would not survive their sentences. Many were comforted and moved by his preaching of the Risen Christ, and over half accepted New Testaments. Podin also visited lepers, who were outcasts as much as the convicts, bringing them medicines as well as ministering to their spiritual needs and baptizing those who so desired. Alongside this work he continued as pastor of the Baptist church in Keila, Estonia, after Estonian independence in 1918, founding a Bible school there and serving as president of the Estonian Baptist Union.

In the capital, St Petersburg, new initiatives were associated particularly with the ministries of Ivan Prokhanov and William Felter. William arrived in St Petersburg in 1907 at the age of 23 as pastor of the small Latvian Baptist congregation, having just graduated from Spurgeon's College in London. Born in Latvia, he spoke fluent Russian and was invited by Ivan Kargel to preach to the congregation established by Lord Radstock and Colonel Pashkov. William became a frequent speaker at meetings in the salons of Princess Lieven and Madame Chertkova, where his impassioned sermons soon began to attract large audiences. So great was his following that the church hired large halls in various parts of the city for his Gospel meetings. These included two theatres, two concert halls and the grand hall of the city council. Every day he would preach to as many as 3000 people. William had an infectious enthusiasm that easily moved his audience. Sometimes he would spontaneously burst into song in the middle of his sermon.

A student, Anna Chekmareva, described one of William Fetler's early meetings in the city:

. . . What a wonderful meeting! Fetler, especially, spoke with such conviction and such power that the whole assembly caught the fire of the Holy Spirit. He called on believers not to sleep, to surrender themselves fully and entirely to the Lord, to repent of their sins and be sanctified, in order to receive the fullness of the Holy Spirit and to be baptized in His power. There was very passionate prayer. Some repented and prayed aloud that they had not glorifed God in their lives and had not been a good light to the world. I was among those who prayed, once more surrendering my whole heart to the Lord . . .

Dr Baedeker's biographer, Robert Latimer, and Dr A. McCaig, principal of Spurgeon's College, testify that times of prayer in Fetler's meetings were full of emotion. Latimer writes:

When the people kneel down to pray . . . the effect is indescribable. Wave after wave of emotion thrills the assembly during the ten or fifteen minutes of intercession. There is no loud voice heard, but there is evident eagerness to join audibly in prayer. Occasionally several voices will be heard softly pleading at one time.

McCaig says:

As each request is read there follows 'silent prayer', which is only silent in the sense that no one in particular leads aloud, but all are praying in a subdued, sobbing murmur, which surges through the building, a veritable groundswell of prayer, and not infrequently sobs and tears accompany the prayers.

As well as being a powerful preacher, William Fetler was a gifted organizer. He established a youth group and Sunday schools, and also initiated revival meetings in the poorest districts of the city. In 1909, with help from Baroness Yasnovskaya, he began to publish a weekly Christian illustrated magazine called *Vera* (*Faith*) - replaced a year later by the magazine *Gost* (*Guest*) - and set up a publishing house with an annual output of between 90 and 180 Christian books and brochures. He was also constantly petitioning the authorities both for permission to extend his own work and on behalf of others. He would go from the Department of Spiritual Affairs to the Parliamentary Commission for Religious Confessions, to the

Ministry of the Interior and to the State Council until his persistence was rewarded with a positive answer.

By 1910 William Fetler's ministry had grown so much that he decided to build a church. He received help from the Baptist Union and friends abroad and within two years the 'House of the Gospel' was completed. Its main auditorium was designed to seat 2000 - though it sometimes held as many as 3000 - and there were two smaller halls seating 600 and 400. It was the biggest evangelical church building in Russia.

The other major figure in St Petersburg evangelical circles was Ivan Prokhanov. At the end of 1904 a group of young people in the congregation led by Ivan Kargel approached Ivan Prokhanov with a view to organizing separate youth meetings. After some thought, and realizing the importance of the spiritual training of young people, he agreed to lead an association of Christian youth alongside the congregation. Their inaugural meeting took place in January 1905. Soon a new congregation was formed by bringing together the youth group and several of the small groups that had been meeting separately from the main congregation, and with whom Ivan had already worked in the early 1890s. A number of people also joined from Ivan Kargel's congregation. By 1908 there were 140 members and in November they were registered by the authorities as the St Petersburg Evangelical Christian Congregation. Prokhanov was elected chairman. One important difference between the two congregations was on the attitude to adult baptism. Ivan Prokhanov's congregation shared the Baptist view that only those baptized on profession of faith could become members and participate in communion, while Ivan Kargel's church held to the view taken by Colonel Pashkov that the issue of baptism should not be allowed to divide believers. All who sincerely believed in Jesus Christ as personal saviour and whose lives bore witness to spiritual rebirth were welcome as members and were admitted to communion. In this they differed not only from Ivan Prokhanov and the Baptist Union but also from most other evangelical congregations in Russia. Another difference was that Ivan Kargel's ministry focused on teaching, while Ivan Prokhanov emphasized an active Christian life.

While agreeing with the Baptist Union on the issue of baptism, Ivan Prokhanov nevertheless had a broad view of evangelical unity and a vision of spiritual renewal leading to a renewal in national life that contrasted with the apolitical attitude of Baptist leaders. During his years in England Ivan had come to believe that diversity of views within an overall acceptance of the basic principles of Protestant Christianity should not just be tolerated but welcomed. In 1896 he had taken part in the jubilee conference of the Evangelical Alliance in London. In his short speech there he had spoken of the need to listen to people outside the Church. This wider concern for society led him to form a Christian political party in 1905 four days after the proclamation of the October manifesto. The Union of Freedom, Truth and Peace, whose founder members were Ivan Prokhanov, Mennonite pastor Peter Friesen, and Vasili Pavlov and Nikolai Odintsov from the Baptists, supported a constitutional monarchy, popular representation with equal universal suffrage and basic rights and freedoms, including equal rights for all denominations and free schooling without class distinction. The Union aligned itself with the Constitutional Democrat Party and merged with it in March 1906.

In January 1906 Prokhanov launched a new magazine, called *The Christian*. It was aimed at 'all who seek the truth and love the Lord' and had three mottos: 'We preach Christ crucified' (I Corinthians 1:23), 'With one mind striving together for the faith of the gospel' (Philippians 1:27) and 'In essentials unity, in secondary things freedom and in everything love'. It had a free supplement, *Fraternal Leaflet*. Later Ivan Prokhanov published a magazine for children *The Children's Friend* and from 1909 a weekly devoted to socio-political themes from a Christian standpoint entitled *Morning Star*. In 1909 he also published a hymn book which contained many of his own compositions and remains one of the most popular collections of Russian hymns.

In August 1906 Ivan Prokhanov wrote to church leaders in St Petersburg proposing the creation of a Russian Evangelical Union. In his letter, he once more emphasized the importance of spiritual renewal for the renewal of society. The aims of the Union, as outlined by Ivan Prokhanov, were to promote spiritual revival in the Orthodox Church and religious renewal on evangelical principles, to link together all manifestations of spiritual vitality, to preach evangelical truth to the Russian people and the other peoples of Russia, to put evangelical teaching into practice and to promote evangelical unity. Anybody who supported the aims and agreed with basic evangelical beliefs could join; there would be freedom in questions of external expression of faith and of church government, so people belonging to different churches would be able to join. In these ways the Union was modelled on the practice of the Evangelical Alliance. In December a meeting of interested individuals issued an appeal signed among others by Ivan Prokhanov, Ivan Kargel and Baron Nikolai. In June 1907 Prokhanov drafted a charter which was approved and signed by a group of 27 Christians from various denominations and of social backgrounds ranging from generals to peasants. In May 1908 the charter was confirmed by the Ministry of the Interior and the Union's founding meeting was held in January 1909. Princess Lieven's son was elected president and Baron Nikolai vice-president. Prokhanov began to publish his magazine *The Christian* in the name of the Union.

Opening the meeting Baron Nikolai spoke of the importance of inner unity:

> The first task of the Evangelical Union and of its individual members is to be peacemakers. Lutherans, Baptists, Evangelical Christians, Orthodox and other believers cannot be members of the Evangelical Union if they have narrow views.

The formation of the Union was welcomed by many, including the leader of the Evangelical Molokans, Dr Baedeker's Armenian guide Patwakan Tarayants, P. M. Friesen and William Fetler. Some Baptists, such as Vasili Pavlov and Vasili Ivanov, were also sympathetic, but others in the Baptist Union leadership, including the president Dei Mazayev, were hostile.

Ivan Prokhanov was also active in developing Christian youth work. On New Year's Eve 1907 there was a united meeting of Christian youth groups in St Petersburg, at which three representatives of a Moscow youth group were also present. It was decided to try to form a national Christian youth movement. In April 1908 a conference attended by 18 representatives from eight cities agreed to create a Union of Christian Youth and elected Ivan Prokhanov as chairman. In May 1909 the second conference, held in St Petersburg, heard that many churches had set up youth groups. It was decided to seek legal registration under the name Evangelical Union of Christian Youth, and Ivan Prokhanov was once more elected chairman. A youth magazine, *Young Vineyard*, was launched, published by Prokhanov.

At the same time the Evangelical Christians were emerging as a separate denomination. In 1906 seven congregations identified themselves in this way. Over the next two years six more congregations were founded as a result of members leaving Baptist churches and groups were formed in at least seven other towns and villages. In 1909 a new Evangelical Christian congregation was established in Moscow and registered with the authorities, bringing together a number of different groups of Christians – followers of Colonel Pashkov, evangelicals who practised infant baptism, Baptists and Evangelical Christians who did not recognize ordained ministry. As with Ivan Prokhanov's Evangelical Christians in St Petersburg the congregation was led by an elected chairman. Some of the Baptists subsequently left to join the Moscow Baptist church founded later the same year.

In 1908 Evangelical Christians from nine congregations in Ukraine held a regional conference in Odessa and in spring 1909 representatives of ten congregations met in Yekaterinoslav. These conferences were largely consultative, with local churches deciding for themselves on matters concerning them directly, but the authority of the conference was recognized in the areas of mission and charity, which were seen as the task of the whole Church. It was agreed to take part in a national Evangelical Christian Congress called by Ivan Prokhanov.

The first All-Russian Evangelical Christian Congress assembled in September 1909 with 24 delegates from 18 churches. This congress saw its decisions as advisory rather than binding. A major preoccupation was Christian unity. An annual day of prayer and fasting for unity was proposed for Good Friday. Baptists were invited to join forces with the Evangelical Christians for the day of prayer and fasting, in youth work, publishing and Bible courses. Letters on unity were sent to the Russian, German, Estonian and Latvian Baptists and also to the Mennonite Brethren. There was also discussion of music in church and Sunday meetings for children. Six-week Bible courses for preachers were to be started in St Petersburg from December. After the business part of the congress participants were addressed by William Fetler and the American Methodist minister in St Petersburg.

At a second congress from 28 December 1910 to 4 January 1911, once more in St Petersburg under the chairmanship of Ivan Prokhanov, there were 47 delegates. The charter for the All-Russian Evangelical Christian Union drafted by Prokhanov was presented for discussion and approved. One of the main principles was congregational autonomy. Prokhanov's magazine *The Christian* became the Union's official publication and he was requested to give special attention to youth and children's work. The new Union was accepted as a member of the Baptist World Alliance and it and the Baptist Union both sent delegations to the 1911 Baptist World Congress in Philadelphia, at which Prokhanov was elected one of the ten BWA vice-presidents.

A year later, the third congress, held from 31 December 1911 to 4 January 1912, was attended by 91 delegates, among them Mykhailo Ratushny, now aged 81. Ivan Prokhanov had to report that he had been unable to organize the planned two-year Bible school or to secure the printing of a small-format edition of the Bible. As at the previous congress, there was a lot of discussion of the legal status of evangelical congregations, with delegates reporting continued harassment and persecution. For example, in Moscow, children from evangelical families were being denied places in grammar schools; the Congress empowered the Union to petition the authorities for permission to establish Christian schools.

The reversal of the freedoms granted in 1905 had begun in October 1910, when the Ministry of the Interior issued new regulations limiting the application of the decrees on religious liberty of 1905 and 1906. On various pretexts the authorities began to ban evangelical worship services. The Baptist Union and Evangelical Christian congresses were held under tight restrictions, and after January 1912 no more congresses could be held. As early as 1909 a criminal case was opened against William Fetler, Vasili Ivanov and others in Moscow for perverting Orthodox Christians and for delivering anti-Orthodox sermons. However, being under investigation did not prevent William Fetler from continuing his work in St Petersburg and building the House of the Gospel, and when the case finally came to court in February 1912 the judge threw it out. In other cases the authorities were more successful: in November 1912 the Vladikavkaz district court sentenced two evangelical preachers to two years' imprisonment, and a third to three years, on the same charges. Vasili Pavlov was twice put on trial during 1913 and together with two others was found guilty of persuading Orthodox Christians to join the Baptists in Odessa between 1907 and 1912. However, he spent a total of only one month and twenty days in prison. In January 1914 he was tried on similar charges for his missionary work in Blagoveshchensk, on the border with China in the Far East. His church in Odessa was closed, as were others in the cities of Moscow, Kharkov, Kiev and Voronezh, not to mention those in a number of villages. In St Petersburg, William Fetler's House of the Gospel was closed from September 1913 to January 1914 on the pretext that building regulations had been violated. In Moscow, the case against him was reopened.

This was also a sad period for the Orthodox Church. During 1905 there had been high hopes that the constitutional changes would allow the Church to become self-governing again and implement long-needed reforms. The Tsar had agreed in principle that a National Church Council should be called, but postponed setting a date for it until the situation in the country had stabilized. The prospect of a Council encouraged those who had already been pressing for reforms to put forward proposals for consideration by the Council and reopened the possibility of restoring the position of Patriarch as head of the Church. However, the Orthodox Church too became a victim of the attempts by the Tsar and his government to halt and reverse the process of reform. The promised Council was never convened and the repression of non-Orthodox denominations in the name of the Church was resumed.

This was the time of the rise in influence of the monk Grigori Rasputin, believed by the royal family to be able to heal the haemophilia of the heir to the throne, the Tsarevich Alexei, but seen by almost everybody else as a charlatan if not a sinister evil force. Rasputin's power extended to church appointments. Metropolitan Antoni of St Petersburg and procurator of the Holy Synod Lukyanov tried in vain to remove Rasputin from the court. Instead, Rasputin secured the appointment in 1911 of a new Procurator entirely under his influence and in 1912, on the death of Antoni, forced the Synod to appoint one of his friends as Metropolitan of St Petersburg. The public scandals surrounding Rasputin and the weakness of the Church in failing to oppose him seriously undermined the authority of the Orthodox Church and hierarchy. Even the conservative political parties were highly critical of the Church over Rasputin as they saw one of the last bastions of the old order being compromised and disgraced. This sorry episode ended only when an outraged aristocrat assassinated Rasputin at a dinner in the palace.

However, despite the submissiveness of the Orthodox hierarchy, the need for reform was still felt very strongly by some parish priests and lay people. One important development within Orthodox Christianity in these years was the formation of a circle of intellectuals who had turned from Marxism to Christianity. Four of them, Sergei Bulgakov, Nikolai Berdyayev, S. Frank and Pyotr Struve, were to make a lasting contribution to Russian Christian thought. Together with theologian Pavel Florensky, they published in 1909 a collection of essays called *Vekhi* (*Signposts*), in which they urged the Marxist and revolutionary intellectuals to consider a programme of reform on the basis of the Christian understanding of responsibility. They countered the atheist materialism typical of the Russian intellectuals at that time with a Christian view of man and the world. Their works were treasured by the young Orthodox intellectuals of the 1970s and 1980s who were seeking a Christian alternative to Communism. Today, in post-Communist Russia, they are as important as ever. As well as urging intellectuals to take Christianity seriously they also brought to the Orthodox Church a strong concern to encourage a Christian response to social issues, echoing the ideas of the earlier Religious-Philosophical Society. However, in the atmosphere of conservatism and intolerance that extended from the state into the Church, they must have felt themselves very much voices in the wilderness.

As the Tsar's government sought to reverse more and more of the 1905 reforms, the Baptist and Evangelical Christian Unions were prevented from holding congresses after January 1912 and even meetings of their national councils and boards were banned. Nevertheless, some projects continued. In July 1912 the Evangelical Christians were given permission to start in St Petersburg a two-year Bible course, which took its first intake of 19 students in February 1913. The Baptists hoped to open a seminary in Moscow, but did not have enough money to finance it and after money was collected at the Baptist World Congress in 1911 they were unable to secure permission. The Baptist Union magazine *The Baptist*, which was suspended during 1913, resumed publication in 1914. In summer 1913 another Baptist magazine, *Word of Truth*, had been launched as a private venture by Mikhail Timoshenko.

Despite the difficulties, growth continued and evangelical congregations were formed in new regions, in particular in Belorussia in the west, and in Central Asia, Siberia and the Far East. One of many remarkable stories of this time is that of Pavel Tikhomirov. Pavel was orphaned at the age of nine when his parents died of typhus during a long journey on the Trans-Siberian railway. They had sold up their farmstead in the village of Sosnovka in Belorussia and were travelling to settle virgin land made available by the government in Siberia. Pavel and his sister were taken to separate children's homes. Pavel soon determined to escape from the appalling conditions and try to find his sister. He managed to escape, but not knowing where to begin searching for his sister he fled into the forest. There he was found by members of a robber band who adopted him. By the time he was eighteen Pavel was a proficient robber and a leader of the band.

One day Pavel and some of his friends ambushed two men on a lonely road. Ignoring their pleas for mercy they killed them, but were disappointed to find that they were carrying just a few roubles. One of them had a small book which Pavel put in his pocket. Back at camp he discovered that it was a New Testament and began to read it. He was devastated by what he read; his early pangs of conscience about living by robbing others had long since subsided and he had become quite used to his way of life. Now he saw the full awfulness of it, and was convinced of God's judgement. His friends, seeing him in a state of shock, enquired what was wrong. As they read the Gospel together they not only realized their wickedness, but understood the possibility of forgiveness and repented. They decided that they must dissolve their robber band and begin new lives. Seven of them, led by Pavel, believed that the only proper course of action was to surrender themselves to the authorities and confess their crimes. Still armed to the teeth they went to see the public prosecutor, told him they were robbers but wished to confess their crimes and laid down their weapons. The prosecutor summoned the head of police who came with a detachment of armed soldiers. Pavel then told their story in detail and explained how reading the Gospel had turned their lives upside down. 'I want to serve God and people,' concluded Pavel. 'I will bear the punishment laid down by the law without complaint. We are now in your hands.' The prosecutor and all those present were visibly moved, some hardly able to suppress their tears. That night the prosecutor read the New Testament himself and by morning had decided to entrust his own life to Christ. He no longer had the heart to prosecute them and therefore resigned from his post.

These strange events became the talk of the town - and of the prison. The Orthodox prison chaplain demanded that the seven be held in isolation to prevent them spreading their beliefs to the other prisoners, but this did not stop their living faith from making a great impression on both prisoners and warders. At their trial the former prosecutor was counsel for the defence and urged leniency in view of their genuine repentance. Nevertheless they were sentenced to ten years' hard labour each, a punishment that they accepted as fully deserved and against which they did not appeal. In open court each of them spoke of their deep regret at the evil they had done to people and of the effect of the Gospel on their lives. Once again their simple testimony made a deep and lasting impression on many of those present. Everywhere Pavel went fellow prisoners were eager to hear his story and some became Christians too. Even the authorities noticed that Pavel's presence somehow calmed the convicts and that there was a marked change in the lives of some of them.

After some years Pavel was released under an amnesty. Together with another member of the band who had served his sentence in the same place, Pavel set off on foot westwards, hoping eventually to reach his home village. They told their story to everybody they met and many were quickened in their faith. In some villages they found evangelical believers with whom they joined in fellowship and Bible study. In one church they spoke to a large congregation at a Sunday morning service with such effect that several dozen people gave their lives to Christ. Arriving in one small town, as was their custom, they asked if there were any believers, and were directed to a neat cottage where they were warmly received by a young couple with two children. As they told their story the wife realized that Pavel was her long-lost brother. She herself had been adopted by a Christian widow, had become an active member of the church choir and had married a Christian husband. Now, with her husband's support, she decided to travel with Pavel to their home village and preach the Gospel there.

They travelled with Pavel's friend as far as Kiev and went on from there to Sosnovka, where they found that they still had uncles and aunts and other relatives. They all thought that the two children had died with their parents and were glad to welcome them into their homes. Conversation soon turned to discussion of the Christian faith and before long about one hundred villagers were gathering for worship at the home of one of Pavel's relatives. This development alarmed the priest, who summoned the police, telling them that some convict had come and was undermining the Orthodox faith. Pavel was arrested and charged with perverting Orthodox Christians. His sister had to return to Siberia without even being allowed to see him, but he wrote to her telling her not to grieve for him:

> I am very glad that no longer as a robber and a thief but as a Christian I am worthy to share the sufferings of my Saviour. I rejoice at this because in prison too there are many dying souls thirsting for the salvation which I will be able to proclaim to them in Christ.

Pavel spent a year in three different prisons before being sentenced to two years' exile in the Yenisei river district of Siberia. On release he returned to his sister's family and dedicated his life to evangelism.

Pavel Tikhomirov's story illustrates well the enthusiasm with which evangelicals shared their faith, the openness with which many people listened to them and the repressive response of the authorities even after the proclamation of religious tolerance and the right to leave the Orthodox Church.

While evangelical revival was spreading to the furthest corners of the Russian Empire, the Pentecostal renewal was beginning in many other countries. The Pentecostal movement struck a chord with many Russian evangelicals, for they were experiencing a similar spirit of revival. William

Fetler invited British Pentecostals to St Petersburg and formed a group called the Brotherhood of the Acts of the Apostles. The spread of Pentecostal ideas provoked a response from Ivan Prokhanov, whose magazine *The Christian* published in August 1908 an article entitled 'Should we expect another Pentecost?' critical of those who claimed to have special power as a result of receiving 'the blessing of Pentecost'. An earlier article criticized believers who tended 'to pay attention only to the first chapters of the Acts of the Apostles'. Pentecostal mission in the Russian Empire began in Finland in 1911 with visits from one of the pioneers of the Pentecostal movement in Europe, Thomas Ball Barratt of Oslo, in response to invitations from Finnish- and Swedish-speaking evangelical churches. Barratt also visited St Petersburg in 1911, but there appears to have been no attempt to bring the Pentecostal message in Russian until 1913, when Barratt began publishing his magazine in Russian.

In 1913 Russian Pentecostal groups began in the Evangelical Christian churches in Helsinki and Vyborg and soon established themselves as separate congregations. By the end of the year there was a congregation in St Petersburg too and in 1914 preachers were sent out to Baptist and Evangelical Christian congregations as far away as Tiflis, provoking warnings against them in the magazines published by both unions. The two leaders were Alexander Ivanov and Nikolai Smorodin. At an early stage they were influenced by the 'Jesus Only' Pentecostals, who believe that the apostles baptized in the name of Jesus only (as opposed to the Trinity); many also reject the Trinity, believing that Father, Son and Holy Spirit are all one person. Ivanov and Smorodin called themselves 'Evangelical Christians in the Spirit of the Apostles', and their followers still keep this name and their 'Jesus Only' and unitarian theology.

Andrew Urshan, the founder of the United Pentecostal Church in the USA and by birth an Assyrian Christian from Persia, visited them when travelling to and from Persia. On his return journey in 1915 he spent two months in St Petersburg – by then renamed Petrograd – holding Gospel meetings in their hall with attendances of up to 200. The converts were so eager to be baptized that baptisms had to be conducted in a hole in the ice on a frozen river. On one occasion the snow was about two feet deep. 'We went there,' recalled Urshan,

and a young lady, who was a sinner, imagined we were foolish, and fanatical, so she followed us to watch the 'fun'. When we reached the snowy spot, the brethren managed to shovel away the snow, and broke a large hole in the ice ... As soon as one young lady stepped into that cold water, God's power fell upon her, and when that young sinner woman saw God's power on her, and others being blessed, she believed too. God's power came upon her to such an extent that she fell on her knees into the deep snow. Rising, she came up running into the frozen stream to be baptized.

The outbreak of the First World War made matters worse for the evangelicals; as non-Orthodox, especially the Baptists with their strong associations with the German churches, they came under suspicion, despite their immediate offers of help in tending the wounded. The members of William Fetler's House of the Gospel in Petrograd set up a hospital in the church, making available the large hall and six apartments; women from the church helped with the care of the wounded. Several other congregations followed their example, either making space available in the church or renting premises for use as hospitals and staffing them with volunteers. A Good Samaritan fund was established by Baptist and Evangelical Christian congregations which made grants for setting up hospitals, sent aid to the families of men killed and wounded and distributed Bibles and Christian literature to troops on their way to the front. In the first four months of the war almost 15,000 roubles were collected. Latvian Baptists organized sewing groups to make warm underwear for the soldiers at the front, and sent two young men to serve as medical orderlies on the battlefield.

However, rumours were spread that Baptists were German agents. According to one rumour Kaiser Wilhelm had made donations to the Russian Baptists, and a booklet published in Petrograd in 1916 entitled *The Baptist movment - a tool for the Germanization of Russia* alleged that the establishment of the Baptists in Russia was planned by the German high command. The Evangelical Christians' Bible School was closed and a number of evangelical preachers were exiled to Siberia without court proceedings, among them Mikhail Timoshenko, whose magazine *Word of Truth* was banned. The authorities withdrew their recognition of William Fetler as pastor of the Petrograd Baptist Church and intended to send him to Siberia. The intervention of highly placed friends ensured that he was banished from Russia instead and sent abroad. His younger brother Robert was exiled to Yakutia in eastern Siberia. Vasili Pavlov was sentenced to eight months' imprisonment for publishing a booklet on baptism and in 1916

Ivan Prokhanov was charged with organizing a revolutionary union (the All-Russian Union of Evangelical Christians), though the case never came to court. In Siberia the order was given to close all evangelical churches and elsewhere services were placed under strict surveillance.

Although suspicions of pro-German sympathies were unfounded, they were fuelled by the evangelicals' strong pacifist tendency. This was manifested in the preference for offering humanitarian aid to the victims of the war rather than active support for the war effort and also in several hundred refusals to serve in the army. From the summer of 1914 up to April 1917, 837 refusals were recorded, of whom 581 were identified as 'sectarians' (mostly Baptists, Evangelical Christians and Seventh Day Adventists and also some followers of Tolstoy); the remainder were not identified by denomination. On a warship in Helsinki in 1915 several Pentecostal converts among the sailors were arrested for refusing to take their positions during an alert and were sentenced to hard labour. Further investigation of the incident led to the arrest of Alexander Ivanov and three other Pentecostal leaders in November 1915; they were exiled to Central Asia.

PART II

Seventy Years
of Communism

FIVE

The Fire of Revolution

'WELL, NOW WE'LL begin a new life,' commented some of the demonstrators who eagerly accepted the gospels offered by members of the Christian student group in Moscow in March 1917. As the revolutionary crowd thronged through the streets in the city centre, full of joy and optimism at the collapse of the old order, the Christian students mingled with the people, handing out small gospels. In those heady days there was complete freedom of speech, the repressive tsarist police simply melted away and the students posted magazines on walls and billboards challenging people to build a new life with Christ. Vladimir Martsinkovsky, a leader of the Student Christian Movement, travelled the country lecturing on 'The Gospel and Freedom' and 'Revolution of the Spirit', attracting large audiences. In his home village in western Ukraine he argued that the new social conditions and the new slogans could only change lives for the better if they were combined with the enlightenment of the Gospel and spiritual renewal. 'Do you understand what I am saying?' he asked his peasant audience. 'We understand and approve,' answered one of the old men.

When the Tsar abdicated in February 1917 few regretted his departure. Even the Orthodox Church declined to come to the defence of the monarchy, turning down the suggestion of the Procurator of the Holy Synod on 27 February that it should condemn the assumption of power by the Provisional Government. One of the new government's first acts was to amnesty all political and religious prisoners. Ivan Prokhanov gave immediate support to the Provisional Government and formed a new Christian-Democrat party, whose slogan was 'Strength and Justice, but above all Love'. The programme called for a democratic republic 'as the most perfect form of state administration and the one that corresponds most closely to Christ's teaching'. In April Vasili Pavlov and Mikhail Timoshenko outlined Baptist expectations of the new government, including separation of Church and state, freedom of speech and assembly and of the press, equality for all citizens regardless of race or religion, freedom of worship and preaching for all denominations and the abolition of laws punishing religious activity. Ivan Prokhanov also called for the separation of Church and state, freedom from state control of the Orthodox Church and equality for all denominations.

Although the Provisional Government was too preoccupied with the war and the growing support for revolutionary parties to take legislative action on religion, there were in practice no restrictions on evangelicals. On return from exile Mikhail Timoshenko resumed publication of *Word of Truth*, and other suspended magazines also began to appear again. Both the Baptist and Evangelical Christian unions were able to hold congresses. Evangelistic campaigns were organized in many cities, with open-air preaching in squares and parks and on the streets as well as in halls, lecture theatres and pubs. A street mission was led in Petrograd by Alexander Karev, a young Evangelical Christian preacher later to become general secretary of the USSR Evangelical Christian-Baptist Union. In Kiev a tent mission was established. Groups of Christian soldiers formed in many places; the group in Moscow was particularly active, holding over forty open meetings for soldiers in a three-month period in the Baptist and Evangelical Christian churches and in a public hall, with a total attendance of over 4,000. Also in Moscow the Student Christian Movement organized public lectures which were well attended.

The Orthodox Church was given the freedom to run its own affairs, though it remained the official Church. The Holy Synod announced in April that a national Council would be convened in August. The last holder of the office of Procurator of the Holy Synod was instructed by the government to assist the Church in calling the Council, hand over his powers to the Council and abolish his own post. The Council opened on 2 August 1917 in the Uspensky Cathedral in the Kremlin in Moscow and was widely representative, with priests and lay people elected from every diocese, and with an absolute majority from the laity. The Council considered extensive proposals for reform, but was overtaken by events and was unable to complete its deliberations and implement many of the proposals. On 26 October, the day after the Bolsheviks seized power in Petrograd, and as Bolshevik forces were already shelling the Kremlin in Moscow, the Council met in St Saviour's Cathedral (later blown up and its site converted into an open-air swimming pool) and elected Metropolitan Tikhon as Patriarch. The new Bolshevik government recognized his election and gave permission for his enthronement in the Uspensky Cathedral – the last service there for over 70 years.

The Bolsheviks acted swiftly, however, to undermine the power of the Orthodox Church with a decree on 23 January 1918 proclaiming the separation of Church and state and Church and school and nationalizing all church property. At a stroke the Orthodox Church was deprived of the lands from which much of its income was derived, and on which the monasteries were particularly dependent, and lost its network of parish schools and the right of priests to teach the catechism in government schools. The Church issued instructions that any attempts to seize its property should be resisted and placed an anathema on all members and officials of the new government who attacked the Church. There were some violent clashes, but the Bolsheviks were soon too preoccupied with their own survival in the civil war to pay much attention to enforcing their will on the Church. For the time being most churches remained open.

For the evangelicals and other non-Orthodox denominations the decree was initially less damaging. The evangelicals in particular had little property and no schools and the separation of Church and state had been one of their main demands of the Provisional Government. They no longer needed to fear persecution instigated by the Orthodox Church and for the first time in Russian history enjoyed full equality with all other denominations and faiths. The first Soviet Russian constitution (July 1918) provided for freedom of conscience, defined as 'freedom of religious and anti-religious propaganda'. As victims of Tsarist repression – some of them had been in exile with revolutionaries – they were regarded at first by the Bolsheviks as natural allies who would not want the old order to be restored in Russia. Indeed, the evangelicals welcomed not only the separation of Church and state but also some of the social experiments. Ivan Prokhanov as early as 1903 had established a Christian agricultural cooperative in the Crimea, a project that was short-lived. Now the formation of communes and cooperatives was a plank of Bolshevik policy, and evangelicals were willing to work along these lines. The first evangelical agricultural communes were established in 1918 in various parts of Russia. Ivan Prokhanov wrote an article in his paper *The Morning Star* in which he described how to set up a commune and published the charter of the first commune. The Baptist Union also supported the principle of agricultural communes and small manufacturing cooperatives.

All the evangelical activity which had begun during 1917 continued with little hindrance and met with an encouraging response. The dramatic political changes and the upheaval of civil war made people open to the Gospel in a new way. However, the chaos of civil war also disrupted the work and prevented national coordination. The whole of Siberia was under the control of anti-Bolshevik forces, whose leader, Admiral Kolchak, under Orthodox pressure ordered the closure of all evangelical churches. The large Baptist church building in Omsk, where the Siberian branch of the Russian Baptist Union was based, was taken over by Kolchak's forces and used as stables. The churches in Ukraine were cut off completely, and for a time suffered at the hands of an anti-Bolshevik government which sought to restore the privileged position of the Orthodox Church. During this brief period of Ukrainian independence Ukrainian Baptists held a conference in Kiev in October 1918 and formed their own Baptist Union. In the Caucasus, Baptists from Georgia, Armenia and Azerbaijan established a separate union in 1919, and during the short-lived Far Eastern Republic in 1921 there was also an independent Baptist Union.

Travel was almost impossible. A Finnish missionary, Nikolai Poysti, got permission to travel with his wife and baby from Petrograd to Tsaritsyn (later Stalingrad) in 1918. The steamer along the Volga reached Kazan before turning back to Nizhni Novgorod, where it waited for hostilities further down the river to cease. Eventually, with food running out, the passengers persuaded the local Bolshevik commissar to let them continue their journey. They were boarded by armed Bolsheviks and soon came under fire. Poysti realized that their steamer was being used as a shield to protect the ship that Trotsky – then commander-in-chief of the Red Army – was using as his command post. Despite the protests of the Bolshevik commissar on board, the passengers signalled to Trotsky's ship and eventually he moved alongside and gave permission for a boat to land to fetch food. At nightfall the steamer proceeded downstream and all the passengers were forced to disembark at a lonely landing stage. There was some shooting and first their steamer and then Trotsky's boat sailed away. By dawn they realized that the Red Army had retreated; the Poystis floated downstream on a raft to Samara, which was now under anti-Bolshevik control. They never did reach Tsaritsyn. As the family moved further east, train journeys that in normal times took one or two days lasted for up to a month.

In these conditions the Russian Baptist Union leadership was unable to meet together and therefore in 1919 the two board members based in Moscow, Mikhail Timoshenko and Vasili Pavlov's son Pavel, formed a temporary board to coordinate the work of churches in the parts of central Russia still under Bolshevik control.

The civil war also brought new dangers to evangelical preachers. In autumn 1919 the members of a tent mission team in Ukraine led by a Mennonite named Jacob Dyck were captured by a band of followers of the anarchist leader Makhno and beheaded. The Bolsheviks, too, were often filled with hatred for religion and in the battle zones were inclined to regard all believers as enemies. In Millerovo, in eastern Ukraine, Cornelius Martens, a member of the Baptist Union Council, was arrested as soon as the Bolsheviks recaptured the town. He had already encountered problems with Bolshevik local authorities before they lost the area to anti-Bolshevik forces. He had planned a series of evangelistic meetings in towns where there were no churches, but had been prevented from hiring halls and had to gather his audiences in the open air.

Now, as an evangelist and a businessman, Cornelius was on the wanted list. Along with his father-in-law and five others he was taken out into the steppe to be shot, but for some reason they were brought back to the prison. His father-in-law was released the next day but Martens was held in a cell with seventeen others. He was, however, allowed to keep his Bible and was able to read it to his fellow-prisoners and pray with them. One day a group of them were taken out to dig a mass grave for thirteen men, but the ground was frozen so hard they were unable to dig deep enough. That night thirteen of his cellmates were shot. Some nights later his own turn came. Martens calmly told his executioners: 'I do not fear to die, for I shall be going home to see Him in whom I believe; but if the Lord has not decided that my hour has come, you cannot do me any harm.' The secret police chief shouted: 'This time I am going to prove to you that your God will not deliver you out of my hands.' He lifted his revolver to fire, but his arm seemed paralysed. After the third attempt to shoot, the chief's fury gave way to fear. 'What has this man been condemned for?' he asked. He was told: 'Don't you know, he's a Baptist? Don't you see that God is fighting for him?' Martens quietly asked if he could go home and he and two other Christians were released. A month later he was once more arrested and sentenced to death. Again he was sent out to dig his own grave, but as he and 48 others were led out at night to be shot he made a dash for freedom. Others followed his example, and in the confusion seventeen got away.

For evangelicals the civil war raised very sharply the issue of conscientious objection to military service. Mennonites had a long pacifist tradition going right back to their roots, and had been granted the right when they settled in Russia not to have to serve in the army. This privilege was recognized by every Tsar. Other evangelicals always had a pacifist minority, but the mood of pacifism was strengthened by the slaughter of the First World War. When faced with the possibility of killing fellow Russians in the civil war, evangelicals became overwhelmingly pacifist. To the surprise of many, the Bolsheviks accepted the sincerity of the Christian pacifists; they believed that the religious minorities were inclined to be more sympathetic to their regime than to the old order, and therefore did not wish to alienate them. In January 1919 the Bolshevik government issued a decree allowing exemption from military service on religious grounds. Mennonites and Dukhobors, along with followers of Tolstoy, were automatically exempted in recognition of their indisputable pacifist traditions. Other evangelicals were able to apply to the courts for exemption on grounds of conscience and many did so successfully. The courts were advised by a United Council of Religious Communities and Groups with two or three representatives of each Nonconformist denomination. Pacifists could either be sent to serve as medical orderlies or be exempted altogether.

However, on the battlefronts the right to conscientious objection was not always easy to secure. The president of the United Council complained in a memorandum to Lenin, Trotsky and Bonch-Bruyevich that during 1919, 25 young men were sentenced to death for refusing to serve in the Red Army. In twelve cases the Council had full details, including names and dates. Six of these young Christians were shot on orders of the Smolensk province revolutionary tribunal on 24 December 1919, almost a full year since the decree recognizing conscientious objection was issued. One of them wrote to his family:

> My dear wife, don't weep for me . . . love all your neighbours, harbour no evil, live in harmony with all my family and teach my and your children to do the same. I'm only sorry I didn't have the chance to say farewell to you, my wife and children. Today, 24

December, I am feeling very subdued, because these are the last
hours of my life. And yet I am in good spirits because I know that
I am dying for the truth.

The civil war also caused economic chaos with transport disrupted and
industry in a state of collapse. There was rampant inflation. In 1917 an
evangelist could be supported for a year for 1200-1500 roubles. By October
1919 the Evangelical Christians needed to raise 600,000 roubles to support
their fifty evangelists (12,000 roubles each) and by December 1921 two
million roubles were needed as the monthly support for each evangelist.

Despite all the difficulties the civil war period was a time of great
opportunities. Vladimir Martsinkovsky, who had begun to work full time
for the Student Christian Movement in 1913 at the invitation of Baron
Nikolai, continued giving public lectures, both in universities and for the
general public. His basic theme was the need for revolution in society to
be accompanied by a spiritual revolution. He told his audiences that
freedom can lead to anarchy if it is given to people motivated by selfishness
and base instincts. It can be properly used only by a person who has been
renewed morally, with new desires, new habits and new understanding of
personality, duty and social welfare. Only the Gospel contains these ideals
in perfect form, and only Christ makes a person able to put them into
practice through new birth into a new life.

Early in 1918 Vladimir spoke on this theme in a large village. The meeting
was well advertised and was held in a large hall above a tearoom. The hall
seated 400, but a thousand squeezed in, with the same number downstairs
hoping to hear something of the lecture. Suddenly word came from
downstairs that the ceiling was beginning to crack and Martsinkovsky saw
that the huge brick-built stove was coming away from the wall threatening
to crush those standing near it. The building was evacuated; undeterred
the audience persuaded Vladimir to speak to them in the village church,
and everybody reassembled at 9.00 the next morning. After the lecture
the people pressed the priest to conduct prayers of thanks that they had
been saved from disaster the previous evening. Then they urged Vladimir
to speak again in the afternoon, as many people had come a long way to
hear him. Finally, in the evening he gave his interrupted lecture on the
Gospel and freedom, in another tearoom, this time with admission strictly
limited to 400 by ticket only. Even the owner of the first tearoom was
content; with his upstairs hall unsafe, he would avoid having Red Army
soldiers billeted there!

Vladimir was invited to give lectures to students and young people in many places within travelling distance of Moscow. In the city of Vladimir he was supposed to speak under the auspices of the department of culture of the city executive committee - the Bolshevik-dominated local government. However, on arrival he learnt that the lecture had been blocked by an atheist teacher. Instead his friends managed to book a hall at the railway depot. They wrote posters and stuck them with home-made glue on advertising pillars along the main street. When they arrived to get the hall ready it was already overflowing; people passed forward their questions on bits of paper and after the lecture there was a lively discussion. The next day there was a favourable report in the local newspaper. Invited to Yuryev-Polsky, near Vladimir, he was detained by the police for pasting up posters without permission, but was rescued in time by one of his hosts.

In the industrial town of Ivanovo-Voznesensk Vladimir's lecture was arranged in a theatre seating a thousand people. As he arrived he saw a huge queue of people trying to buy tickets winding round the square. At the end of the lecture he invited any who were interested to come the next day for a more detailed study of a Bible passage. They expected a maximum of fifty or a hundred people, but once more the theatre was filled to capacity. Following this, Vladimir was invited to give a special lecture for youth, which was arranged at the girls' school. This time the authorities intervened, and cancelled the meeting by putting the school under quarantine. Instead, the 500 young people who had turned up set off in a procession to find another venue, thus turning the occasion into a public witness on the streets of this leftist town.

Many of those involved in the Student Christian Movement, including Vladimir Martsinkovsky, were Orthodox Christians. They received a mixed response from the Orthodox Church. In Samara, where they held a congress of student Christian groups in spring 1918, they approached the local bishop to explain their work. Unable to talk with them himself, he nominated a group of priests to meet them. One was a 'missionary' responsible for working against evangelicals and other 'sectarians'. He said that study of the Scriptures by lay people always led only to heresies and sects. The students responded that they wanted to work with the blessing of the Church and under the guidance of its pastors. One of the students, a graduate of the St Petersburg Theological Academy, spoke forcefully of the responsibility of pastors to their flock from Ezekiel: 'You are doomed, you shepherds of Israel! You take care of yourselves, but never tend the sheep.' (Ezekiel 34:2). As a result of the meeting several of the priests expressed their support and subsequently invited Vladimir Martsinkovsky and other student movement leaders to preach in their churches. Vladimir on another occasion met the 'missionary' privately, and reminded him of the words of one of the most respected of the church fathers, John Chrysostom: 'heresies and a corrupt life spring from ignorance of the Scriptures'. One of those who gave support was the priest at the Cathedral who was a very open and tolerant person. He had once been approached by a parishioner who asked whether it was permissible to go to Baptist meetings. He responded with a question: 'What do they do at their meetings?' 'They read the Word of God.' 'Well, that's a good thing. Of course you can go.'

Vladimir Martsinkovsky had many friends in the evangelical churches, including Vasili Pavlov, by now an old man. He thought extensively about baptism and came to the conclusion that baptism should follow commitment to Christ. He wrote a paper on the subject which he presented to the Patriarch. In a personal interview he asked the Patriarch if he could be baptized on profession of faith in the Orthodox Church. The Patriarch replied that the Orthodox Church recognized only one baptism and could therefore not rebaptize him. Half-joking, the Patriarch suggested Vladimir should go to the Baptists, but nevertheless requested him to prepare material for discussion by the Council. Later, while visiting Mennonite friends, Vladimir requested baptism, to which they readily agreed, but he never formally left the Orthodox Church to join another denomination.

For a short time in 1918 Samara was the seat of the anti-Bolshevik government consisting of some members of the Constituent Assembly. Vladimir Martsinkovsky had been a member of the prison philanthropy committee and used this position to try to give talks in the prison. In fact, his efforts only came to fruition after the Red Army had reoccupied the city. At Christmas he received permission to speak to the non-political prisoners and to take a choir into the prison. In Samara he was invited to give one of the inaugural lectures when the Pedagogical Institute became a university, and subsequently spoke often there and in public halls.

Nikolai Poysti, stranded in Samara, and staying with a Christian doctor, Yuri Grachev, who had been in the student Christian circle in St Petersburg, attended one of Vladimir Martsinkovsky's lectures and met there a representative of the American YMCA, who invited him to take charge of the development of YMCA work in Samara. A centre was opened with a restaurant and library; relief work for the needy, regardless of political affiliation, was accompanied by evangelistic lectures. Poysti was astonished at the response. He wrote:

> The Russians as a nation have never been morally lower than other nations. It was the World War and the Revolution that lowered them . . . Every country that was drawn into that terrible war suffered like results. At the 'Y' we decided to hold special lectures on this topic. The first and all the succeeding meetings were so crowded that we could not find in our spacious hall room enough to accommodate the eager listeners. One such lecture was divided into two parts. During the first half a medical doctor spoke on social diseases; in the second half I addressed the assemblage on the subject 'How can a youth safeguard his purity' . . . At the end of my talk I pointed them to the living Christ who gives us victory over all sin. I saw tear-filled eyes. Not intending to hold an after-service, I went to my study immediately, but that was not to be – the young men crowded into my study asking for further explanations. Most of them were students from the University of Samara. I had not expected to find such a response in their hearts.

As the Bolsheviks advanced the Poystis moved further and further east, first to Yekaterinburg in the Urals, then to Irkutsk in Siberia and finally to Vladivostok on the Pacific coast. Alongside the YMCA relief work Poysti was able to continue evangelism in personal conversations and in public meetings and services. In Yekaterinburg a man came to his first meeting, saying he was the only evangelical Christian in the city. There were many opportunities to speak to soldiers and to prisoners of war returning from Germany, who were recipients of YMCA relief, and the nucleus of an evangelical congregation was formed. In Irkutsk, Poysti had the opportunity to conduct a Bible School programme for 25-30 preachers at the Baptist church.

Another of Vladimir Martsinkovsky's initiatives in Samara was to begin a Sunday School for the street children, who had grown more numerous following the deprivations of war and then civil war. They were allowed to use a school building for two hours on a Sunday. It was so popular (and not just among street children) that a second Sunday School was opened in another part of the city, and 300 children attended regularly. In the corner of the classroom there was an ikon of Christ blessing the children; following Orthodox custom the children faced the ikon when they prayed. One Sunday, after the Bolsheviks had reoccupied the city, the ikon was missing: in accordance with the Bolshevik policy of separation of Church and school, all religious items had been removed from the schools. Some of the children asked how they could pray when there was no ikon. One of the Sunday School teachers was blind and said to them: 'Children, what am I to do? I'm blind, so I cannot see any ikons. Does that mean I cannot pray?' After some thought, one boy replied: 'God is in the soul.' 'There you are,' said the teacher, 'Jesus says: "God is spirit" and the Bible says nobody has ever seen God.' The children understood, and prayed with their usual enthusiasm, having learnt from the Bolsheviks' move to secularize the schools that they could turn to God in any circumstances.

The Bolsheviks began to sponsor anti-religious talks and debates. The question of God's existence, and the value and relevance of Christian morality and ethics, were hotly debated in the press, and at lectures and public meetings, and were of greater interest to many than political and economic issues. Vladimir Martsinkovsky inevitably found himself clashing with proponents of atheism. In the winter of 1918-19 in Samara he gave a series of lectures on ethics and religion, which were so popular that students from the university petitioned for a course on ethics to be included in the syllabus of the philosophy faculty. The professorial council, eager to demonstrate its academic independence of the Bolsheviks, voted to appoint Vladimir as lecturer in ethics. One topic that was popular with the students was brotherhood. Vladimir argued that people can become brothers only when they have found a common father through Christ. On one occasion he spoke on this theme at the post office club, but afterwards the subject was banned on the grounds that 'the lecture is not in the spirit of the times'.

His outspokenness was not without dangers. At a hall at the university he gave a talk entitled 'Can we live without Christ?', in which he denounced the authorities for promoting atheism.

> The atheist can say only that in his experience and in his soul there is no God. But he has no logical or moral right to assert that God does not exist at all or in the experience of others. To proclaim that there is no God is a criminal lie. By depriving the people of faith in God, you are destroying its soul, cutting off the branch on which you are sitting and undermining the basis of the social ideal

which you preach - thus you are yourselves promoting the failure
and collapse of socialism in Russia.

After the lecture Vladimir was approached by a man in military uniform
who asked him: 'Comrade lecturer, how did you get permission to give
this lecture? Do you have permission?' Despite showing their permit from
the police, Vladimir and two of his friends were obliged to accompany
him to the Cheka, the political police, accused of agitation against the
Soviet authorities. After spending the night in an improvised basement cell
they were released, but Vladimir had to sign an undertaking not to leave
Samara without permission, and to come immediately to the Cheka if he
was summoned. He was, however, still allowed to give lectures.

In Moscow, Vladimir Martsinkovsky several times debated with Anatoli
Lunacharsky, the People's Commissar for Education and the Bolsheviks'
foremost anti-religious speaker at the time. After hearing him lecture for
the first time, on 'Why one should not believe in God', Vladimir sent up
a note asking to be allowed to speak. When Lunacharsky put the matter
to the vote the majority of the audience of some three thousand approved
giving Vladimir ten minutes. He criticized Lunacharsky for concentrating
on primitive religions, which he agreed were irrational, and not saying
anything about Christianity, which was a faith shared by many great
scientists. He concluded:

> Our life itself, full of sufferings, is a testimony against godlessness.
> Without God we cannot create and generate. We can only destroy.
> Without faith we perish, and Christ's words 'Without me you can
> do nothing' are confirmation of this.

Lunacharsky proposed a full debate, in which he would reply to his
opponents. When the debate was arranged, Lunacharsky said he did not
have time to come, so Vladimir lectured on 'Why one should believe in
God' and then threw the floor open to other speakers. Six spoke against
religion and thirteen for.

After a while posters appeared announcing another of Lunacharsky's
lectures, with the same title, but Vladimir was surprised not to see his
name included in the list of opponents. He arrived early and was told:
'We wanted to invite you, but we couldn't find your address.' 'In that case,
you can include me now,' replied Vladimir. Lunacharsky was over an hour
late, apologizing that he had been delayed on government business, and

proposed that a chairman be elected. Much to his own surprise, Vladimir was proposed from the floor and elected by a clear majority. Lunacharsky's atheist views were opposed by six speakers, including the Chief Rabbi and Vladimir Martsinkovsky himself. As chairman, Vladimir received notes from the floor. One of them reproached Lunacharsky for his atheist 'sermon': 'I came here with a crushed spirit, and I am leaving feeling even more crushed.' It was signed: 'A seamstress'. Vladimir passed the note to Lunacharsky, who read it and then threw it away.

On the next occasion, Lunacharsky was so late that Vladimir, who wanted to speak after him in order to respond to his points, had no opportunity to speak at all. There was a sharp protest that Lunacharsky was constantly late, thus depriving the opponents of atheism of the right of reply. He was also asked to speak more respectfully of religion, and subsequently he began to speak positively of Christ as a person, calling him one of the first socialists. Another prominent lecturer was V. Posse, who had made a public conversion to atheism, having earlier spoken in favour of Christianity. One day Vladimir Martsinkovsky saw an advertisement for a lecture by Posse on the theme 'With or without God', and discovered that he was listed as an opponent, although nobody had asked him if he wanted to speak. Posse spoke very sincerely: 'I renounced faith in God . . . Don't think that it was easy for me . . . I often don't sleep at night.' The other opponents in the debate attacked Posse sharply, but Vladimir spoke more gently: 'Atheism is an illness of the spirit . . . That, incidentally, is why it causes sleeplessness . . . And since it is an illness I do not want to condemn it, but to sympathize with it, as one sympathizes with any suffering.' Afterwards Posse thanked him very warmly for his words.

As well as erudite lecturers such as Lunacharsky and Posse there were also speakers who were much more primitive and simply mocked religion and religious people. Christians of humble background were among those who spoke for religion, and their straightforward and practical faith disarmed the arguments of their opponents. The harder the atheists tried to promote their views the more people became interested in religion and it was gradually realized that the debates were counterproductive: they merely stimulated interest in religion. The debates were phased out, but for a while Christian lectures could continue. In spring 1920 Vladimir Martsinkovsky began a series of lectures on 'Science and Religion' in a student canteen in central Moscow, but was unable to complete it as the local Communist cell got his talks banned. Later in 1920, when he returned to Samara, he was able at first to lecture in the University, but his talks were the target of scurrilous press attacks. His replies to the papers were not printed. The Student Christian Movement had been barred from holding meetings on University premises, but as a lecturer of the University Vladimir was entitled to give lectures. Before returning to Moscow in autumn 1920, he planned three open lectures, two of which took place in the University. However, for the third he could not secure a University auditorium, and it was held in the Cathedral instead.

At this time Vladimir Martsinkovsky noted an increasing interest in the end of the world, the Antichrist and the second coming of Christ. He began to speak on the theme 'Christ coming in glory'. In the godlessness and immorality of Soviet Russia people clearly felt the spirit of the Antichrist. At one lecture a question was passed up and read out by the chairman: 'Comrade lecturer, is Lenin not the Antichrist? According to the Scriptures the Antichrist will take his seat in the temple like God. And Lenin is in the Russian temple, i.e. the Kremlin.' An expectant hush fell over the hall, as the thought flashed through Vladimir's mind whether the question was a provocation; he prayed for wisdom as he answered:

> Lenin is not great enough to be the Antichrist. The Antichrist will perform miracles, but Lenin has no miraculous powers over the famine. In speaking of the temple, the word of God means the temple in Jerusalem and not some other temple. But if you mean not the Antichrist himself, but the spirit of the Antichrist, i.e. opposition to Christ, then that applies to each of us who is not with Christ; for Christ said: 'Anyone who is not for me is really against me; anyone who does not help me gather is really scattering.' Thus everybody who is not with Christ has the spirit of the Antichrist within him.'

The bloodshed and cruelty of the civil war caused many to become disillusioned with revolutionary change, including communists and Red Army soldiers. In 1920 Cornelius Martens was a travelling evangelist in the Caucasus. Everywhere the audiences were so large that at the close of every meeting he would announce a special meeting only for those who wanted to seek peace and a new life in Christ. Often the Communists who became Christians were the ones who personally had been involved in massacres. One Communist confessed to having murdered thousands of innocent people and told Cornelius: 'The day before yesterday I became firmly convinced of the Gospel and have firmly resolved to follow the Lord and will not share any longer in the life and filth of these men, and I will not wear the sword any more. I believe in Jesus and believe He has forgiven me my sins.' He was expelled from the Communist Party, but as a result of his conversion five other Communists and many Red Army soldiers also found Christ. Cornelius had to flee for his life from that place and some of the converted Communists were arrested and imprisoned. In another place a teacher denounced Cornelius, telling him: 'Be quiet, for uneducated people can offer nothing to me.' But the next day the same man returned and asked: 'What must I do to find peace? For 25 years I have been a teacher in St Petersburg, an atheist, and have instilled the atheistic poison into thousands of students. Is there any possibility of grace left for me?' Cornelius assured him that God could forgive even him.

In the next town the authorities allowed the use of a hall seating two thousand, but even this was insufficient for the crowds who flocked to hear Cornelius. So it was announced that only those would be admitted who were prepared to give themselves to the Lord. Not surprisingly, many who attended became Christians, including many Red Army soldiers. Another evening two Red Army colonels were present. Of the whole audience only they and a few others remained unmoved. At five minutes to midnight Cornelius addressed them: 'Do you wish to be lost eternally? You have five minutes left.' To their laughter he responded: 'Your laughing shall be turned into weeping; now we will close the meeting.' During the closing hymn first one colonel and then the other stood up and throwing their revolvers on the ground came forward to ask: 'What shall we do to be saved?' After praying with Cornelius both found peace. When later they were baptized, the banks of the river were filled with Red Army soldiers. Here too the Communists attempted to arrest Cornelius and one of his helpers, but they escaped to a Cossack village where they continued their ministry.

The change of mood of many Communists and Red Army officers is illustrated by the story of Jacob Vagar. Brought up as Lutheran in Latvia, he trained as a teacher in Russia and was called up into the Russian army, where his education before long brought him promotion. In the First World War he was a lieutenant, and when the Bolsheviks seized power he willingly transferred to the Red Army, for he was thoroughly disillusioned with the Tsarist government that had so mismanaged the war, and the Communist slogans of equality, justice and brotherhood appealed to his idealism and his experience as a member of an oppressed nation.

It was not difficult for him to accept the atheism expected of a Red Army officer, for he saw the Lutheran Church as a tool of the oppressive class. He was full of enthusiasm to make the Communist ideal reality. For those who were loyal to the new regime everything was permitted – there was no sin – and Jacob was not slow to indulge in the pleasures of the world.

But Jacob also saw at first hand the brutality of Communism in those violent times and the greed and selfishness that was let loose in its name. He grew uneasy and dissatisfied. His life had lost its purpose and meaning. Like many others he became disillusioned with the new regime and with Communism and atheism, and, like many others, saw suicide as the only way out. One night, in despair, he was ready to take his own life. He already had his revolver in his hand, when an inner voice spoke to him: 'You have tried everything in the world, and nothing satisfies you. One thing you have not tried. You have not tried living according to the Gospel. Try it and you will be satisfied.' Childhood memories flooded back, and verses learnt in Sunday School came to him. Putting aside his revolver, he rummaged in his trunk for the Latvian New Testament his mother had given him when he left home and which he had never read. Now he prayed that God would reveal himself through his Word and began to read. It was not easy. For four months he read and prayed, seeking the truth, until one Sunday, reading alone in his room, he came to faith. He soon realized the incompatibility of his allegiance to Christ and his oath of allegiance to atheistic communism. He could not keep his faith a secret, he wanted to share the joy in salvation that he had experienced. For an officer to speak openly of his faith would be considered counter-revolutionary, but he could not simply leave the Red Army. He therefore applied for discharge on grounds of his Christian faith. When his case came before the court he convinced the judges of his sincerity and, with the civil war drawing to a close, he received his discharge. Alone in Odessa, he sought out fellow-Christians and soon found a small Baptist church which he joined.

One of the consequences of the civil war was a severe famine in the Volga region in the winter of 1920-21. Evangelicals supported the government's efforts for famine relief. The Russian Baptist Union appealed to foreign Baptists to put political considerations to one side and respond to the human need. Local congregations formed relief funds, meeting the needs firstly of the needy in their own midst and when possible giving aid to those outside the congregation. When foreign relief supplies of food and clothing began to arrive in the Volga region the Baptist church in Saratov offered its premises as a distribution centre for Saratov and surrounding provinces. Much of the aid that was sent from abroad to the Saratov church was passed on to the state famine relief committee for distribution.

The Orthodox Church also contributed many of its valuables for famine relief, but the Bolsheviks exploited its refusal to hand over consecrated items in order to launch an attack on it. The government accused the Church of not caring about the starving and ordered the confiscation of valuables. This resulted in many bloody clashes as the faithful resisted the desecration of churches. Lenin personally ordered the confiscations to be carried out in such a manner as to provoke resistance in order to provide an opportunity to crush the Church. In some places Orthodox faithful, priests and monks and nuns were shot as they tried to protect the churches and monasteries. Many churches were looted and vandalized and closed for worship, and some were put to secular use. Clergy, from parish priests to bishops, were arrested and charged with inciting the people to civil strife. Among those convicted and executed on these charges was the young and popular Metropolitan of Petrograd, Veniamin. In 1922 the Patriarch himself was arrested.

The Bolshevik government further sought to undermine the Orthodox Church by facilitating the formation of a pro-Communist 'Living Church', led by some within Orthodoxy who welcomed the demise of the old order, supported ideals of Christian socialism and wished to see more far-reaching reforms within Orthodoxy than the 1917-18 Council had approved. The 'Living Church' grew out of the Renovationist Movement, led by Father Alexander Vedensky, who had a close relationship with the Petrograd Bolshevik chief, Zinoviev. With government support the Renovationists took over the patriarchal chancellery and 20,000 parish churches. In 1923 they called a Council which passed resolutions supporting the Soviet regime, withdrawing the anathema on the Bolsheviks, removing Tikhon as Patriarch and recognizing married bishops and the right of widowed priests to remarry. Facing the possibility of schism within the Orthodox Church, Tikhon secured his release from prison by agreeing to issue a confession that having been brought up in a monarchical society he had been influenced by anti-Soviet circles to have a negative attitude to the Soviet regime; he distanced himself from counter-revolutionary movements in Russia and abroad.

Evangelicals, however, did not face such systematic pressure. In January 1921 the People's Commissariat of Internal Affairs issued a special instruction banning Sunday schools. Some congregations had established

Sunday schools soon after 1905, and by 1921 virtually all churches had them. The People's Commissariat of Justice ruled that the religious education of children under the age of eighteen could take place only at home; at the request of parents the teaching could be undertaken by Sunday school teachers, but only in groups of no more than three. After negotiations with the authorities, who remained immovable, the leaders of the Baptist and Evangelical Christian Unions were obliged to accept these restrictions and recommended local congregations to conduct religious education only privately until there was a change in the law. In May 1921 42 participants in the seventh Congress of Christian Youth in the city of Tver, including Ivan Prokhanov, were arrested and Ivan and eleven others were sentenced to terms of between one and three years in the Tver forced labour camp. Following petitions to the central government, the twelve were released after about three months, but not before Ivan Prokhanov had signed an open letter of support for the Soviet regime.

Vladimir Martsinkovsky was arrested with a friend in March 1921 and taken to the Cheka headquarters in the Lubyanka. That night two women leaders of the Salvation Army were brought to their cell, having also been arrested. Vladimir had sometimes spoken at their meetings. The Cheka were particularly annoyed that two of their women agents had been converted at a Salvation Army service. From the Lubyanka Vladimir was taken to a temporary prison in a block of flats commandeered by the Cheka; the owner was one of those imprisoned there. Their 'cell' was a five-room flat holding 60-70 prisoners. On the Sunday morning Vladimir's friend announced that there would be a religious talk. One of the prisoners came up to Vladimir and said: 'I heard a lot about your lectures and for ages I had intended to go to one, but I never had the time.' 'Well, now I've come to you,' laughed Vladimir; 'there's plenty of time now.' He read the parable of the prodigal son, asking whether this was not the story of Russia and of each person there. He concluded by asking whether his cellmates would like to meet again on a Sunday to read the Bible. 'Why only on Sundays?' came the response. 'We can meet on weekdays too.' And so on Sundays a service was held and on Saturdays Vladimir gave a talk followed by a discussion.

In April Vladimir was moved to the Taganka prison where he was held until his release in October. This was a prison for common criminals, but because of the overcrowding at Butyrki prison quite a few political prisoners were brought here while their cases were being investigated.

During Vladimir's stay the prisoners included two metropolitans of the Orthodox Church, an archbishop, three bishops, two abbots, priests, a professor of theology and a former Procurator of the Holy Synod, as well as an Evangelical Christian and an Adventist, not to mention members of opposition political parties, officers, soldiers and sailors.

The prison's director of education, a Communist, heard that Vladimir was a lecturer and invited him to give a lecture to the prisoners. He chose to speak on the topic of beauty, and asked for a pianist friend to be allowed to come to the prison to play music to accompany the lecture. The lecture summary was submitted to the censor for approval. In the first half of the lecture Vladimir spoke of how beauty points us to God, and quoted Russian poetry on this theme. At the interval the director of education came to him in some alarm and begged him not to talk about religion. Vladimir continued his lecture by saying he had no intention of talking about religion but he wanted to talk about God. 'Only God through Jesus Christ can make our life beautiful,' he said. This was the experience of great prisoners who underwent a spiritual transformation in prison, among them Dostoyevsky. 'Prison can maim us, but it can also make us deeper and stronger. This happens if we are with God, if through Christ and the Gospel we turn from sin and darkness to light, truth and love. This is what Dostoyevsky did when he read the Gospel.'

His talk drew tremendous applause from the prisoners, including the criminals. But the chairman of the prison's party cell, thinking that Vladimir had been invited from outside along with the pianist, demanded that he should be arrested. 'How can we arrest him?' someone commented. 'He's already under arrest.' In consequence he was called to the governor's office and threatened with punishment by the commissar of the punitive wing. Vladimir cited his constitutional freedom of religious and anti-religious propaganda. 'Yes, but not in prison,' replied the commissar. 'There are special regulations for prisons. It is forbidden to preach about Christ here.'

There were no more lectures, but as prisoners were free to move about within the prison Vladimir had many private conversations and established an extensive ministry of comfort. He even got permission to visit prisoners on death row. After his release, Vladimir was able to continue giving lectures for over a year, but in December 1922 was summoned to the political police (now no longer the Cheka, but renamed the GPU) for interrogation about his activities and his views, especially on military service, from which he had been exempted on grounds of conscience. In

January he was informed of the decision of the investigative commission: he was to be exiled to Germany for three years. He asked if instead he could go to prison and remain in Russia, but this was refused. He was told that he was accused of undermining the Red Army, because some soldiers who had become Christians through his work had refused further military service. Later he discovered that he was being exiled on the orders of the 'commission to purge higher education of bourgeois ideology'. He and two others were the last to be sent abroad: from then on 'undesirables' were exiled to the far north of Russia, to Siberia or to Central Asia.

The Bolshevik government, however, continued to support the establishment of Christian agricultural communes and other cooperatives. In 1921 the People's Commissariat of Agriculture set up a special commission to help Christians to settle on state farms, virgin land and the estates of former large landowners. One of the members of the commission was Vladimir Bonch-Bruyevich, the Bolsheviks' expert on religious minorities and a long-standing defender of evangelicals against Tsarist persecution. The commission called on Christians to organize communes on vacant land, noting the advantage if communes were formed on the basis of religious communities that already enjoyed a spirit of unity. They were invited to apply to the commission for an allocation of land. By 1924 there were 24 evangelical agricultural communes. There were also Christian manufacturing and commercial cooperatives including bakeries and a shoemaking workshop. In Moscow one Christian cooperative ran a chain of six cafeterias, one of which was on the ground floor of the All-Russian Central Executive Committee, the precursor of the Supreme Soviet, or Russian parliament.

One of the smaller evangelical groups which was particularly active in forming communes and cooperatives was the Moscow congregation of Temperance Christians. Their leader, Ivan Koloskov, as a young man worked with the leader of the temperance society in St Petersburg, Ioann Churikov. Ivan moved to Moscow and began preaching to the heavy drinkers of the city's taverns. In 1907 he organized a society called The Sober Life. His call to repentance and sobriety was heeded by many. Vladimir Martsinkovsky, who knew of his work at that time, commented on his remarkable ability to persuade people to make a new start. In 1911 Ivan was excommunicated from the Orthodox Church and imprisoned for a year. On his release he continued his work through his Sober Life society. For a while he was strongly influenced by the religious teachings of the writer Tolstoy, then he became friendly with Ivan Prokhanov, and finally drew close to the Pentecostals. Under the influence of Prokhanov he accepted adult baptism and formed the Christian Temperance congregation. Soon the movement had two churches in Moscow and three in nearby towns. The Temperance Christians organized a labourers' cooperative, two agricultural communes in Moscow region, a commune for orphans and four vegetarian cafeterias in Moscow.

However, evangelicals soon came under pressure on the issue of conscientious objection to military service. The government complained that young men were joining evangelical congregations in order to evade military service and proposed that young men of conscription age should be subject to a period of probation for at least a year before congregations admitted them as members. The issue was put on the agenda of the Baptist and Evangelical Christian congresses in 1923 and 1926. Before their 1923 congress the Council of the Evangelical Christian Union issued a letter accepting the principle of military service, which was published in the government newspaper *Izvestiya*. There was a stormy debate at the congress, with supporters of the right to conscientious objection accusing the leadership of departing from the truth. In Moscow some of the delegates who had been at the congress left the Church over this issue, and about 400 went with them to form an independent congregation. The Baptist Union Council sent out a letter at the beginning of 1925 recognizing that the government was correct to verify the credentials of anyone calling himself a Baptist who was called up for military service.

In September 1925 a new law on military service tightened up the provisions for exemption, which could be granted in the case of deeply held religious convictions. This meant that those who had been brought up in families whose beliefs did not permit armed military service could still be exempted, but other young men from Christian families, or who had been brought up by non-Christians, could not. The following year the Baptist Union congress passed a resolution stating: 'We consider ourselves obliged to perform military service when the government requires it of us.' The Pentecostals, Seventh Day Adventists and finally even some of the Mennonites adopted similar resolutions under strong pressure from the authorities. Thus, although the provision for exemption from military service on religious grounds was not withdrawn until 1936, it became practically impossible to secure exemption, as the authorities could claim that the official position of all the denominations was to recognize the obligation to serve in the armed forces.

Evangelicals also came under pressure to pass resolutions expressing loyalty to the Soviet government and support for its policies. Since the religious policy was generally acceptable to evangelicals and more favourable to them than Tsarist policy, such declarations of loyalty were not particularly difficult, but their fulsomeness suggests that they were required by the authorities rather than passed spontaneously and voluntarily. In 1923 Ivan Prokhanov was imprisoned in Moscow for several months until he agreed to put his name to a circular to the Evangelical Christian congregations drafted by the authorities, condemning propaganda against military service and calling for the issue to be placed on the agenda of a conference. Before the text was finalized and actually signed by Prokhanov and the other members of the council the circular was published in the government newspaper *Izvestiya*. It stated:

> We must . . . concentrate all our forces and all our knowledge in order to strengthen and support the Soviet government . . . We urge all our brethren to work honestly and in absolute submission and obedience to Soviet institutions, both civil and military and equally to serve in the Red Army.

The Evangelical Christian Congress in October after stormy debate accepted the explanation of the circular as an invitation to discuss the issue, and recognized military service as an obligation, while insisting on the right of a Christian to determine the form of military service - under arms or in a medical or labour unit - in accordance with his own conscience.

Later the same year the Baptist Congress passed a resolution stating:

> This congress reaffirms the unalterably loyal attitude of the Baptists to the Soviet government from the first moment of its existence and . . . considers it inadmissible for Baptists to participate in unions and organizations aiming at the overthrow of the existing regime, or to take part in any kind of anti-governmental activity whatsoever . . .

Furthermore the Congress condemned William Fetler for signing a loyal address to the Tsar in November 1914, declaring that he had 'discredited himself in the eyes of the world', and expressed its gratitude for the 'proclamation of religious freedom'. This echoed the report by Pavel Pavlov on behalf of the Russian Baptists to the Baptist World Congress in

Stockholm in August 1923, which stated that 'full religious freedom' had been proclaimed and that any constraints were not systematic and were due to the conditions of civil war. Pavlov noted that the Soviet flag was not flying with the flags of the other nations represented and insisted that this be rectified.

Despite these pressures to conform to the requirements of the Soviet government the evangelicals were not a particular target of anti-religious efforts during the 1920s. The brunt of persecution was borne by the Orthodox Church, whose hierarchy was decimated by arrests. When Patriarch Tikhon died in 1925, not only was the Church prevented from convening a Council to elect a successor but Tikhon's nominee as acting head of the Church, Metropolitan Peter, was arrested. Two of the three metropolitans whom he nominated to succeed him in this role were also arrested. The third, Metropolitan Sergii, continued Tikhon's efforts to secure official registration for the Orthodox Church, but was himself arrested in 1926. Three months after his release he issued a statement in which he wrote that 'the most fervent adherents of Orthodoxy can be faithful citizens of the Soviet Union, loyal to the Soviet government'. He continued: 'The Soviet Union is our motherland, whose joys and sorrows are our joys and sorrows, whose misfortunes are our misfortunes.' Sergii remained acting head of the Church and finally, in 1943, a year before his death, was permitted by Stalin to be elected Patriarch.

The Catholics also found themselves the targets of concerted attacks by the Bolshevik government. The Roman Catholic Archbishop of Petrograd, Jan Cieplak, was put on trial in March 1923, along with the exarch of the Eastern-rite Catholic Church in Russia, Leonid Fyodorov, thirteen Catholic priests and a seventeen-year-old student. The archbishop, the exarch and eleven of the priests were accused of conspiring between 1918 and December 1922 to found a counter-revolutionary organization with the aim of instigating a revolt against Soviet laws on religion. They were also accused, together with the other three defendants, of resisting the government's confiscation of church valuables for famine relief. The court hearings took the form of a show trial with maximum publicity. The trial concluded on Palm Sunday 1923, and Archbishop Cieplak and Mgr Konstantin Budkiewicz, the Dean of St Catherine's, the main Catholic church in Petrograd, were sentenced to death, Bishop Fyodorov and four of the other priests received ten-year sentences and the eight remaining priests three-year sentences, while the student was given a suspended sentence of six months and was freed. Fr Budkiewicz was executed in the

Lubyanka, but Archbishop Cieplak's sentence was commuted to ten years' imprisonment in order not to make a martyr of him; later in the year, without being informed of what was happening to him, he was deported to Latvia.

The monastery on the Solovetskie Islands in the White Sea off Archangel was turned into the Bolsheviks' first concentration camp and many imprisoned bishops and clergy of various denominations were sent there. In the beginning lay people were usually more fortunate. Members of the Signposts group, with their ex-Marxist background, were particularly unwelcome to the Bolsheviks. Most of its leaders, who had kept their teaching posts through the revolution and civil war, were exiled or forced to emigrate during 1922. Father Pavel Florensky, who remained in Russia, eventually died in one of Stalin's labour camps.

For Protestants, however, the end of the civil war brought political and economic stability and relative toleration. The Lutheran Church, much depleted by the independence of Finland, Estonia and Latvia, was permitted in 1924 to call a general synod, the first in the whole of Russian history. A new church structure was put in place, and a theological seminary opened in 1925, as a result of which the number of clergy increased despite the death of many elderly pastors.

Especially for the evangelicals the 1920s were a golden age. Their numbers increased dramatically, publishing was expanded and seminaries and Bible schools were established. Evangelism and missionary work could be conducted openly, since the Bolsheviks believed that the work of the 'sects', as they labelled the evangelicals, would undermine the authority of the Orthodox Church.

Among those who took advantage of the opportunities were the Pentecostals. The Pentecostal churches established on the eve of the First World War had been left without a national leadership as Alexander Ivanov died in exile in Central Asia during the war and Nikolai Smorodin moved to newly independent Poland at the end of the civil war. However, the Pentecostal movement received a new impetus with the arrival in Odessa in 1921 of Ivan Voronayev, a former Baptist preacher in Siberia, who had emigrated to the United States and there become a Pentecostal. Ivan was a gifted preacher and organizer and was at first made welcome in the Baptist and Evangelical churches. Soon he had sufficient following to establish his own congregation under the name of Christians of Evangelical Faith. His revivalist approach attracted a lot of interest and many evangelicals came to Odessa from elsewhere in Ukraine to see his work for themselves. Those who became Pentecostals under his influence took the new teaching back to their own churches and the pattern of new Pentecostal congregations emerging from existing Baptist and Evangelical Christian congregations was repeated in many towns and villages.

The division caused in many congregations by the new movement caused considerable bitterness and hostility towards Ivan Voronayev and the Pentecostals among Baptists and Evangelical Christians, but soon all three denominations were growing rapidly through conversion of those with a non-evangelical background instead of competing with each other. One of Ivan Voronayev's evangelists was Ivan Slavik, a Czech prisoner-of-war who had joined the Bolsheviks and remained in Ukraine when most of his fellow-countrymen were repatriated. He had become an officer of the Cheka, and in 1926 came to a service at the church in Odessa intending to kill Ivan because his wife had become a Christian and a member of the Pentecostal Church and was bringing their young daughter there. As he listened to Ivan preaching he repented of all the violence he had committed, went forward, laid down his gun and confessed his evil intent. He was arrested several times before being exiled in 1933 to Alma-Ata in Kazakhstan, where he continued to work as an evangelist.

The opportunities were so great that perhaps the rivalry among the different evangelical groups was no great hindrance to growth, but the rivalries certainly persisted. Pentecostals claimed that they had the secret to revival and that with the spread of their movement the other evangelical unions would crumble. Baptists and Evangelical Christians had been on the brink of unity in 1920 when both their unions held simultaneous congresses in Moscow with as many of the sessions combined as possible. Although joint activities continued locally in some places and in some instances evangelists were jointly employed, the two structures remained separate and the attitudes of the leaders were clearly divergent. The Baptists insisted on a congregational structure with a clearly defined leadership of ordained ministers. The Evangelical Christians on the other hand, with their Brethren roots, had always rejected the idea of an ordained ministry, preferring an elected leadership. Their only ordained ministers were those who had joined them from the Baptists. In 1924, however, Ivan Prokhanov bowed to increasing pressure from within Evangelical Christian ranks and agreed to be ordained. His hostility to the Russian Baptists, though, was so great that he went to Prague to be ordained by the Czech Baptists.

Ivan Prokhanov had a vision for the renewal of the whole of society through the evangelical movement and regarded the Baptists as too narrow to achieve this. He pursued contacts with the 'Living Church' wing of the Orthodox Church, pointing out that proposed reforms within Orthodoxy were largely superficial and urging a thorough Biblical reformation. As a result he was invited to preach in Orthodox churches in Moscow, and in return invited the head of the Living Church, Metropolitan Antoni Vedensky, to speak to an Evangelical Christian congregation. In March 1923 Prokhanov was invited to address the Living Church congress and was well received, though the delegates rejected any formal alliance.

These friendly contacts with part of the Orthodox Church increased suspicion of Ivan Prokhanov among the Baptist leaders, who accused the Evangelical Christians of prostituting their beliefs. In 1925 the Baptists drew up a list of complaints against the Evangelical Christians, citing 80 congregations that had received into membership Baptists who had been excommunicated, and had spread slanders about the Baptists, sowing discord in Baptist congregations and trying to destroy them. Ivan Prokhanov was accused of wanting to destroy the Baptist Union and take over its churches; Baptist leaders alleged that he said in 1923 that he would not die before he had stepped over the corpse of the Russian Baptist Union. At the end of 1925 the Baptist Union formally broke off all relations with the Evangelical Christians.

The only Christian publication to survive during the civil war period was Ivan Prokhanov's *Morning Star*, which appeared sporadically from 1917 to 1922, when it ceased publication. From 1924, once the economic situation had stabilized, both Baptist and Evangelical Christian Unions had extensive publishing programmes, with a number of magazines and regular editions of song books, Bibles and New Testaments. A concordance was published for the first time in 1928. Some of the publishing work was enabled by subsidies from evangelicals abroad, but much of it was self-financing through the income from sales.

To establish formal theological education was, however, financially more demanding. In the early 1920s most training was carried out through short courses arranged in local churches. In 1923-4 a joint Evangelical Christian-Baptist Bible course lasting nine months was held for fifty students from each Union at the main Evangelical Christian church in Petrograd (renamed Leningrad after Lenin's death in January 1924). This grew into a regular Evangelical Christian Bible School with a one-year programme. From its inauguration in January 1925 until the summer of 1929 about 400 preachers and evangelists studied there. The Baptists finally established their own full-time Bible school in December 1927 in Moscow, with fifty students embarking on a planned three-year programme.

Many of those who completed Bible courses were employed as evangelists by individual local churches, regional associations and by the Baptist and Evangelical Christian Unions nationally. From 1926 evangelistic activity was intensified. The Ukrainian Baptist Union alone supported 56 evangelists, and 53 evangelists were serving in Siberia. Some evangelists were commissioned especially to work among the minority peoples of the country. By the end of the 1920s the Baptist Union had seven missionaries working among Muslims, and others preaching to Georgians and Armenians. A small hymn book in Georgian was published in 1926. Small churches were founded with members drawn from the Tatar, Chuvash, Udmurt, Mari and Mordovian peoples living along the Volga and the Yakuts in Siberia. In March 1928 the Evangelical Christians held a special congress in Kazan for Christians from the Volga peoples.

By the mid-1920s the Baptist Union had grown to over 3,000 congregations with an average membership of 100. Another 1,000 Baptist congregations were believed to exist independently in districts where there was no Baptist Union structure, making a total membership of some 400,000. By 1927 spokesmen were claiming 6,500 congregations and 500,000 members. No overall statistics are available for the Evangelical Christians, but they had 2,000 congregations and groups in Ukraine alone and their total membership was believed to be close to that of the Baptists. The Pentecostals, who established a Ukrainian Union in 1926 and a National Union in 1927, had 350 congregations, mostly in Ukraine, and possibly as many as 80,000 members. Full church members therefore numbered about one million, a five-fold increase when compared with the total of 150-200,000 in 1917. If children and adults who attended worship but had not become full members through baptism are taken into account the evangelical community numbered several millions; Ivan Prokhanov on one occasion even estimated ten million. Both Baptists and Evangelical Christians had strong youth movements that competed directly with the Communist youth movement, the Komsomol (abbreviated from Communist Union of Youth). Even the names adopted by the evangelical youth movements were a challenge to the Komsomol: the Bapsomol (Baptist Union of Youth) and the Christomol (Christian Union of Youth). Towards the end of the 1920s, it was claimed, their combined strength was greater than Komsomol membership.

However, by the end of the 1920s the popularity of the evangelicals

among the working class and the strength of their youth movements began
to cause considerable disquiet and there were increasing calls to find
effective ways of countering their influence. The Union of Militant Godless
was formed in 1925 and under its influence newspaper articles warning
of the ever-growing activity of the evangelicals began to appear in 1926.
By 1928 religious groups were accused of being tools used by the remnants
of the former ruling classes to exert a political influence over the workers.

Even before the late 1920s there was some persecution. Cornelius
Martens, by now one of the full-time evangelists, was arrested in 1923.
His greatest offence, he was told by his interrogators, was his work among
children. After five months, during which he was offered all kinds of
inducements to work for the secret police, he was placed in a cell with
dangerous criminals, in the hope that they would murder him. Instead,
learning that he was a Christian, the leader of the prisoners told the others
not to touch him. For two weeks, which he afterwards described as the
happiest time in his life, Cornelius was able to share the Gospel with his
cellmates. One confessed to having murdered eighteen people and asked
whether it was possible for him to experience forgiveness. Counselled by
Cornelius he found peace. Then Cornelius was told that he was to be
banished to the Solovetskie Islands in the far north, but instead he was
released. He believed that this change in fortune was the result of
representations made by the British government at the request of the
Archbishop of Canterbury and other church leaders. However, for the next
few years he constantly moved from place to place under threat of arrest,
until in 1927 he emigrated to Latvia.

SIX

The Gates of Hell

THE 1930s IN the USSR were the era of the infamous 'midnight knock', when NKVD (secret police) prison vans, often disguised as bread or meat delivery trucks, went from house to house in the early hours of the morning picking up suspects. Many thousands of evangelicals (one estimate is 22,000) were sent away to Siberian labour camps, many never to return. Their families have vivid memories of tearful partings. Vera Shchukina was nine when her father, a member of the Pentecostal church in Alma-Ata, was arrested in 1937. She recalls:

His arrest took place on a night which was one of terror for many families. On 25 December 1937 a police van drew up quietly in one of the narrow streets of 'Moscow', as the shanty-town district of Alma-Ata where we Christians lived was facetiously known. 'Is Yefrem Mikhailovich home?' My father heard the familiar voice of the pastor of the church Konstantin Korneichuk . . . They had arrested him not long before that dreadful night.

My father thought that he had been released and was filled with joy. But in fact things were very different. They used Korneichuk to arrest many people that night. He had been badly beaten in an attempt to force him to betray the Church and cooperate with the authorities and finally after dreadful torture in an electric chair the poor man had broken and now pointed out the houses where the members of his church lived . . . 'Yes, I'm at home, brother Konstantin,' Father replied joyfully. He quickly opened the low door of our one-room home, but . . . two men in militia uniform were standing on the doorstep. Strong hands pulled Korneichuk aside into the darkness and the 'keepers of law and order' burst into our hut. Terrified, we all leapt from our beds. 'Are you Yefrem Mikhailovich Shchukin?' 'Yes, I am,' our father replied tersely. 'Get your things together, you're under arrest.' In our room everything was turned upside down, they felt in every corner of the mattresses, the pillows, the patched blankets, our clothes. The only thing they didn't do was dig up the earth floor. We were sobbing. 'Perhaps you will let me pray for a last time with my wife and children.' 'All right then, pray, maybe your God will help you!' said a militiaman sarcastically. We all fell on our knees, wept and sobbed, feeling the presence of the Spirit. 'That's enough now,' the militiaman broke in anxiously. 'We haven't much time.'

That's how my father was arrested; for his faith in Christ he got ten years. Many others were arrested that night and here are the names of those who never returned to their families: Svinarenko, the choir-leader; Serdyuk, a preacher; Kvasha, an elderly preacher; Levkovich – a young preacher whose wife had only just given birth to a baby boy; Slepov, an old man, also a preacher; Mikhail Pishchenko, a preacher; and Rybak, also a preacher, who left three children, the youngest, Luke, still a baby. All of them, arrested on the same day, never saw their children again, and Korneichuk was not spared either: he died in a concentration camp.

Stalin had succeeded Lenin in 1924 as the leader of the Bolsheviks and gradually removed his opponents, both real and potential, and later imaginary, within the Bolshevik party and in society at large. He was to rival Hitler as the greatest mass murderer in world history. Stalin began by removing Trotsky, who had masterminded the Bolshevik seizure of power in October 1917 and under whose leadership the Red Army had won the civil war and reconquered Ukraine, Georgia and Armenia which had declared independence. Soon after Stalin came to power, the USSR was formed as a centralized state. As Stalin's grip on power tightened he began to implement plans to strengthen the Soviet Union through a crash programme of industrialization.

In Stalin's new Soviet Union religion was to have no place. 1928 saw the beginning of new restrictions on Christian activity. The Bibles and New Testaments published in that year were the last Scriptures to be printed in the Soviet Union until 1956. Christian publications were forced to cut their print-run and most did not survive beyond the end of the year. The Pentecostals' magazine, launched only at the beginning of the year, survived for just eight issues before folding altogether when its paper supply was cut, and Prokhanov's *The Christian* was suspended with the November or December issue, its print-run having already been cut from 15,000 to 5,000. The Ukrainian Baptist Union's magazine also ceased publication with its November issue.

In the summer the two Bible schools in Leningrad and Moscow closed, while Ivan Voronayev's plan to open a Pentecostal Bible school in Odessa came to nothing. Ivan Prokhanov, who received a passport to attend the Baptist World Congress in Toronto, was advised not to return to the Soviet Union as he was likely to be arrested. He took the advice and lived in exile until his death in 1935. His last great project, to build a new evangelical city, to be known as *Yevangelsk* (Gospel City) or City of the Sun, got approval from the People's Commissariat of Agriculture and a site was allocated at the confluence of two Siberian rivers. In the summer of 1927 Prokhanov took part in a tree-planting ceremony at the site, but the plans got no further before the government withdrew its support.

The optimism of the evangelical leaders began to be replaced by caution. In 1926, Nikolai Odintsov, president of the Baptist Union had estimated a membership of 500,000 with a total Baptist community of one and a half million. Now he spoke of just 200,000 Baptists. The Pentecostal leader, Ivan Voronayev, exercised similar caution, writing in his magazine of a total membership of 17,000, an average of fifty per congregation. This was a minimum figure, as Ukrainian legislation did not permit the registration of congregations with less than fifty members. Other estimates indicate that there may have been as many as 80,000 Pentecostals. Already the evangelicals understood that it was diplomatic to understate their success.

Government support for Christian communes and cooperatives was withdrawn and they either collapsed or were forcibly merged with collective farms under Communist leadership. They were denounced as 'false communes' in which the ordinary members were allegedly fleeced by the church leaders. For the first time under the Soviet regime, evangelical churches were closed by the authorities. On 3 March 1929 the main Temperance congregation in Moscow held its last service in its own building before the authorities' closure order took effect. In the first part of 1929 three of the Evangelical Christians' meeting halls in Leningrad were also closed. One of the Lutherans' main churches, St Michael's in Moscow, had been closed in January 1928.

The gradually deteriorating position of the churches took a sharp turn for the worse in April 1929 with the enactment of the Law on Religious Associations. The new law severely curtailed church activity and pushed religion to the fringe of society. In keeping with Marx's adage that 'religion is the opium of the people', religious believers were treated as though they were registered drug addicts: pending a cure for their religious faith they were allowed to 'satisfy their religious needs', as the law put it, in worship services held inside a registered church building, but they were not permitted to do anything that might spread their addiction to others.

A legal commentary on the new law summed up the restrictions as follows:

> Thus, the activity of all religious assocations is reduced to the conduct of the cult (prayer, carrying out rituals etc.). Activity which falls outside the satisfaction of these needs is not allowed.

The aim was to emasculate the churches completely, and all forms of evangelistic or social outreach and fellowship activities were specifically banned. Article 17, listing all the prohibitions, reads like a checklist of all the things that an active, caring congregation should be doing:

> Religious associations are forbidden:
>
> a) to establish mutual-aid funds, cooperatives, production associations or in any way to use the property at their disposal for any purposes other than the satisfaction of religious needs;
>
> b) to provide material support for their members;
>
> c) to organize either special prayer meetings and other meetings for children, young people or women, or general meetings, groups, circles or departments for Bible study, literary activity, handwork, other work, the teaching of religion etc., and also to arrange excursions and children's playgrounds, to open libraries or reading rooms, to organize sanitoria or medical aid.
>
> In prayer buildings and other accommodation, the only books that may be kept are those that are required for the conduct of the given cult.

Other regulations in the new law limited the activity of the congregation to the place of residence of its members, thus banning any kind of mission in areas where there was no church, and gave the authorities the right to veto nominations to the congregation's executive committee, a group that the law required each congregation to elect. The authorities could thus in effect choose which members of the congregation they would deal with.

An early victim of the new restrictions was Christian publishing in all forms. Of the Christian magazines only *The Baptist* appeared, until the summer, and not a single religious book was listed in the Soviet national bibliography for 1929, compared with 15 published in 1928 and 22 in 1927. On the other hand the number of anti-religious books grew from 61 in 1927 to 84 in 1928, jumping to 202 in 1929. The equality of religious and anti-religious propaganda that was guaranteed by the Russian constitution was clearly contradicted by the new law, and in May 1929 the constitution was amended to guarantee 'the freedom of religious confessions and of anti-religious propaganda'. This amendment was interpreted to mean that people who were already religious could worship together, but that any form of activity aimed at attracting new converts or teaching the Christian faith to children was religious propaganda which was not permitted under the constitution and might therefore be considered a criminal offence.

The churches soon found that they were entirely defenceless against arbitrary decisions by the authorities. The first Soviet law on religion of January 1918 had deprived the churches of the right of juridical person, that is, although they existed legally they could not act as legal entities. They had no right, for example, to take any dispute to the courts or defend their interests, or to own property: all church property had been nationalized, although congregations were allowed to use some of it. Subsequent regulations had introduced procedures for the registration of religious congregations, so that their existence was legally recognized. The new law permitted local authorities to register congregations of more than twenty adults and to lease them places of worship but did not oblige them to do so. This provision enabled the authorities to refuse registration or the use of a church building without giving any reasons and with no right of appeal.

Congregations soon became victims of a campaign to close places of worship; within ten years no more than a few hundred churches of all denominations were left open. According to one Evangelical Christian leader only four evangelical churches remained open at the end of the 1930s. One of those remaining open was the former Reformed Church in Maly Vuzovsky Lane in Moscow, which now housed an Evangelical Christian congregation. This church was never closed and since the Second World War has been well known to foreign visitors as Moscow's central Baptist church. Often decisions to close churches were 'legitimized' by transfer of the premises for more 'socially useful' purposes. This is well documented in the Smolensk Communist Party archive, which was captured by the invading German army in 1941 and shipped back to Germany where it survived the war and was taken to the United States and made available to scholars.

Local meetings were held which passed resolutions calling for the closure of places of worship and the use of the premises for some more worthy purpose. A collection of some of these from Belorussia has been published. As early as November 1928 it was reported that the Jewish population of Krucha decided to close the synagogue and ask the local authorities to open a school in the building. In October 1929 workers in Minsk demanded that the city council confiscate one of the synagogues to be used as a club; a more sinister note crept into the newspaper report, which stated that such a move was all the more necessary because the worshippers at the synagogue were surreptitiously engaging in anti-Soviet agitation and setting the black-market exchange rate for the dollar. Synagogues were not the only targets: from December 1929 to February 1930 meetings of workers and villagers passed resolutions to close nineteen Orthodox and Catholic churches (as well as more synagogues) to be used as clubs, schools, medical centres and even as an electricity sub-station. There were also meetings that called for the closure of all places of worship in Minsk and the district town of Senno. Furthermore, in several instances the resolutions demanded the confiscation of church valuables and the melting down of church bells for the benefit of the industrialization drive. These resolutions ignored the wishes of those who wanted to continue to worship, though one village meeting did record that the decision to close the church and use it as a club and school was passed by 35 votes to 18 with one abstention. One of the saddest reports dates from June 1929, when the Lutherans in Mogilev decided to hand their church over to the city council and urged other parishes to do the same. Earlier, when elections had been held for a new parish church council none of the parishioners had been willing to stand for election – a measure of the general intimidation felt by religious believers.

By the end of 1930 all but one of the Baptist churches in Leningrad were closed and turned over to secular use, and of seventeen Evangelical Christian meeting places only one remained open; the same happened in Moscow. One Evangelical Christian pastor who fled to China in August 1930 estimated that 60 per cent of churches had already been closed. In Ukraine the situation was particularly severe. A law passed in 1927 had deprived clergy, including lay pastors, of their civil rights and many evangelical ministers had resigned in order to protect their families. With no official leaders many congregations lost their registration and as early as 1929 the number of evangelical churches open in Ukraine fell sharply. By March 1930 in the Crimea the Mennonites had lost four churches, the Evangelical Christians three and the Baptists and the Adventists two each, while the Pentecostals apparently had no churches left open. By 1931 there were no more than ten evangelical churches in Ukraine that were still officially registered.

In Mariupol, in eastern Ukraine, some of the thirteen churches of all denominations had been closed as early as 1925, and the remainder were all closed in 1930. In nearby Taganrog, across the border in Russia, of twelve Orthodox churches nine were closed between 1922 and 1938, when the remaining three were destroyed. The Armenian church was closed in 1934, the Lutheran in 1935 and the Catholic in 1938. The two prayer houses of the Baptists and the Adventists were also closed during the 1930s. In Ingermanland, the district between Leningrad and the Estonian border, there was a small union, affiliated to the Evangelical Christians, consisting of fourteen churches made up of Christians from the native population of the area, ethnically related to the Finns and the Estonians. In 1933 most of their churches were closed and their president, Heinrich Piiparinen, was deported to Finland.

The closure of churches was in many instances accompanied by the arrests of priests, pastors and preachers. The first reported arrest of an evangelical leader came at the end of 1928, when A. M. Bukreyev, the secretary of the Ukrainian Baptist Union, was charged with espionage. The Ukrainian Baptists' treasurer, F. G. Kosolapov, was arrested in 1929 and fell ill during a lengthy period of pre-trial detention in Kharkov prison; he was freed and died at home soon after. Pavel Ivanov-Klyshnikov, vice-president and secretary of the Federal Baptist Union, was arrested in March 1929 and exiled to Alma-Ata for three years. The leaders of the Temperance Christians in Moscow were all arrested in 1929. All the Lutheran pastors in Leningrad were arrested in December 1929 and banished to the Solovetskie Islands. Ivan Voronayev and other Pentecostal leaders were arrested in January 1930, Voronayev receiving a six-year sentence. All the council members of the Far East branch of the Baptist Union in Vladivostok were arrested in March. By the summer of 1930 it was estimated that 40 per cent of full-time evangelical workers had either fled the country or been arrested.

By 1933 only 41 of the 90 Lutheran pastors who had been in office in 1929 were still at liberty, and most of them were unable to conduct any meaningful parish life. Some of the elderly pastors managed to emigrate to Germany. In 1934 the number fell further to 24, and in 1935 to eight. The last pastor in western Siberia was sentenced to imprisonment in 1935, the pastor in Vladivostok disappeared in 1936 and the last pastor in Moscow was arrested in 1937.

During 1929 the regional Baptist Unions were forced to close and in December the Federal Baptist Union suspended its activity. The National Council of the Evangelical Christians was disbanded in May 1930, and the Pentecostal Union was banned. The offices of the Baptist Union were closed in May 1930 and 10,000 Bibles that had been printed but not yet bound were impounded. However, the Baptist and Evangelical Christian leadership was able to resume limited activity for a while, the Baptist Union being reconstituted in 1930, though now as a centralized organization rather than as a federal body; in August 1931 the Evangelical Christians held a conference, which elected a new Council, with Ivan Prokhanov as honorary president. The Evangelical Christians were charged a prohibitive rent for their offices in Leningrad and moved their headquarters to their church in Moscow, where at least one member of the new council managed to provide continuity of leadership throughout the 1930s. The last leaders of the Baptist Union were arrested in March 1935 and their one remaining church in Moscow closed.

Ironically, Ivan Prokhanov in exile in Berlin did live to see the demise of the Baptist Union. However, it was not his efforts to persuade the Baptists to accept his ideas or attempts to bring reconciliation between members of the rival unions but the savage attacks of the Soviet authorities that finally brought the evangelicals together. As churches were closed, leaving at most one still open for worship in each town, Baptists, Evangelical Christians and Pentecostals forgot their differences and began to worship together.

In the early 1930s the persecution was not uniform. Some churches that remained open continued their activities relatively unhindered, with services crowded with Christians whose own churches had already been closed. In the summer of 1930 many churches in Ukraine were still baptizing new converts. Other congregations continued to meet in private homes. One such 'underground' church is reported to have baptized 60 people and another church 150 in 1932-3. At first those arrested were full-time Christian workers and usually received prison sentences of three or five years at most. Despite rapidly deteriorating prison and camp conditions many survived to return to their congregations. Others were sentenced to exile in Siberia or Central Asia, where for a while new congregations were established and existing ones flourished. In Alma-Ata, capital of Kazakhstan, there was a growing Pentecostal congregation that even managed to build a church in the early 1930s. Membership expanded rapidly, from a small group in 1929 to 100 in 1931, and reached 300 by 1934, as exiled leaders were joined by members of their congregations. The Baptist congregation in Tashkent, capital of Uzbekistan, also grew rapidly at this time, swelled by an influx of refugees from persecution in European Russia and Ukraine.

Rural churches were disrupted by the social upheaval of collectivization and industrialization, as a result of which many peasants left their villages to work in the cities or on the new industrial projects. Christians are known to have moved to the new industrial city of Magnitogorsk in the Urals, to the mines of eastern Ukraine and Kazakhstan and to other industrial developments in Central Asia. On one of those projects, the construction of a dam and hydro-electric power station on the Dnieper in Ukraine, according to a report in an atheist magazine, there were in 1931 hundreds of active evangelicals, secretly holding small prayer meetings all over the site. Some meetings were held in the large hostels that had been built, more often three or four workmen would gather in one of the small huts that they had built for themselves. In the collectivization drive, in which the wealthier peasants were branded as *kulaks* (literally *fists*, i.e. people who brutally exploited their poorer fellows) and expelled from their homes and their land, some Christians were also forcibly resettled. Sometimes their frugal life style meant that they were indeed more prosperous than average, in other instances they were deported on suspicion of being opposed to collectivization.

In the village of Ilanskaya, in Siberia, the pastor of a lively Evangelical Christian church was soon arrested, as was his elected successor. Nevertheless, a third preacher was willing to be elected as pastor. Yegor Baturin was a poor peasant with a small piece of land and a cow and a horse. As soon as the authorities discovered he had been elected as the minister of the church he was deprived of his civil rights. When the collectivization campaign began, farmers who had been deprived of civil rights received demands to deliver large quantities of produce to the state. Yegor's quota for grain was 80 per cent higher than what he actually harvested! For failing to deliver enough grain he was arrested and ordered to send his cow to the slaughterhouse to boost the meat quota and to do forestry work for a month with his horse. However, his horse had been stolen while he was in prison, so he was unable to fulfil this demand either, and he was soon exiled. In 1934 he was released from exile and in 1935 was able to gather his family together again and settle in the city of Krasnoyarsk.

Most of the leaders who were not arrested were unable to continue in full-time church work and took secular employment. By and large the church became invisible, meeting secretly in members' homes. Although some members undoubtedly fell away during the 1930s many continued in fellowship or, if they had lost touch with other members or moved to a new city where they knew of no other Christians, kept their faith alive in their own homes through family prayers and Bible study. In prisons and camps the arrested preachers were not inactive either. In the early 1930s one Pentecostal pastor is said to have converted many of his fellow prisoners in camp before being moved to prison where he also found opportunities to share his faith. A Baptist preacher from Ryazan, F. I. Konkin, was exiled to the Siberian city of Kuznetsk for five years. As a result of his witness people there were converted. He was re-arrested and sentenced to ten years' imprisonment in camp.

The notorious purges of the mid to late 1930s, in which Stalin removed all real, potential and imaginary opposition to his rule, struck a further blow against the churches. The remaining clergy and many ordinary members of all religious denominations were prosecuted under the catch-all Article 58 of the Russian criminal code, which covered all forms of 'counter-revolutionary activity'. As early as 1930, the atheist magazine *Bezbozhnik* (*Godless*) had written that anyone engaging in religious propaganda should be prosecuted under this article. The Special Department of the NKVD secret police compiled lists of people who for one reason or another were suspected of being in opposition to the regime. They were categorized under various headings, which included 'AS' (Anti-Soviet), 'Ts' (Tserkovnik – active Church member, i.e. Orthodox, Catholic and Lutheran) and 'S' (Sectarian – member of a religious sect, i.e. Baptists,

Pentecostals etc.). When Lithuania was occupied by the Soviet Union in 1940 the suspect part of the population amounted to 23 per cent. Overall, throughout the USSR it is estimated that during the purge period of 1936-9 between five and six per cent of the population were arrested. Now ten-year sentences were routine, and many were summarily sentenced to be shot. In any case, mortality in the camps was high, as prisoners were used as slave labour until they were so exhausted they could do no more work, so imprisonment amounted for many to a suspended death sentence.

Arrests came in waves. For example in Frunze (now Pishpek), the capital of Kirgizia, in 1933, the leaders of the Baptist congregation were arrested and the church closed. Although there were no services members of the church continued to meet for prayer when they had the opportunity, despite a strict prohibition by the authorities and extensive surveillance. In 1937 there was a fresh wave of arrests. In Krasnoyarsk, Evangelical Christian pastor Ivan Belkin was arrested in autumn 1935 for refusing to forbid Yegor Baturin from preaching. In April 1936, just after Easter, the midnight knock came at the Baturins' house. The secret police claimed they were searching for weapons, and worked till dawn turning the house upside down. But the only weapon they discovered was the Word of God – a Bible, a New Testament and Christian magazines and brochures. Only one item survived, a pocket New Testament and Psalms which Yegor managed to hide on a shelf in the bathroom during the search. In the morning Yegor was arrested. Their case was decided in Moscow and in the autumn the verdict reached them in Krasnoyarsk: Yegor and dozens of other preachers from the two evangelical churches in Krasnoyarsk were sentenced to three years each and Ivan Belkin to five. However, Yegor never came back: in 1938 the family stopped receiving letters from him, and when she enquired about his fate his wife was informed that he had been sent to a remote camp without the right to receive visits or write letters. Only in 1958 did they learn that he had died in 1941.

In Tashkent, too, the church was closed and there was a first round of fifteen arrests in 1933. Many Christians, including some of the older preachers, were deterred from meeting. But the young people continued to meet together, with sometimes 40-60 gathering in a small room. They prayed for a revival and saw many more young people come to faith. These young people were aflame with a desire to hear God's Word and to serve him. In 1937 a new wave of arrests was much more extensive than the first. Leaders and ordinary congregational members were arrested. In some families father and son were arrested together and in others both parents were taken. Yet young Christians continued to meet in small groups around the city, despite close surveillance, which sometimes made it impossible for people to get to a meeting when they could not shake off their pursuers in time to reach the secret meeting place.

In Alma-Ata members of the Pentecostal church were arrested in 1933, 1937 and 1939. In the Krasnogorsk district of Bryansk region eleven Evangelical Christians received ten-year sentences in November 1937: only two of them were leaders, the others were ordinary members. Even the wives and children of Christian leaders were not spared. Pentecostal leader Ivan Voronayev's wife Yekaterina was arrested in 1933 and sentenced to three years' exile. The wife of Fyodor Sanin, Evangelical Christian chairman in the North Caucasus, who had been arrested in 1930, was herself arrested in 1935 and exiled to the Dzhambul region of Kazakhstan. Ivan Belkin's wife was arrested in 1937 in Krasnoyarsk, along with several other Christian women, while the wives of several prominent Baptists were arrested in 1941. The sixteen-year-old son of Baptist leader Fyodor Sapozhnikov was sentenced to ten years' imprisonment in Magadan.

Although 'religious propaganda' and unregistered religious activity were considered anti-Soviet in themselves, the NKVD often tried to embellish cases to show how well they were seeking out 'saboteurs' and 'spies' who were undermining the Soviet regime. Thus, two of the Pentecostal preachers in Alma-Ata were alleged to have been sent there from abroad by foreign intelligence in order to subvert the military might of the Soviet Union by persuading young men to refuse to serve in the army. They were said to have made special efforts to contact young people working in defence industries. Other details were intended to discredit those arrested: Mikhail Timoshenko, one of the Baptist Union leaders, was claimed to have collected so much money from believers that he didn't know what to do with it all, so he spent it by taking baths in eau-de-Cologne!

The story of Leonid Kozyarsky illustrates well the escalating repression. He was first arrested on 31 December 1930 at the age of sixteen with thirty other members of the youth group of a village Pentecostal church in Ukraine. They had met to celebrate the new year, but their service was soon interrupted by armed Komsomol members who dragged them off to prison in Pervomaisk. There they were beaten up and released a couple of days later with a warning of a worse fate if they were caught again meeting for worship. In March 1931, threatened with exile to the far north because their father refused to join the collective farm, the family moved to Batumi. Less than a month later Leonid and his father were rounded up and sent to a concentration camp in Central Asia until the autumn. A few months after returning home his father was arrested again, this time never to return. In 1933 the family moved again, to Alma-Ata, as the state farm where they worked had sacked all the Christians for asking to have Sunday as their day off. The government had introduced a six-day week, in which everybody was to work five days and then have one day off. In that way on any one Sunday only one sixth of the workforce had a free day, and each worker had a day off on a Sunday only once every six weeks.

In Alma-Ata fellow Christians found Leonid a job at the brickworks, but he hadn't even received his first wages before he was arrested along with other members of the congregation. Because he was still only nineteen, Leonid got the lightest sentence, of two years, but the others received sentences of up to ten years. Ten months after returning home from this sentence he was arrested again by the NKVD and given a ten-year sentence.

As the arrests escalated, those who had already served sentences earlier in the 1930s were not spared. Pentecostal leader Ivan Voronayev was rearrested in 1936 and sentenced to ten years' imprisonment without the right of correspondence. He is believed to have died in a concentration camp in the Far East after being mauled by guard dogs when he became so weak he couldn't keep up with the other prisoners. Nikolai Odintsov, president of the Baptist Union, released in 1936 on completion of a three-year sentence, was arrested once again in 1938 and died soon after. Little is known of the heroism of these martyrs, but many of them maintained a faithful witness to the end and some had opportunity to worship together secretly even in a concentration camp. An ex-prisoner describes the atmosphere in a Siberian camp at Easter 1936:

> On Easter Day all the 'religiozniks' of our camp were united by a shared joy in Christ: an Old Ritualist bishop and Orthodox priests, nuns and laypeople, Catholics and Lutherans, Baptists and Pentecostals. In unison, in shared spiritual exultation, we glorified God.

For Christians to witness to their faith in camp or to meet together was dangerous, as it could lead to incarceration in the punishment cells, where many died of the cold or became so ill that they couldn't work and faced a slow death by starvation. Or they might be rearrested for 'anti-Soviet agitation' and condemned to an even longer sentence. When Baptist preacher Sergei Golev was arrested in 1937 and sentenced to ten years' imprisonment, he hoped that he might somehow survive by keeping his faith to himself. One November morning after he had been in camp for a year he was ending a night shift when the camp commandant came to inspect. He found that one of the cauldrons in which they made pitch from timber had burnt through. Sergei got the blame and was ordered to the punishment cell. The outside temperature was minus fifteen and the cracks were so big that it was hardly less cold in the cell. Sergei was sure that in his light clothes he would freeze to death on the first night. He reflected on how he had sought to save his life by keeping quiet about his faith, and now faced death for something that wasn't even his fault. Now as he prayed, he confessed his faithlessness and cowardice and repented of his decision not to preach the Gospel in camp. At nine o'clock in the evening he was released from the cell and allowed back to his barracks. There he had a dream in which Jesus forgivingly laid his hand on his head and he felt his former fear disappear. When he awoke Sergei felt strengthened and for the remaining nine years of his sentence he was never afraid to speak to people of God and he saw people come to faith.

Soon after, Sergei was transferred to another camp. On the train he met another Christian. As soon as they arrived at the new camp they were taken to the bathhouse. The attendant there was one of the prisoners and they heard him humming a hymn tune. They asked him: 'Are you a brother?' Through the hymn tunes that he hummed this elderly Christian helped newly arrived Christian prisoners to identify him, so that they could then be introduced to other Christians. They could even meet together in the boiler-room where he worked.

The onset of the Second World War brought some respite from new arrests, although the prisoners were not released. However, as a result of the August 1939 Molotov-Ribbentrop non-aggression pact between the Soviet Union and Nazi Germany, the USSR was given a free hand in eastern Poland and the Baltic states. Soon the NKVD turned its attention to the western regions of Ukraine and Belorussia, which were seized from Poland in September 1939, and to Lithuania, Latvia, Estonia and Moldavia, annexed in 1940. The churches felt the full weight of Soviet restrictions and religious leaders and active Christians were among the 'undesirables' rounded up and deported to labour camps in the interior. Especially in the Ukrainian villages in eastern Poland there had been a strong evangelical revival during the 1920s and 1930s with hundreds of Baptist, Evangelical Christian, Church of Christ and Pentecostal congregations being established in an area that had previously had only a very small evangelical presence. Here, in contrast to Soviet Ukraine, where the other evangelical denominations had enjoyed a head start, the Pentecostals were the largest single evangelical movement in many districts.

SEVEN

War and Revival

T HE SITUATION changed dramatically with Hitler's invasion of the
Soviet Union in June 1941, which took Stalin completely by
surprise. Not only in the western areas so recently invaded by the
Soviet Union, but also in other parts of Belorussia, Russia and Ukraine
rapidly occupied by the advancing German army, people welcomed the
Germans as liberators. They soon became disillusioned, however, for the
Nazis regarded the Slavs as a sub-human race, with even their name
thought to be derived from the word 'slave'. The Germans refused to allow
the break-up of the hated collective farms, for Ukraine was an important
source of food for Germany. Ultimately they intended to settle these lands
from the crowded parts of Germany.

In one important respect, however, Nazi policy differed from the
communist dictatorship: provided churches stayed out of politics their
existence was tolerated. In the occupied territory there was a massive
spontaneous revival of religion. In some villages in Ukraine the first thing
local people did, within hours of the arrival of German troops, was clean up
the village church and hang in it a few ikons that had been hidden away, even
buried. In the towns and cities, among the first requests received by the
military administration was permission to reopen churches and hold
services. In Rostov-on-Don an Orthodox church that had been damaged in
the fighting and was filled with rubbish from its previous use as a workshop
was restored to working order in two days by hundreds of volunteers.

At first, even German army chaplains were mobbed by villagers begging them to solemnize their marriages and baptize their children. Lutheran field services held for the troops in Borisov in Belorussia and in Smolensk were attended by many local people, somewhat to the consternation of German military intelligence, alarmed at the possibility of fraternization between the troops and the civilian population. Before long the Gestapo banned the chaplains from serving civilians and ordered that field services should be attended only by military personnel. Parts of southern Ukraine were placed under Romanian administration and Romanian priests baptized 200,000 people, with Romanian soldiers often acting as godfathers. As the German armies moved forward across Ukraine and into the Caucasus in 1942, in eastern Ukraine and the Don region mothers taking their children to be baptized in newly reopened churches often asked German soldiers to be godfathers.

Evangelicals in Germany managed to give some help to their Ukrainian and Belorussian brethren, although the Nazi authorities tried to prevent contacts. At first German missions secured permission to work in camps for prisoners-of-war and among forced labourers brought from the East to work in Germany's war industries, but soon they were banned from visiting the camps. Ukrainian Gospels and New Testaments printed with official permission in Warsaw were confiscated by the Gestapo in May 1942, though most were later released to the Ukrainian Orthodox Archbishop of Chelm, who passed them on to the Baptists. However, it was forbidden to import the Scriptures to Ukraine. Nevertheless, Christian soldiers and officers risked their freedom to take parcels of Bibles, New Testaments and hymn books as they returned from leave in Germany or Poland and passed them on to trusted contacts in Ukraine. Sometimes Christian railway workers were able to deliver larger consignments. One of the Ukrainian Bible couriers, Vladimir Husaruk, received copies of the Scriptures in Rovno (administered as part of Poland) and tried to find ways of sending them further east. He was arrested in June 1944 carrying 52 Ukrainian New Testaments from Warsaw to Vienna for distribution to Ukrainian forced labourers and spent the rest of the war in concentration camps.

Everywhere church services were full. In some places the elderly predominated, and often when younger people attended they clearly did not at first know the services. Soon in many places people of all generations were attending church, including former members of the Komsomol and relatives of Communist officials, though usually women and children made up as much as eighty per cent of those present. It appeared that the Bolsheviks had succeeded in persuading younger people to reject the Christian faith only in some of the highly industrialized districts. German military intelligence reported that the majority of people had kept the faith alive through teaching within the family and prayers at home. In Orthodox homes, ikons that had been carefully hidden were once more displayed. Religious festivals had been marked throughout the time of Bolshevik rule, sometimes under cover of associated folk celebrations. German officers reported that even long-standing Communist Party members were seen to pray before they were executed.

The German military authorities readily gave permission for the reopening of churches and the holding of services. An official army announcement in September 1941 proclaimed religious liberty. The civil administration that followed the military was less generous, allowing only churches that had already been reopened to apply for registration and forbidding the establishment of church administration above regional level. A decree of the Reichskommissar for Ukraine of 1 June 1942 governed the legal status of religious organizations and an order specifically regulating the Baptists was issued on 19 October 1942. Evangelicals were encouraged to hold regional conferences uniting Baptist, Brethren, Evangelical Christian and Pentecostal churches, though each denomination also developed its own structures. Pentecostals in central Ukraine reestablished 350 congregations and elected a new leadership. Further east, Ukrainian territory remained under military administration and the evangelicals enjoyed particular freedoms. They were allowed to use public halls for evangelistic rallies and on one occasion two hundred new Christians were baptized together.

In Belorussia too, the civil administration on 18 June 1942 introduced regulations similar to those in Ukraine. Nevertheless, evangelical congregations were re-established and denominational unions were registered. In November 1942 Ivan Panko, who had played a leading role in the Pentecostal Church before the Soviet occupation of eastern Poland, applied to the German authorities and received permission to organize the Pentecostal churches into a union. He was elected bishop. The churches in the western districts (formerly Polish territory) had lost a relatively small number of leaders during the less than two years of Soviet occupation since September 1939, and they provided the impetus for new mission work in the east of Belorussia. In one mass baptism on 27 June 1943, 262 people were baptized. The number would have been still larger, but some were prevented from attending by the partisans and a separate secret baptism had to be held at night.

On the Soviet side of the front line the German invasion prompted a rapid change of policy towards religion as Stalin's government did all it could to foster national unity and patriotism. The Orthodox Church was quick to demonstrate its loyalty and patriotism by urging the faithful to defend the Motherland. On the very first Sunday after the German attack Metropolitan Sergi, as acting Patriarch, delivered a rousing sermon in the Patriarchal Cathedral and broadcast to the nation recalling that Russian Christians had always rallied to the defence of their country against foreign invaders. It was only several days later, eleven days after the invasion, that Stalin came out of self-imposed isolation to broadcast an address to the nation himself. The few remaining open churches were thronged with people and had to hold multiple services even on weekdays to cope with the crowds. The church launched an appeal for funds to equip a tank regiment, which was dedicated to St Alexander Nevsky, the Russian prince who had defeated the Teutonic knights in the thirteenth century.

In Moscow the number of open churches grew rapidly from fourteen to forty. At Easter 1942 the curfew in the city was lifted so that people could attend midnight mass. Candles, unavailable in the shops, were in abundant supply in churches. Throughout Russia churches were reopened and priests reappeared in their parishes. On a lesser scale the evangelicals also re-emerged. By May 1942 a number of surviving Baptist and Evangelical Christian leaders had been released from concentration camps. Together with the few who had been spared imprisonment, they formed a temporary joint council and sent out a letter urging believers to support the war effort and do everything possible to bring victory closer. Although many men served in the armed forces, the evangelicals' inclination towards pacifism was manifested in activity aimed at relieving the suffering of the victims of war. Church groups organized collections of clothing and other necessities for the families of soldiers killed in action and worked as volunteers caring for the sick and wounded in hospitals and orphans in children's homes. The churches collected funds to buy an ambulance plane, named the Good Samaritan, to fly out severely wounded soldiers from the front.

Fellowships that had survived underground came out once more into the open, and began to grow as they were joined by those who had lost touch with fellow Christians and by new members who found comfort and support in the close-knit Christian communities. Elsewhere, new fellowships emerged, as seemingly chance encounters brought together isolated Christians who had been displaced by the traumas of the 1930s or evacuated to work in new factories well away from the front line and who had previously not known one another. Evangelicals were often able to recognize one another by their sobriety – most abstained from all alcoholic drinks – and their avoidance of swearing. In the mining towns of the Altai mountains near the Chinese border several churches came into being as Christians met for the first time in works canteens when they noticed each other silently saying grace over their meal; they then resolved to gather together for fellowship, prayer and worship.

The change in official policy was not just towards toleration of religious activity. Anti-religious propaganda was soon halted and the League of Militant Godless disbanded. Early in the war the League's magazine *Bezbozhnik* (*The Godless*) shared the fate of its religious opponents in the late 1920s: its publication was suspended on the grounds of an alleged shortage of paper. Instead, the former Orthodox Church press on which atheist propaganda had been printed once more began to produce church publications. Behind the lines, Communist partisans insisted that the Soviet government would now actively support religion, 'put up crosses, reopen churches, even import priests'. In occupied Belorussia German intelligence noted that the partisans were pursuing a decidedly pro-church policy, organizing local people to erect new wayside crosses and even bringing in Orthodox priests. In one Orthodox Church in spring 1943 a partisan leader came to a service, knelt before the priest and said:

> In the name of the Father, the Son and the Holy Ghost. Brothers and sisters, God is and will be. We were for a while bewildered because we despised God. One must pray to God. Pray for us, for all soldiers and partisans. Amen.

In September 1943 acting Patriarch Sergi and the two leading Metropolitans were brought to Moscow. Sergi was given the mansion of the German ambassador as his official residence. The next day they were summoned to see Stalin in the Kremlin. Invited to present the Church's needs, they asked for many more churches to be opened, for the opportunity to train priests and for permission to hold a council to elect a patriarch. According to one account, when Stalin asked why there was a shortage of priests (many of them had perished in his concentration camps), Sergi replied that one reason was that 'when a man had been trained in a seminary he became a marshal of the Soviet Union'. Stalin, the seminary student turned revolutionary, appreciated the joke, and no doubt Sergi's tact.

There were immediate positive results of this meeting. A Synod of nineteen surviving bishops was called and unanimously elected Sergi as Patriarch. More churches were opened, permission was given to publish a church magazine, the *Journal of the Moscow Patriarchate*, and there were promises that seminaries could be reopened as soon as the war was over. At the same time a new state body was established, the Council for the Affairs of the Russian Orthodox Church, to provide a link between Church and state and a channel for government assistance to the Church. With the help of the Council, bishops and priests were tracked down in concentration camps and released and funds made available to get churches and monasteries back into working order. The Council, headed by a former NKVD (secret police) officer, also had the function of exercising control over the Church on behalf of the government. However, for the time being it was expedient to respond generously to the Church's patriotism and loyalty and to allow the people freedom to express their faith in worship.

In July 1944 a parallel state body, the Council for the Affairs of Religious Cults, was established in order to deal with all of the non-Orthodox denominations and religions. With help from this Council, the Baptists and Evangelical Christians were encouraged to hold a conference in October 1944 at which they formally merged into one denomination and created the Union of Evangelical Christians and Baptists. By this time much of the Soviet territory occupied by Germany had been reconquered and representatives from these areas were also present at the conference. Superintendents were appointed for the main republics and for some regions and these men helped the church leadership in Moscow to establish contact with the newly emerging fellowships and build a new union out of the ruins of the two old ones. In January 1945 the new union was also permitted to begin publishing a church journal, the *Fraternal Herald*.

The Soviet military command maintained a friendly attitude to the churches as the Soviet armies pushed the Germans back. Churches re-established during the German occupation were allowed to continue to function, and many of them took immediate steps to show their loyalty to the Soviet regime. In November 1943 the central Pentecostal church in Dnepropetrovsk held a congregational meeting at which it was decided to organize a special collection for wounded Red Army soldiers. The leaders declared themselves willing to work within the framework of Soviet legislation and recognized military service as a Christian duty. Clergy of all denominations were exempted from military service and in Belorussia, for example, the exemption extended even to Pentecostal pastors, whose church had no official government recognition. In November 1944, after the western regions of Belorussia were reconquered, the Pentecostal leaders elected during the German occupation travelled around the churches issuing certificates to the ministers, including preachers, deacons and choir-leaders, with which they were then able to secure exemption from military service.

The work of the churches was not simply to try to restore what had been before. Both Orthodox and evangelical communities had been changed by the school of suffering. The faith of those who had remained loyal to Christ had been deepened during the preceding decade of persecution. At the same time the hardships that had been endured by almost the whole people during the collectivization of agriculture and the rapid industrialization process, followed by the deprivations, grief and pain of war, made many open to the words of comfort offered by the churches and to the deeds of mercy carried out by groups of Christians and by Christian neighbours. Certainly many who had drifted away from the churches, or whose faith had cooled when there was no longer any opportunity to worship in church, once more began to attend church now that there was an apparent religious freedom.

Nikolai Baturin was only eight when his father was arrested in 1936. As all the other preachers in and around Krasnoyarsk had been arrested at the same time, the churches had been closed and there were no more services. By the age of thirteen at the outbreak of war Nikolai was outwardly a tearaway, but inwardly he felt a desire to change and began to read the Bible and pray for strength to live as a Christian. In 1942 evangelical services began again in Krasnoyarsk, and Nikolai soon came to a personal knowledge of God. In October 1945 he was baptized along with forty other young people in the first baptism in their church since the mid-1930s. In the next four years a large number of young people came into the church in Krasnoyarsk, many of them students, and the single congregation grew to be bigger than the combined membership of the three that had been closed in the 1930s. Nikolai was to go on to become preacher, pastor and church leader, suffering many years in prison and labour camps along the way and finally dying of a heart attack soon after completing his last sentence.

Another future church leader who became a Christian in the hard war years was Ivan Antonov, an officer in the medical corps of the Red Army. Ivan was taught to believe in God by devout Orthodox parents and at the age of twelve had a dream in which an angel told him: 'Son, if you want to be a good person and study well, you must believe in God and pray.' From then on, right through the 1930s, he maintained a personal prayer life using the Orthodox prayers he had learnt. In summer 1941 he managed to get a Bible and read it from cover to cover. As a result, like the Stundists seventy years earlier, he ceased to regard the ikons as holy and no longer prayed through them.

The outbreak of war soon changed Ivan's life. In 1938 he had entered medical school in Moscow, but in 1942, without having the chance to complete his course, he was drafted into the army as an officer. His spiritual path was also interrupted. In the face of the horrors of the battlefield and the deprivations of life at the front line he began to drink and was soon enslaved to alcohol. Although as a doctor he tried to help others with a drinking problem, he could not help himself. Twice one of the men he used to drink with tried to shoot him and he was so depressed by his powerlessness to change himself that he contemplated suicide. At this time he went to a fortune-teller, who accurately described his past life and predicted that he would go to prison, though she did not know that he would be imprisoned as a Christian. She even invited him to learn from her to become a fortune-teller himself, but this suggestion reminded him of God's injunctions to the people of Israel to shun fortune-telling and prompted him to begin to pray again.

In June 1944 Ivan met some young Christian women and through the witness of their lives and words he sought to know Christ in a personal way, repented of his sins and found forgiveness and release. He was mocked for his new-found faith by his commanding officers and colleagues, but he quietly explained how he had become a Christian. To his joy a number of soldiers also became Christians. But the tolerance of the Soviet military to the churches did not extend to Christian work inside the army. Within six months Ivan was arrested and sentenced to ten years' imprisonment for anti-Soviet agitation.

Once the war had ended the churches were able to consolidate their position. The Orthodox Church reopened eight seminaries and the total number of churches open for worship reached 22,000. This was still less than half the number of parishes that had existed before the revolution (there had been over 50,000 parishes, not to mention 20,000 additional chapels in schools, hospitals etc.), but a vast improvement on the few hundred churches remaining open in 1939. However, a disproportionate number of these churches were in western Ukraine and in other areas that had been occupied by the German army. In Ukraine 1165 evangelical congregations, with 82,000 members, had been registered by the end of 1946. Throughout the Soviet Union 3000 were registered by 1946 and the number of congregations in the Union grew to 3500 in 1947 and 4000 in 1948. Total membership was put at 350,000. Later a figure of 500,000 members in over 5000 congregations was regularly quoted by Union leaders, though this estimate has recently been shown to have been inflated. In any case, the number of congregations was still much lower than before the persecution began when as many as 10,000 existed within the Soviet Union with another 2000 or so in the territories annexed in 1939-40.

This increase in the number of churches is not in itself an indication of a continued revival: it is more a reflection of the slow process of re-establishing contacts and securing official recognition for congregations. The Evangelical Christian and Baptist (ECB) Union also grew from the absorption of smaller denominations which failed to secure official recognition from the authorities as separate entities. These denominations faced the choice of being subsumed within the ECB Union, and thereby gaining registration for their congregations, or of continuing independently but illegally, with all the risks and hazards that might be involved.

The largest denomination to face this choice were the Pentecostals. Four of their leaders, two each from Ukraine and Belorussia, met with the ECB leadership in August 1945. The old hostility led to severe restrictions being imposed on the Pentecostals, who had to agree not to speak in tongues during public worship and not to speak to non-Pentecostals about their specific beliefs and to abandon the practice of foot-washing as part of their communion service. Although the four leaders signed a unity agreement on this basis, only about 40 per cent of congregations followed their lead, mostly in the western regions of Ukraine and Belorussia where foot-washing was not widely practised. The two senior Pentecostal leaders – one of them, Dmitri Ponomarchuk, was a surviving member of Voronayev's Union in Ukraine and the other, Ivan Panko, had been elected bishop of the Belorussian Pentecostals during the war – were appointed as deputy superintendents in these two republics and others were appointed superintendent or deputy superintendent in some of the western regions.

The earliest Pentecostal denomination, the Christians in the Apostolic Spirit, still led by Nikolai Smorodin, joined the Union in 1947, as did the Temperance Christians.

At the same time that the Pentecostals were negotiating with the Union leadership, Baptists from the Baltic republics, and from the western regions of Belorussia and Ukraine annexed from Poland and Romania, were also gathering in Moscow. They too had little choice but to abandon their independence, though, of course, there were not the same doctrinal obstacles to unity. Also in western Belorussia and Ukraine about 70 Churches of Christ came into the Union. In Ruthenia, or Transcarpathian Ukraine, annexed from Czechoslovakia in 1945, the Free Christians (Brethren) formed the strongest evangelical denomination. In 1946 they too agreed to join the Union, and for a while their leader served as superintendent in the region. Methodists could not formally amalgamate with the ECB Union as they did not practise adult baptism on profession of faith. In Latvia and western Ukraine their churches were closed and many of their members agreed to be baptized and joined ECB churches, while their pastors in Latvia mostly transferred to the Lutheran ministry. Only in Estonia were the Methodists registered.

Of all the believers the most difficult situation was that of German Christians, whether Lutheran, Catholic, Baptist or Mennonite. After Hitler declared war on the Soviet Union the German population of Ukraine and the Volga region were deported to Siberia as potential defectors to Germany. Almost all of their churches had already been closed, but in the process of transportation to the east their communities were totally disrupted. In Siberia they were virtually interned, living under close supervision in special camps with a strictly enforced curfew; they were deployed where needed in agriculture and industry in the so-called 'labour army'. The wartime freedom of religion did not reach them, for they could not establish congregations or build churches. After the war they continued to live under the same restrictions, as a conveniently captive labour force. Only a small proportion of Germans escaped this treatment. Some were not deported because Hitler's advance was so rapid that the top Communists had time only to evacuate themselves and their families; these Germans were resettled in Poland or eastern Germany and when recognized by the advancing Red Army as Russian-Germans were arrested and incarcerated in concentration camps or deported to the far north.

The conditions under which the deportees lived were appalling. They were constantly hungry, for they were at the mercy of Russian officials who were often corrupt and took the best things for themselves, secure in the knowledge that their victims were totally without any rights. For many of the Germans their Christian faith was their only comfort, but opportunity for fellowship was rare. In Novosibirsk, where the German families had more freedom than in remote villages deep in the forests, Jakob Esau heard his call to be a preacher. All the Christian leaders had been imprisoned or deported and so Jakob was pressed into service visiting the sick and dying and conducting funerals. As a young Christian, Jakob often felt that he received more encouragement from the witness of those who had preserved their faith through much suffering than he was able to give them. And his first attempts at preaching at funerals were much criticized! But there was nobody else, there was no going back and he felt the Lord's calling and blessing.

Even in their poverty Christians helped one another and Christian love also crossed the boundaries of nationalism and hatred. In 1947 Jakob Esau was admitted to hospital with a fever. Without his wages his parents could not bring him any food, and the hospital rations were so meagre that his recovery was very slow. He was helped to get back on his feet by Russian Christians who brought him food in hospital. One day after he had been discharged his mother announced that there was just one piece of bread left in the house. Should they eat it now or save it for the next day? Jakob replied that they should eat, because God would provide for the next day. He read his Bible and was comforted by the knowledge that the Lord had supplied the needs of those who trusted Him. Jakob didn't know how God was going to provide, but he was calmly sure that He would. A knock at the door brought the answer: Dusya, a Russian Christian who explained that she had gone to see Jakob in the hospital with some food and not finding him there had come round to his home. Jakob and his parents were speechless as Dusya unpacked fish, groats, sugar, lard and bread. Then Jakob explained that they had no food left at all. 'Now I know,' said Dusya, 'why I felt no peace until I decided to come to you. Actually I don't have the time, but I couldn't resist my inner voice.'

The luckiest were Germans in the Urals and West Siberia who were far enough away from the front line not to be considered a risk. It was only in this area that German villages remained intact and some restoration of religious life was possible. One of these German villages, Waldheim in West Siberia, was reawakened to Christian faith through a young man named Jakob returning home from a winter spent working beyond the Arctic Circle in Vorkuta. There he had met Christians who were experiencing a revival and deepening of their faith. Under their influence he became a Christian and before returning home he managed to obtain a Bible. On the evening of Jakob's arrival in Waldheim, without any announcement, curious neighbours gathered at his family home. Jakob read them a few verses from the Bible, spoke briefly and haltingly about his own experience of becoming a Christian, fell to his knees and spoke a simple prayer: 'Lord, I pray to you that each person gathered here will be converted tonight, amen.' A woman pushed her way towards Jakob and asked him to help her to pray. Both dropped to their knees and the woman began calling on God to be merciful to her. Within seconds everybody in the house was on their knees screaming to God for mercy. Jakob had to calm the people and tell them not to scream out, as God could hear their prayers. Herdsmen in the field heard the noise and came in to find out what was happening. People ran home to wake their families: 'Come quickly, the whole village is getting converted tonight.' Jakob's prayer was answered literally.

In another village the news was passed from person to person that in the neighbouring village someone had a Bible and dared to read from it in public. The villagers found the house packed with an expectant crowd, with just one candle burning to enable the Bible to be read. Everyone spoke quietly for fear of attracting unwelcome attention. A few there remembered some hymns and sang them, then followed reading from the Bible and a time of prayer, during which people begged God for forgiveness for their sins. Even hardened people wept like children.

Especially among the exiles in Siberia and Central Asia and in Ukraine, revival spread. Mass conversions were reported in the Central Asian cities of Tashkent, Dushanbe, Chimkent and Dzhambul. Some large churches baptized over one hundred new converts each year - in Novosibirsk it was reported that 195 people were received into membership in 1946-7. Throughout the country Christians who had drifted away were renewed in their faith and returned to the churches.

EIGHT

Christians in the Gulag

'*I*F THE LORD had said to us, 'Go to the far north and preach the Gospel,' I don't think anyone would have dared to go. I would not have gone to the north willingly. I would have said, 'Lord, You know I am afraid of the cold, the hunger and the hard work! Send somebody else!' But the Lord worked it out. We were arrested, sentenced and transported free of charge up to the north . . . We were well guarded, so that we could not run away. When the prophet Jonah should have gone to Ninevah he fled, but we could not flee, and so living churches came into being in the far north!''

Thus Jakob Esau became a missionary in the Gulag, arrested in 1949 and sentenced to 25 years' imprisonment for his activity as a preacher. One evening one of the prisoners called Jakob over to him and asked him what kind of a person he was. Jakob couldn't understand what he meant, but the man explained that he had been watching Jakob and had seen that he was quite different from the other prisoners. Jakob was amazed that his way of life had been noticed and was able to testify freely that he believed in Jesus Christ and that Jesus had changed his whole life. He realized that he had been observed by the other prisoners and without any words had been a witness for Jesus. Then and there Jakob asked God to give him the strength to be a blessing to others through his path of suffering. From then on he was conscious of God's calling to minister in camp. Later he commented:

> The more the believers are persecuted, the more the Gospel is spread throughout this great and godless land. It is amazing that even in the far north, beyond the Arctic Circle, the Gospel is being preached.

The wartime toleration of the churches had soon proved to be hollow. The authorities refused to register many of the churches, halting new registrations completely after 1948. In most cities where there were congregations belonging to the different denominations that had joined the ECB Union only one combined congregation was allowed to exist. The Union leadership was obliged to present this as a voluntary process of reconciliation and an expression of new Christian brotherhood, but the result was to close neighbourhood churches and reduce the scope for public witness. In Kiev the central church was confiscated and the congregation forced to merge with two others. Sometimes the situation was not altogether negative: in the Estonian capital Tallinn the new combined ECB congregation, formed in 1950 by the merger of eight existing churches, was allowed to use a thirteenth-century cathedral, St Olaf's (Oleviste) church, on condition that the church members themselves repaired the damage inflicted on the building during the war. This solution had advantages for everyone: the city council got an ancient monument lovingly restored at no cost to itself; the Council for the Affairs of Religious Cults had only one congregation to deal with; and the congregation had the use of a church building that was a famous landmark dominating the city centre skyline where all who wanted to come to worship with them would have no difficulty finding them.

Churches found themselves hedged about by restrictions. In 1949 the ECB Union was denied permission to continue publishing its journal and all official contact with Christians abroad was cut off. Active Christians soon faced arrest once again. The criminal code was amended with the maximum sentence for 'anti-Soviet activity' raised from ten to 25 years. One of the many who were condemned to this virtual death sentence of 25 years was Neonila Korolkova, the girl who had led Ivan Antonov to Christ: she had continued with evangelism among young people, but the fact of leading an army officer to the Lord was a particularly damning piece of evidence against her. The number of young people attracted to the

Krasnoyarsk ECB church began to concern the authorities. In 1948 the pastor was arrested and sentenced to 25 years. A few months later three of the most active young people, including Nikolai Baturin, now aged 20, were imprisoned. Nikolai's indictment read as follows:

> The accused N. G. Baturin did not sing Soviet songs, did not read Soviet literature and did not go to the cinema, the theatre or clubs. On the contrary, he read and preached the Gospel, attended Baptist meetings, sang religious songs and glorified life after death, thus distracting himself and others from social and political life, i.e. committed the crime defined by Article 58, point 10, part II – anti-Soviet agitation – and point 2 – committed by a group.

He and his co-accused received ten-year sentences.

It was not just local pastors and youth workers who were imprisoned. Arrests also struck church leaders, especially the Belorussian Pentecostals. Their leader Ivan Panko, deputy superintendent for the ECB Union in Belorussia, was arrested in 1948 along with several other Pentecostals, including a regional superintendent. He was accused of collaboration during the war with the German occupation authorities because he had secured official recognition of the Pentecostal Church; he was also charged with helping Pentecostal pastors and preachers to evade military service in the Red Army by issuing fraudulent exemption certificates. Sergei Vashkevich, who had been Panko's deputy during the war and was a co-signatory of the unity agreement with the ECB Union, had emigrated to Poland in 1947, but at the insistence of the Soviet authorities he was also arrested there in 1950 and imprisoned on similar charges.

In Ukraine many Pentecostals quickly became disillusioned with the ECB Union. Not only was the Union forced to bow to restrictions on Christian work imposed by the authorities, but because of Baptist mistrust Pentecostals found themselves strictly monitored by the Union leadership. They complained that they were discriminated against within the churches and often passed over when pastors and superintendents were appointed. As a result, in 1947, Afanasi Bidash led a Pentecostal walk-out from the Union. He was the fourth Pentecostal signatory of the unity agreement and himself had a legitimate complaint of discrimination as he was the only one not to be appointed as a superintendent. In his home region of Dnepropetrovsk 38 per cent of Pentecostal churches in the Union followed him and united with the unregistered Pentecostal churches that had never gone into the Union. Together with other leaders, Bidash began to organize an independent Pentecostal Union and to petition the authorities for registration.

The new wave of persecution in the late 1940s was part of a reimposition by Stalin of the terror of the 1930s, this time implemented by the infamous Lavrenti Beria. Once more people from all walks of life, from the Jewish wife of Politburo member Vyacheslav Molotov downwards, were arrested on suspicion of opposition to Stalin. Politburo member Bulganin once commented to Khrushchev:

It has happened sometimes that a man goes to Stalin on his invitation as a friend. And when he sits with Stalin he doesn't know where he will be sent next, home or to jail.

Unregistered churches were hit particularly hard. Women and young people and those against whom there was little evidence sometimes escaped with a ten-year sentence, but most were condemned to 15 or 25 years' imprisonment. In the case of Christians the charges were to some extent based on fact in that they really were church members, but the evidence that their churches were anti-Soviet organizations was usually flimsy in the extreme. In Barnaul, in the Altai mountains of Siberia, Yevfrosinya Kalabukhova, a war widow who became a Christian in 1944, was sentenced in 1949 to ten years' imprisonment on the grounds that the Pentecostal Church was a branch of American intelligence; the 'evidence' for this was that Pentecostalism originated in the USA. Two Germans, Heinrich Wiens and Dietrich Klassen, drafted to work in a uranium mine in Kirgizia, gathered a small fellowship together and after a while an evangelical church was formed. In 1951 Wiens and Klassen and five other men from the congregation were arrested on charges of espionage, for which Wiens was subsequently executed. Despite the arrests the congregation continued to meet for worship and submitted an application for registration. The authorities' response was to arrest nine more men on charges of anti-Soviet activity: they were all sentenced to 25 years' imprisonment and five years' exile.

Afanasi Bidash and other independent Pentecostal leaders, like Ivan Panko, were charged with wartime collaboration with the enemy because they had registered their churches with the occupation authorities. Although this was true, so had all the other denominations, and they had never sought to hide it. These charges were a convenient way of arresting them and trying to discredit them when the political wind changed.

It was not only evangelical Christians who were imprisoned at this time. All denominations were affected, especially in the three Baltic countries of Estonia, Latvia and Lithuania, which were annexed in 1940 and reoccupied in 1944-5. As part of the programme of subjugation of these countries, tens of thousands of people were deported to Siberia, including priests, ministers and active lay people. In Lithuania virtually the entire Catholic hierarchy and hundreds of priests were imprisoned or exiled. From Estonia alone, with a population of little over a million, 20,000 were deported in 1945-6 and a further 40,000 in 1949. Alexander Kuum, minister of the Methodist church in Tallinn, was one of many to be sent into Siberian exile simply because he was a Christian leader. He later joked that the crisp Siberian cold cured his rheumatism, but he was one of the lucky ones who returned to his homeland after Stalin's death. In 1948 the authorities began once more to arrest Orthodox priests, though not on the same scale as in the 1930s. Orthodox layman Anatoli Levitin was arrested in 1949 and met many other Christians during his seven years in camp.

The Ukrainian Catholic Church was the victim of particularly harsh treatment. This church was formed at the end of the sixteenth century when some Orthodox bishops agreed to accept the supremacy of Rome in return for the right to continue to use the Slavonic liturgy and maintain many Orthodox practices, including having married priests. The Russian Orthodox Church had always resented this union of part of its flock with Rome and Stalin distrusted the Ukrainian Catholics because of their loyalty to the Vatican. The Soviet authorities ordered the amalgamation of the Ukrainian Catholics with the Orthodox Church, which the Orthodox genuinely welcomed as a reunion. None of the Catholic bishops agreed and all were arrested. A small group of priests and laypeople called a council, without the authority to do so, at which it was resolved to go into self-liquidation and reunite with the Orthodox. The majority of priests refused to accept this decision and were arrested. Several million church members, many of whom outwardly accepted Orthodoxy, remained loyal to their roots and participated in clandestine Catholic life, thus forming the largest underground church in the Soviet Union.

The concentration camp network known as the Gulag once more filled up with political prisoners. The Christians among them often saw themselves as having the opportunity to continue their ministry within the prison system, to which they would otherwise have had no access. Priests found in the camps a flock greatly in need of comfort and for many of whom the candle of faith was all that gave them the will to live. Father Walter Ciszek, a Polish American who was arrested as a 'Vatican spy' and served his sentence in the camps of Norilsk, in the far north of Siberia, conducted secret masses in the corner of barracks or during the lunch-break on the building site, perhaps in a shack used for storage or hidden by the wall of an unfinished building. In the nearby camp at the coal-loading depot in Dudinka he had met another Polish priest, who by his own example encouraged Father Ciszek to work as a priest among the prisoners. Being able to serve others as a priest gave him new strength.

> I thanked God daily for the opportunity to work among this hidden flock, consoling and comforting men who had thought themselves beyond His grace.

There was no need to look for his flock:

> The moment it became known in a new brigade or a new barracks or a new camp that a man was a priest, he would be sought out. He didn't have to make friends; they came to him instead. It was a very humbling experience, because you quickly came to appreciate that it was God's grace at work and had little to do with your own efforts . . . To realize this was a matter of joy and humility. You realized, too, that this imposed on you an obligation of service, of ministry, with no thought of personal inconvenience, no matter how tired you might be physically or what risks you might be running in the face of official threats.

In every camp where Father Ciszek served there were also Orthodox priests and monks and evangelical preachers. The evangelicals rarely had anything to do with the Catholics and formed a close-knit group. They held regular prayer meetings and recited the Bible from memory. The camp officials were particularly severe on them, trying to break up their groups.

Nikolai Baturin spent a year in a small prison near Moscow where the prisoners - mechanics, technicians, engineers and even professors - were engaged in a research project. One of his fellow-prisoners, with whom he had made friends, became a Christian and Nikolai was placed under surveillance. His notebook with Christian poems and songs was discovered and he was threatened with a new sentence for 'agitation'. However, instead, he was transferred to a hard-labour camp in Vorkuta, in the Komi republic in the far north of Russia. In transit he met a pastor and preacher from Novocherkassk on the way to the same camp, and on arrival they found two more Christians, one of whom had a Bible, which they took turns to read. Nikolai copied out much of it for himself. Although the climate and work in Vorkuta was harsh, life in the camps there was relatively free and the Christians were able to enjoy fellowship together, praying and even singing. However, early in 1952 the camp regime was tightened up and Nikolai lost his handwritten Bible. Undeterred, he began to copy from a New Testament that some Orthodox prisoners had managed to keep hidden.

Prisoners who were released were not allowed to leave the district and thus an evangelical church began in Vorkuta. Its first pastor Grigori Kovtun, on completion of his sentence, continued to work in the timberyard of the camp and was able to meet Nikolai, give him encouragement and learn of the needs of the Christian prisoners. Another ex-prisoner worked as a driver and was often sent to the camp and was able to bring Christian literature for the prisoners. On release Nikolai was warmly received in the Vorkuta church, which was made up almost entirely of ex-prisoners and exiles of Russian, Ukrainian and German nationality. It was a strong, lively and caring fellowship where Christians rejoiced at being free to worship after so many years of imprisonment and were united in love for Christ and each other. Prisoners who had become Christians in camp gladly joined the church when they were freed and were baptized into membership.

Ivan Antonov also served his sentence in the Komi republic. Amidst terrible atrocities that he witnessed, he knew that God was protecting him and giving him the strength not only to survive but to witness to others about God's love. He wrote afterwards of these years: 'What indescribable joy filled my heart when souls turned to the living God and found comfort in Him!' For his work for the Gospel in the camps he was threatened with prosecution and a new term of imprisonment, but in August 1954, three months before the end of his sentence, he was released under one of the amnesties for political prisoners that followed the death of Stalin. Within a month he had found the Baptist fellowship in the locality of the camp and been baptized in the chill Arctic waters. The following year Neonila, the girl who had led him to Christ, was amnestied - having served five years of her 25-year sentence - and they were married.

One man who became a Christian in the camps was Dmitri Minyakov.

He was arrested in 1944, accused of collaboration with the enemy during the German occupation. He had never encountered Christians before he ended up in camp, and he recalls how the Christians were mocked and taunted by many of the prisoners. However, through their patient and loving witness Dmitri became a Christian himself in 1949. In his camp there was an evangelical congregation, even with a pastor, and the Christians were able to meet together for worship. Right there in the camp Dmitri was baptized into membership of the church. When the following year the pastor was transferred to another camp, Dmitri was elected to lead the services. On his release in 1952 he continued to serve as a lay preacher, later becoming pastor of an unregistered church and a leader of the unregistered Baptist movement.

Another future pastor who became a Christian in camp was Nikolai Savchenko. At the age of seventeen, in 1943, he was called up into the army straight from school and sent to the front line. In 1945 he was arrested and sentenced to eight years' imprisonment. In the camps he met many believers, one of whom had a New Testament and read it with him. Nikolai recalls the impact of God's word:

> I listened, soaking up every word and it was as though I was in a different world. My thoughts flew away from the earth; something new and amazing happened to me.

Nobody pressed him into conversion, but his own consciousness of his sins grew and as he repented of them he felt liberation and cleansing. The camp authorities responded to his new-found faith by trying to bully him into becoming an informer, but he steadfastly refused. As a result he was sent to the most remote branch of the camp. His fellow Christians collected some money for him and gave him a New Testament, which he hid in a pocket. He wrote:

> This was the first miracle in my life. I took off my sweat-shirt for inspection with the New Testament in the pocket. The guard picked it up by the collar and looked right through it, as though it were tranparent. He turned it round and threw it to one side. He carefully felt the rest of my things and confiscated a lot from me, but I had no regrets – I had the New Testament! How happy I was! With my own eyes I had seen the all-powerful hand of God and I knew that He loved me and was blessing me.

NINE

Khrushchev's 'Thaw'

ONE DAY WE heard that a real pastor had come to the city and some already knew where he lived ... We empowered a man and a woman to contact the pastor and invite him to hold a divine service the following Sunday, a real service with communion! It turned out that the pastor was willing to hold the service. He was working on road construction at the time.

Berta Steblau was one of that little group of Christians in the city of Tselinograd (Akmolinsk) in Kazakhstan. Pastor Eugen Bachmann, the only graduate of the short-lived Leningrad Lutheran seminary still in the Soviet Union, never realized what he was letting himself in for when he accepted their invitation. Berta takes up the story:

The news concerning the imminent worship service to be conducted by a pastor spread rapidly among the Germans in the city, and on Sunday about a hundred persons assembled, so that all the rooms of the house were filled to overflowing ... We eagerly waited for the pastor ... I can no longer remember the text of the sermon – I was probably too excited. But one thing I know – I was so stirred by the sermon that I thought I would lose my composure!

A new church was born in distant Kazakhstan that Pentecost Sunday of 1955.

Stalin's death in March 1953 had brought genuine grief to many people who had believed the propaganda about Stalin being the wise father of the nation and the great leader who had saved the country from the Nazis. But for others hope was born that a nightmare had come to an end. Even to his close colleagues on the Politburo Stalin's death brought an immediate sense of relief. They knew Stalin's machine of terror might engulf any of them at any time. Already Stalin's suspicion had fallen on Politburo members Molotov and Mikoyan, and at the time of his death the Supreme Court was about to begin a trial of Kremlin doctors on evidence that Stalin's colleagues suspected was totally fabricated and based on confessions extracted under torture. The trial was stopped and within two months the doctors were free. Stalin's head of secret police, Beria, was arrested and disappeared without trace, probably executed without trial like so many of his victims. In the power struggle that followed Nikita Khrushchev emerged as first secretary of the party. Like Stalin before him, he was able to use this position to outmanoeuvre his colleagues and become prime minister as well.

Prisoners' hopes of freedom, or at least improved conditions, were raised and the camp system was rocked by strikes, unrest, rebellion and mass break-outs. Resistance was quashed by a mixture of concessions and force, but the authorities recognized that in hundreds of thousands of cases the sentences were unjust and excessive. In 1954-5 general amnesties released from the camps most of those who had been imprisoned for alleged wartime collaboration and for anti-Soviet activity, and reduced the sentences of others. A review of all cases involving political charges was commenced and families had the opportunity to enquire about the fate of missing relatives who had been arrested: often only now were they able to discover that their loved ones had died in a concentration camp 10, 15 or even 20 years earlier. In December 1955 the restrictions on the German population were lifted, although they were not allowed to return to their homes on the Volga or in Ukraine.

Conditions in the camps got rather easier. After the camp rebellions, Father Ciszek was the only priest among the 1000 prisoners in Camp 5 in Norilsk, many of whom were Catholic Poles and Lithuanians. On top of work every day on a building site in the city, he was in constant demand as a priest. He did a lot of spiritual counselling and was even able to organize retreats. In the next camp he was moved to, there were already three other priests. Father Ciszek received the occasional warning about 'subversive activity', but on the whole nobody paid any attention to the work of the priests. The more relaxed atmosphere encouraged more of the prisoners to admit to religious beliefs and Christmas and Easter were major celebrations. The guards knew well what was happening, but would turn a blind eye, just telling the men not to be too boisterous. For these major festivals each denomination would arrange to use a separate barrack: the Orthodox in one, Catholics in another, Ukrainian Catholics in yet another and Baptists in another. Here in a crowded barrack, Father Ciszek celebrated mass for the first time virtually in public since the Soviet occupation of Eastern Poland and his arrest.

The ECB Union grew steadily through the mid-1950s, with between 7,000 and 12,000 baptisms reported each year. The Union had resumed publication of its journal in 1953 and in 1956 printed 15,000 hymn-books and in 1957, 10,000 Bibles. It also distributed a gift from abroad of 100 concordances. The Orthodox Church too published its first edition of the Bible since the 1920s in 1956, although neither church was allowed to print any more until 1968. German Christians also took advantage of their new freedom to travel in search of Bibles, to evangelize and to build up links between congregations.

The release of Christian prisoners, and of political and criminal prisoners who had become Christians in the camps, gave a new impetus to the churches and stimulated a second wave of revival which was even stronger than that of the 1940s, especially in the districts around the camps in Siberia and Kazakhstan where many of the released prisoners first settled. Many of those who had been imprisoned had been strengthened in their faith and were more determined than before to continue Christian work. Susanna Herzen, daughter of a German Baptist preacher arrested in 1937 never to return, recalls how in 1955 her mother came back convinced of the urgency of evangelism after serving four years of a 25-year camp sentence for leading children's and youth meetings in her home. She explained to her children:

If I had been released from prison instead of being sentenced, I would probably have assumed that it wasn't the right time for evangelism. But after I had seen in labour camp the misery of prisoners perishing without God, I had to confess to the Lord that I was wrong. I can't be silent. As long as God's Spirit is at work on earth we must tell sinners that salvation is found in Jesus Christ!

One of those who experienced a dramatic conversion was Rudolf Klassen. Born in a German Christian family in Ukraine in 1931, like many of his generation deprived of fellowship in a congregation, Rudolf drifted away from the faith of his parents. In 1950, simply because he was a German, he was arrested and deported from Novosibirsk to Yakutia, in eastern Siberia, where he was even more removed from any Christian influence. When he returned to his family in 1956, he found that almost all of them had become Christians. Very unwillingly, Rudolf went to church on Sunday with his elder brother David. After the morning service the young people gathered for lunch. Rudolf felt very out of place. He agreed to go to the evening service only on condition that he was left in peace. He sat in the furthest corner at the back. The leader of the congregation preached on Saul's conversion and concluded with an appeal: 'Yes, there are Sauls like that here today, kicking against the goads, unwilling to surrender their hearts to the Lord. They are putting up resistance. If there are Sauls like that here, turn to God and your whole life will be changed!' Rudolf understood that he was one of those Sauls and was aware of an inner desire to go to the front of the church and repent. But he couldn't see how he would be able to make his way through the packed congregation. 'But all of a sudden I could contain myself no longer,' he writes, 'and, I don't know to this day how, suddenly I found myself in front of the pulpit . . . There was a call for prayer and I knelt down, but was unable to pray - I just wept, and that evening the Lord gave me peace in my soul. When I rose from prayer, the whole world had changed for me.' The revival continued with many other young people coming to faith and the young Christians visiting surrounding villages and towns preaching the love of Christ and seeing many turn to God.

Much of the revival was in unregistered fellowships, such as that in Dedovsk, near Moscow. Like many new congregations the Dedovsk church did not choose to be unregistered - the authorities did not wish to register any more evangelical congregations and the ECB Union offered them no help. Indeed the young church experienced more obstruction from the Union leadership than from the Soviet authorities, who at first ignored their activities. It is not clear whether the authorities chose to put pressure on the Dedovsk church indirectly, through the denominational leaders, or whether the Union leadership was simply extremely cautious and tried to stop any Christian activity that might provoke repression from the authorities. In any case, the Moscow ECB church leadership urged the congregation to disband. The only result was to alienate the Dedovsk congregation from the official church. Instead of identifying themselves with the ECB Union the members deliberately chose to be independent. Elsewhere, other unregistered churches had similar experiences and also distanced themselves from the officially recognized Union.

Independent Pentecostal activity resumed with vigour as Afanasi Bidash and other leaders were released from prison. They travelled across Ukraine and beyond, organizing the churches into a new Union and collecting signatures to a petition to Khrushchev in which they requested to be allowed to register separately from the ECB churches. They claimed to have the support of 90 per cent of Pentecostals, of whom about 100,000 had refused to join the ECB Union and were in unregistered congregations. In January 1957 Bidash led a delegation to Moscow to present the petition. Once more the authorities' response was repressive. He and four others were arrested for anti-Soviet activity and once more sentenced to long periods of imprisonment. A wave of arrests followed in Ukraine with pastors and preachers sentenced in Nikolayev, Zhdanov (Mariupol) and Zaporozhe during 1957.

In Siberia, Kazakhstan and Central Asia, German Lutherans began to rebuild a church life. Gradually little groups began to gather and pieced together what they could remember of the teaching and practice of their Church. At first it was the women who began to meet, often at the bedside of a sick or dying friend to offer comfort through God's word, prayer and singing. Hymn books were reconstructed from memory and people met to read from the Bible. The first congregation to be founded was Eugen Bachmann's church in Tselinograd (Akmolinsk), Kazakhstan. It took two years of petitions to secure official registration and for ten years it was the only legally existing Lutheran church apart from those in the Baltic republics. After the first service at Pentecost 1955, Pastor Bachmann was asked to hold a service the next Sunday in another district of the city. He decided that this service should include communion: for most people who were there it was their first communion for 20-25 years. Right through the summer he held a service every Sunday, always in a different home and always with communion and baptisms. To make space for all who wanted to come the hosts would take all their furniture outside, and it would literally be standing room only.

As autumn approached the congregation began to look for a building to use as a church. Two families who were sharing a house had decided to move to a warmer part of Central Asia and secretly money was collected to buy the house from them. In one half all the dividing walls were removed to make a chapel and Pastor Bachmann moved into the other half. The church was consecrated on Advent Sunday. Every Sunday, worship would begin at 9.00 A.M. and even before one service was finished the next congregation would be waiting to get into the chapel. It would be late in the afternoon before Pastor Bachmann could take a break. By next spring the chapel was too small and it was decided to demolish it and build it larger. Money was quickly raised for the building materials and the men and women of the congregation, joined by the young people in the confirmation class, did all the work themselves. The whole project was completed with such enthusiasm and speed that the church was closed for only one Sunday and the first service was held in the new chapel at Pentecost, just one year after Pastor Bachmann's first cautious service.

Word spread and Pastor Bachmann was invited to towns in the region, where he organized new fellowships, took services and appointed preachers. As the only surviving German pastor he was also invited by groups of German Lutherans thousands of miles away in the Ural mountains and in the far north. He usually acted with great caution, not knowing what the reaction of the authorities might be. In some villages the chairman of the village council, who was always appointed by the Communists, turned a blind eye to the holding of services, providing they were held in the evening and therefore did not disrupt work on the collective farm. Some told him openly that if the Communist Party ordered the services to be stopped they would be obliged to comply, but otherwise they would not interfere. One village chairman even drove Pastor Bachmann home in his official car! In one village, however, the local Christians were too open in their preparations and the local Communist Party secretary enquired why benches were being brought to a house in the centre of the village. Not satisfied with the explanation that there was going to be a celebration, he continued to observe and got the village chairman to stop the proceedings. Pastor Bachmann had managed only to baptize all the children brought by their parents, and the main service had to be abandoned.

One one occasion, in February 1957, Pastor Bachmann was invited by Lutheran congregations in villages in the forests of Udmurtia, northeast of Moscow, where Russian Germans arrested in Germany at the end of the war were working in forestry or digging peat. The local authorities had given permission for the visit and so he was able to travel openly from village to village for a whole week, baptizing, confirming, marrying, visiting the sick, celebrating communion and giving advice to the elders. In a

German village in West Siberia he was reported to the authorities by the leader of a religious sect who hoped to be able to convert the Lutheran flock. However, the situation was turned to good: Pastor Bachmann was summoned to the village council to meet a senior official from the district administration, who questioned him in detail about where he had preached and which villages he still intended to visit. Understanding the malicious intention of the sect leader, the official let the pastor go with the words: 'Good, you may travel to all those places.'

All this time the congregation in Tselinograd was unregistered and therefore illegal. As soon as they had opened the first chapel, Pastor Bachmann and one of the church members went to the authorities in the Kazakh capital Alma-Ata. They were told they had to apply for registration through the local authorities, but got no response. After the new chapel was built, officials gave them severe warnings for acting without permission, but hesitated to take any action against them. Meanwhile Pastor Bachmann had established contact with Lutherans in East Germany, who sent the congregation Bibles, hymn books and other religious literature and even a harmonium. On Maundy Thursday, 1957, a KGB officer and the city fire chief came and ordered the church closed for violation of fire-safety regulations. The congregation had to obey the order, but continued to worship in a barn. The authorities' action, however, prompted them to renew their petitions for registration. Finally, after a visit by a member of the congregation to the Supreme Soviet (parliament) in Moscow, Pastor Bachmann was summoned to Alma-Ata. After four days of negotiations, registration was finally granted, but only under strict conditions. He was told that as pastor in Tselinograd he was not allowed to serve any other congregations or to engage in pastoral work beyond the city; teaching religion, confirmation classes, children's services and youth work were all forbidden, as was any charitable activity; they were not to help other congregations; children and schoolchildren were not allowed to attend services; and the cross on the church should face the yard, not the street, so that passers-by would not recognize the building as a church.

Released in 1955, Father Ciszek found that there was already a lively Catholic parish in Norilsk led by two priests who had been released earlier than he had. Within a few weeks he had organized a Polish parish in another part of the city, holding services in a barrack of a former concentration camp: the barbed wire had been removed and the barracks were now part of the city housing stock. After Sunday mass he conducted baptisms and weddings in ever-increasing numbers as word of his work spread. In the laboratory where he worked it soon became known that he was a priest and staff would seek him out for advice and counselling. A young woman, a member of the Komsomol and married to a Communist Party member, confided that she had been reading a Bible she borrowed from time to time from an old lady; as a result of her reading she wanted to be baptized, and wondered whether as a priest he knew how to do it. On discovering that he did she asked eagerly: 'When can I be baptized?' He told her: 'When I find out what you know about God, about baptism, about salvation and a lot of other things. Also I have to make sure how sincere you are.' He sent her away with a list of Bible passages to read and arranged to meet her regularly. 'Working with Nina, night after night,' he wrote, 'I could actually sense the grace of God at work - in her sincerity, in her enthusiasm and in the change which had come over her.'

However, the watchful eye of the authorities was never far away. Before long Father Ciszek was summoned to an interview with the KGB. 'Who gave you permission to do missionary work? You know that requires Moscow's approval.' He told them he was not agitating or advertising, but if people came to him as a priest he couldn't turn them away. They argued for an hour and finally dismissed him with a warning to 'watch out'. Through the summer and autumn of 1956 the three priests worked even harder, but at the beginning of 1957 they were summoned again and given a 'final' warning. Father Ciszek's two colleagues felt that it was indeed time for them to move on and after Easter 1957 he was left as the only priest in Norilsk. A year later he himself celebrated his last Easter there. On the Wednesday after Easter he was summoned again to the KGB. 'Your missionary work here in Norilsk is not needed. You have ten days to leave Norilsk; and never think of coming back.' Ordered to live in Krasnoyarsk, Father Ciszek was refused permission to serve a parish whose priest had just died. Soon he was moved on to Abakan, and finally was allowed to return to the USA.

TEN

'I'll Show the Last Christian on TV'

'**D**ON'T BRING YOUR children,' said the deacon guarding the door of the church to Georgi Vins one Sunday in 1961. 'Only adults are allowed into the services!' Sadly Georgi's wife told him to go into church while she took the children home. Soon after there was a commotion as two boys dashed past the deacon and ran to the front of the church with the deacon in hot pursuit. When he tried to eject the boys there was uproar in the congregation, and the pastor indicated that they should be allowed to remain. They had come in to the city church in Kiev from one of the villages where their church had already been closed down. Meanwhile several parents had slipped in with their children. However, the pastor insisted that in future all children would have to be barred from attending, because the authorities were insisting on it.

The situation of all the Churches had taken a sharp turn for the worse in 1959 when Nikita Khrushchev launched a much more active anti-religious policy. Churches were closed, Christians of all denominations were imprisoned, and anti-religious propaganda was stepped up. The campaign was part of the programme to establish a fully Communist society by 1980, by which time religion would be entirely superfluous. Religion would be relegated to museums as a relic of the past and Khrushchev boasted that he would show the last Christian on television.

Paradoxically, Khrushchev was regarded as a liberal in most other respects. He had shocked many people in the Soviet Union in 1956 by denouncing Stalin's repressive methods, and inaugurated a 'thaw' in political life, in the world of the arts and in international relations. Khrushchev personally authorized the publication of Alexander Solzhenitsyn's story of the Gulag, *A Day in the Life of Ivan Denisovich*. New criminal codes introduced in 1959-60 in each of the Soviet republics abolished the infamous catch-all Article 58 on anti-Soviet activity and replaced it with a section of more narrowly defined 'crimes against the state'. The maximum sentence was reduced from 25 to 15 years, though some political prisoners regarded as being particularly dangerous opponents of the Soviet system were detained for the whole of their 25-year sentences imposed under Stalin.

The new campaign against religion, however, did not necessarily conflict with Khrushchev's anti-Stalin drive. Firstly, Khrushchev's denunciations were of Stalin's treatment of the party and of Communists rather than of his reign of terror over the people. Khrushchev passed over in silence the brutality of the collectivization of agriculture and the horrors of the man-made famine in Ukraine in 1933. Secondly, Stalin's compromise with religion during the Second World War and his toleration of the consolidation of the officially recognized churches after the war could be seen as a deviation from the policies laid down by Lenin.

Even the reform of the criminal codes, which put an end to wide-scale arrests on political grounds, had an anti-religious twist. Instead of charging active Christians with anti-Soviet activity under the discredited Article 58, the authorities now had the opportunity to use a new non-political article, 'Infringement of the person and rights of citizens under the guise of performing religious rituals' (Article 227 in the Russian Code). This article was originally designed to provide a means of prosecuting leaders and active members of banned religious groups like True Orthodox Christians, Pentecostals and Jehovah's Witnesses, but was later applied to Baptists and on at least one occasion to an Orthodox priest. The maximum sentence was five years' imprisonment followed by five years' exile. Admittedly this was a much less severe penalty than the previous 25-year sentences, but the new article was specific to religious activity and therefore much easier to apply with the appearance of legitimacy.

Khrushchev's anti-religious campaign was directed at both the registered and the unregistered churches. The number of legal places of worship was cut drastically by using any pretext to withdraw registration and close churches. Precise statistics are not yet available, but it is believed that in the five-year period of the campaign, from 1959 to 1964 when Khrushchev was deposed, about half the registered churches were closed. Almost all the male monasteries and most of the women's convents were closed, as were five of the eight Orthodox seminaries. The two government councils for religious affairs at every meeting approved proposals from local authorities for the closure of scores of churches. The volume was so great that far from examining each case in detail, as required by the law, the two councils could do no more than rubber-stamp local decisions.

There is much concrete evidence of extensive church closures. The Komsomol newspaper announced in June 1961 that 500 places of worship had been closed in two regions alone. In Rostov region half the Baptist churches were closed during 1960, and Baptists calculated that throughout the USSR 300 of their churches had been closed in the first half of 1961. In Kherson and Nikolayev regions, which had been the birthplace of the Ukrainian evangelical movement, virtually all the village congregations were closed. These closures were achieved through pressure on the ECB superintendent: in some villages there were no local atheists to campaign to get the church closed. Often 'neighbouring' churches were merged, usually at great inconvenience to the members of the church that was closed. In Brest, on the Polish border, the large central congregation was in 1960 amalgamated with a small congregation in the village of Vulka. If it was a case of rationalization, the least inconvenience would have been caused by closing the smaller village church, but in this instance it was the other way round. Only about 100 members of the central church agreed to travel to Vulka for services and the remaining 280 began worshipping in private homes. In Leningrad the ECB congregation was evicted from its city-centre building and rehoused in a small disused Orthodox church on the edge of the city.

Pressure was put on the official church leaders to assist in restricting religious life. The Orthodox Church's council of bishops agreed to remove the parish priest from the position of head of the parish, leaving all administrative matters in the hands of the parish executive committee. This committee was more easily manipulated by the authorities, who bullied its members into submission or used their veto over membership to get a compliant committee. Often local officials simply imposed non-believers who acted on their instructions. As a result hundreds of churches were closed on the initiative of their own executive committees.

Fearful that resistance to the demands of the authorities could lead to the destruction of the Church, the leaders of the ECB Union seemingly caved in to government pressure. At the end of 1959 they drafted a new constitution taking away many of the rights of local churches and sent a circular to all regional superintendents instructing them to ensure that local congregations adhered strictly to government limitations on their activity, including banning children from church and not permitting visiting preachers to speak in church. The letter went even further than the requirements of the law by urging them to keep the baptism of young people aged under 30 to a minimum and discouraging 'unhealthy missionary tendencies'. The latter phrase in particular was seen by many as an indication that the instructions were literally dictated by the atheist authorities. The ECB leaders no doubt felt that their policy was vindicated by the fate of the Seventh Day Adventists, who shared their church building in Moscow. The national council of the Seventh-Day Adventist Church refused to submit to the authorities. In 1960 it was accused of breaking the laws governing religious life and disbanded.

In Tselinograd Lutheran pastor Eugen Bachmann faced increasing harassment after 1959. He and his congregation were particular targets, with a smear campaign aimed at preparing the ground for his arrest and the closure of the church. There were attempts to install listening devices in his home and constant provocations. He was called into the city council and shown a thick file of workers' resolutions condemning him and his 'harmful activity'. As Pastor Bachmann left the room the council chairman called after him: 'We will do everything we can to close your church.' The brave pastor responded vigorously: 'And we will do everything we can to keep it open!' He endured many other unpleasant interviews with officials and anonymous telephone calls which were obviously officially instigated, as they continued even when he had his phone number changed. The congregation took a petition with over 500 signatures complaining at the persecution to the Council for the Affairs of Religious Cults in Moscow, which sent an official to investigate. Since the congregation, as the only registered German Lutheran church, was well known in Germany, the official obviously advised the local authorities to halt their campaign in order to maintain the appearance of religious freedom in the USSR.

In Dedovsk, persecution against the unregistered Baptist church also began in 1959. Over the next two years many of the men of the church were repeatedly arrested and fined. A criminal case was compiled against five of the preachers and in September 1961 they were sentenced to exile in the Krasnoyarsk region of Siberia. They were accused of starting a church, holding services in a private home and organizing children's activities and youth work in the church. Among the evidence was a statement from the ECB Union's regional superintendent for Moscow testifying that the Dedovsk congregation was not a part of the Union and its leaders and activities were not sanctioned by the Union.

All over the country leaders and preachers of unregistered evangelical congregations had similar experiences: they were arrested and fined, their homes were searched, and they were put on trial. Some of the trials took place in court, but many of them were show trials, with the court sitting in cinemas, theatres and factory sports halls in order to make the maximum local impact. Many active Christians were summoned to 'comrades' courts' at their workplace or to community meetings in the districts where they lived, at which they were denounced as antisocial elements. The meetings would pass resolutions urging the authorities to expel them from the town or to prosecute them. On the basis of such resolutions the local council was empowered to revoke their residence permit by administrative order and force them to move elsewhere.

One of the earliest show trials was of Pentecostal leaders in Moscow region in April 1961. The central figure in this trial was a young preacher named Ivan Fedotov, who was alleged to have incited one of the church members to kill her daughter as a sacrifice. In a carefully stage-managed event a group of valiant Komsomol members rescued the girl as she was being brought to Ivan for him to carry out the alleged ritual killing and he was arrested. He was also accused of driving a young woman to suicide and committing acts of 'hooliganism' when requested by the authorities to stop holding open-air services. Ivan later revealed that the first investigator assigned to the case refused to proceed with it on the grounds that it was a fabrication. The second investigator had fewer scruples. The trial was held in a large factory hall in the town of Drezna near Moscow. The entire proceedings were filmed and the resulting documentary widely screened in cinemas. A full-page report appeared in the major weekly writers' newspaper *Literaturnaya gazeta*, which normally avoided publication of blatantly propagandistic material. Ivan was sentenced to ten years' imprisonment, and his five co-defendants to terms ranging from two to seven years.

An interesting aspect of this case was the persistence of Ivan Fedotov's lawyer in protesting his client's innocence. Normally Soviet defence lawyers limit their defence to pleading extenuating circumstances, as questioning the prosecution case, especially in politically sensitive trials, is seen as an attack on the competence of the state prosecution service. At worst this could be viewed as subversive and unprofessional and lead to being barred from practising as a lawyer; at best it is likely to halt any progress in the legal profession. Six years later Ivan's lawyer, S. Ariya, tried to get the case reopened with a strongly worded appeal against the decisions of the Moscow regional court and the Russian Supreme Court. Ariya alleged that Ivan's conviction could be explained only by the need to find him guilty for propaganda purposes. On the two major charges the evidence simply did not stand up to scrutiny and he believed that this must have been obvious to the trial and appeal court judges. Aside from the inadequacy of the evidence, Ariya pointed out that there was no legal basis for citing 'religious fanaticism' as an aggravating circumstance in the alleged incitement to murder. Since the supposed victim came to absolutely no harm the imposition of the maximum sentence was totally inappropriate, argued Ariya. He concluded:

> The Fedotov case at the time it was being examined played an important role as an instrument of anti-religious propaganda. The hearing took place in circumstances which hindered an objective and critical evaluation of the evidence for the guilt of the defendants. I presume that it was this which caused serious mistakes in the verdict and the appeal court decision. Now that Fedotov has served more than half his sentence and the case has been fully exploited for educational purposes, it is necessary to reopen it and re-evaluate it from the perspective of respect for the law.

Ariya's efforts were, however, unsuccessful, and Ivan served the full ten-year sentence, though towards the end he was transferred to an open prison for good behaviour.

Two of Ivan Fedotov's co-defendants were sentenced under the new Article 227. Cases under this article were relatively simple to prepare. Evangelical groups could easily be portrayed as 'antisocial' with their emphasis on 'separation from the world'. Many Christian parents discouraged their children from joining the Communist-organized youth organizations, the Young Octobrists, the Pioneers and the Communist Youth League (the Komsomol). Thus, it was alleged, they deprived them of the joys of childhood and brought them up alienated from the society in which they lived. Refusal to have televisions or go to the cinema was seen in the same light. Adult members were discouraged from joining the trade unions, which were Communist-dominated, but which were also the channel for the provision of some social security benefits such as sick pay and visits to health resorts. In this way, it was alleged, the church leaders deprived members of their social rights. Sometimes adult baptism was portrayed as endangering life or health when conducted outdoors except in the summer months. With Pentecostals there was also another aspect to the accusations of being damaging to health: their form of worship itself, with the practice of speaking in tongues, was claimed to provoke mental instability and even breakdowns. It was not difficult for a prosecutor to collect 'evidence' of this kind and to prove the identities of those who were leaders or particularly active in the life of the churches.

Altogether hundreds of Christians were imprisoned under Article 227 during the Khrushchev anti-religious campaign. Precise figures are not available, but the Baptists alone documented almost two hundred cases and an analysis of the Soviet media at the time reveals many more trials involving Baptists, Pentecostals, Adventists and others. There were also some other cases similar to the Fedotov trial in which universally recognized criminal charges such as rape were brought. A more common method of discrediting Christians was to bring charges under Article 227 and to allow all kinds of allegations to be made in court - ranging from hypocrisy, dishonesty and ruthless exploitation of believers to child sacrifice. These allegations were fully reported in the media as though they were facts endorsed by the court when in fact they did not relate to the substance of the charges. Sometimes the press reports glossed over the basic charges arising from the activity of the defendants as church leaders, for the official propaganda line was that there was freedom of religion in the Soviet Union and that those on trial were charlatans and criminals and not genuine believers. The media were quite successful in instilling this distorted image of evangelical Christians, reinforcing a deep-seated prejudice which persists to this day.

Although the authorities' aim of a drastic reduction in the number of places of worship was achieved, the policy of intimidating Christians into submission was less successful. In February 1960 the head of the Russian Orthodox Church, Patriarch Alexi, addressing a peace conference at the Kremlin, spoke out on the attacks and denunciations to which the Church was being subjected and declared that 'the gates of hell shall not prevail against it'. In the same month the Church's journal announced the excommunication of five priests, including a theology professor, who had publicly renounced their faith and joined the anti-religious campaign. These counterattacks led to the removal and house arrest of the Patriarch's right-hand man, Metropolitan Nikolai – and quite possibly his death in unexplained circumstances in September 1960 – and the transfer of church administration to the more compliant Bishop Pimen. The chairman of the Council for Russian Orthodox Affairs was dismissed, accused of having cooperated too much with the Church.

The strongest resistance was encountered in the evangelical churches. They could look back on past repressions and see how God had preserved His Church. On the surface the Church had been wiped out, but it had lived on in the hearts and homes of thousands of faithful Christians and when the persecution had eased there had been renewal and revival. Although thousands had perished in the concentration camps, especially those arrested during the 1930s, some had returned unbroken to their families and churches after Stalin's death. These ex-prisoners were an example and an inspiration to many, and the faithfulness of those who had died was remembered with love and respect and a determination that their death should not be in vain. Unregistered congregations refused to bow to repression. New leaders stepped forward to replace those who were arrested and worship continued in homes or forest glades. Some, especially Pentecostals, went 'underground', meeting as unobtrusively as possible in small groups, cautiously approaching their hosts' home one or two at a time. Others found quiet places in the forests where the whole congregation could gather without drawing too much attention. Others still tried to be as open as possible in continuing their life of worship. As many as two thirds of evangelical congregations and groups were unregistered because they had never had the opportunity to register.

The example of the unregistered churches demonstrated to many that compliance with the wishes of the authorities was not necessary in order to ensure survival. Even before the full force of the anti-religious campaign was unleashed on the churches, there was resistance to leaders who were seen to compromise with the authorities by trying to restrain the most active Christians. Already by 1958 independent Baptist groups had broken away from registered churches in a number of cities from Tashkent in Central Asia in the east to Brest on the Polish border in the west. The authority of the ECB Union leadership slipped as they invariably supported the discredited local or regional leaders. As pressure to restrict the activities of the churches grew, more and more active Christians protested and either left the registered churches or were expelled.

Nikolai Baturin, after completing his sentence, had at first been refused permission to move away from the far north, but after his marriage and the birth of their first child he and his wife were allowed to move to the town of Shakhty, Rostov region. The young people, ex-prisoners and some of the older members received them warmly, but the pastor had been very cool toward them. They soon learnt that he had been intimidated into forbidding any meetings, especially youth meetings, which would encourage church growth. He had threatened the young people that he would have to report them if they held meetings in homes and that they were risking imprisonment. The atmosphere was quite different to the freedom, joy and unity in Christ of the Vorkuta church. However, some people felt the need for deeper fellowship and met in small groups in each other's homes. Soon after Nikolai arrived, to the pastor's displeasure, a Bible study group began to meet and its members also gathered for prayer and fasting on Fridays. Nikolai and some of the other preachers led the Bible studies; there were lively discussions and the young people began to be actively involved. The pastor, afraid of the reaction of the authorities, did all he could to dissuade them, although, reluctantly, under pressure from the membership, he did allow Nikolai to preach from time to time.

In 1959 the church was closed by a health and safety commission which declared that the building was in a state of disrepair and therefore unsafe and that the toilets violated sanitary rules by being too close to the meeting room. At first the members attended neighbouring churches, but as more and more churches were closed Nikolai and the others who were in the prayer and Bible study group began to seek guidance on whether they should begin to hold services in their homes. Finally a group of twelve became convinced that the Lord was leading them and began holding services. More and more Christians in Shakhty joined them, but apart from one deacon all the old leaders stayed away. The pastor accused Nikolai and his friends of ruining any chance of reopening the church by their irresponsible actions.

People in hundreds of other churches had similar experiences. Ivan Antonov had moved to Kirovograd, Ukraine, on completion of his sentence in 1954, became a preacher in the ECB church and was elected secretary of the preachers. The local official of the Council for the Affairs of Religious Cults had insisted on the appointment of his own nominee as a deacon and through this deacon controlled the life of the congregation. All lists of candidates for baptism had to be submitted to him and he would delete the names of all young people. When Ivan refused to accept this he was dismissed as secretary of the preachers. In 1960, when the Letter of Instructions was circulated, he objected to its provisions and was barred from preaching. Soon he and other members who protested were expelled from the congregation. Ivan was elected as leader of the independent unregistered congregation that formed as a result.

Before long about two thirds of Baptists were in unregistered congregations and groups. Many of these were in churches that had never been registered, but they were joined by thousands whose churches lost registration or who left or were expelled because of their opposition to the new restrictions. There was a similar movement away from membership of registered ECB churches among Pentecostals, groups of whom defected from forcibly combined congregations to worship independently or to join up with already existing unregistered Pentecostal congregations.

The circulation of the new statutes and the Letter of Instructions among the ECB churches had an effect opposite to the one intended by the authorities. It crystalized the growing unease with the ECB Union leadership into a widespread movement to bring about reform in the Church by calling a national church congress which would debate the issues and elect a leadership accountable to the members. This proposal was first put privately to the Union leaders, but when they refused even to seek permission from the authorities for a congress, an 'initiative group' of reformers in August 1961 sent out a letter to all ECB congregations asking them to press for a congress. The supporters of change became known as '*initsiativniki*' (supporters of the initiative group) or 'Reform Baptists'. The reformers made a detailed critique of the church statute, proposing extensive amendments. When the leadership still refused to accept any change the reform group announced the excommunication of the entire Union leadership and some of the regional superintendents, promising to issue supplementary lists as other superintendents and local pastors were excommunicated by assemblies of local Christians. The two men who emerged as leaders of the reform movement were Gennadi Kryuchkov and Georgi Vins.

Gennadi Kryuchkov had personal experience of the attitudes of the Union leadership. As a young preacher in the congregation at Uzlovaya, near Tula, he had in 1956 been considered for nomination for study abroad. There was no doubt a genuine desire to encourage promising young preachers, but without the consent of the KGB nothing could be done. The KGB could block the advancement of anybody who would not cooperate with them. Kryuchkov confided to the Union's general secretary, Alexander Karev, that he was being constantly summoned by KGB officials, who wanted to know details about the life of the church. Karev gently told him that such questions were inevitable and he should not be afraid to answer them: if he didn't, then somebody else would and he would simply be pushed aside from his position in the church.

Georgi Vins had seen for himself what kind of person was at that time sent to study abroad, along with the sons of the Union leaders. At the church in Kiev that he attended, a young man named Alexei Stoyan was welcomed at a service as a new member, allegedly from a congregation in Moldavia. It was announced that he was on his way to study theology in England. After the service the young people of the congregation eagerly gathered round and plied the newcomer with questions. To their amazement, he could not answer the simplest question about his faith and they rapidly came to the conclusion that he was not a believer at all. Nevertheless, he completed his studies and for many years ran the international department of the Union, controlling the foreign travel of Baptist leaders and organizing the programmes of the Union's foreign guests. He was widely suspected of being a KGB plant, acting not only as an informer, but also as a channel for KGB instructions.

For the Vins family and others in the Kiev central church the last straw was when their children were turned away from church. Georgi Vins and about one hundred of the members wrote a letter of protest to the ECB Union in Moscow. However, all the signatories were called in by the pastor and deacons and warned that they would be expelled from the church if they did not renounce their letter. Each of them was also summoned by the KGB, who told them: 'Children and young people belong to the government, not to you. The Soviet authorities do not permit religious upbringing of children or teenagers.' Soon Georgi and twenty others were expelled from the congregation and they and other members decided they must organize their own fellowship. Georgi's daughter Natasha recalls her disappointment at not being able to go to church any more, and her exitement one Saturday evening when her grandmother told the children to go to bed early, in order to be able to get up very early to go to church. They couldn't believe it. 'Granny,' she asked, 'are you sure that we can go too?' The next morning they took a train out of Kiev and walked from a small station along a forest track. In a clearing, people had spread out blankets on the grass. Natasha couldn't understand where the church was, but when the service started and she heard the familiar hymns, she realized that this was just as much church as the services she had been used to. And so she grew up in the 'forest church'.

The response of the authorities was to begin a crack-down on unregistered congregations and on the leaders of the reform movement, making extensive use of Article 227 to imprison the most active Christians. A wide range of other measures was applied in seeking to break the spirit of the unregistered congregations. These included detention of participants in services, 50-rouble fines (then over an average week's wages), and 'administrative arrest' for periods up to 15 days. In some places the break-up of services was accompanied by violence; in others children were taken away from their parents and placed in boarding schools.

One of the most fiercely persecuted congregations at this time was an independent Pentecostal congregation in Chernogorsk, Siberia. Its members were subjected to all these forms of attack and on more than one occasion the authorities attempted to disperse their meetings by calling in the fire-truck from the local mine and driving worshippers out of their prayer house with high-pressure hoses. Children from Christian families were mocked and denigrated at school, so that some parents decided to withdraw them from school. Some of the children were then taken away by force to be brought up in state children's homes. In desperation, in January 1963, 32 men, women and children of the congregation travelled to the American Embassy in Moscow to request help in emigrating in order to escape persecution. They were persuaded to leave the embassy and were escorted by the Soviet authorities back to Chernogorsk, but they left extensive documentation of their persecution at the embassy. Five members of one of the families involved, the Vashchenkos, together with two members of the Chmykhalov family, returned to the embassy fifteen years later and spent almost five years there before finally receiving permission to emigrate. They became famous throughout the world as the 'Siberian Seven'. Two of the Vashchenko daughters, Lida and Lyuba, were among those who had been held in a children's home in 1963.

When the authorities saw that these attacks were having no effect and that on the contrary the ECB reform movement was growing stronger and stronger, they modified their policy. By depriving many churches of registration and tightening controls on the registered ECB churches to such an extent that many members found the restrictions unacceptable, the authorities had in fact lost control over the greater part of the ECB churches. Hundreds of small groups and even large congregations were worshipping freely, ignoring official restrictions and limitations and electing their leaders without the authorities being able to exert any influence. Unlike the registered congregations, these unregistered fellowships were not afraid to proclaim the Gospel openly and to urge people to accept Jesus Christ as their Saviour. They were therefore seeing people come to Christ and were growing. The authorities decided it was necessary to ease some of the restrictions in order to encourage a return to the registered churches and permitted the Union to call a national conference in October 1963. However, it was too late: the gulf between the leaders of the reform movement and the Union leadership was too great to bridge. The reformers sent three observers to the conference who refused to participate in the proceedings.

The conference was, however, in many ways a success. It voted to constitute itself as a congress, empowered to enact changes in the Church's statute. Although debate was limited, the Union leadership had already accepted many of the amendments put forward by the reformers. The resulting statute was a huge improvement over the 1959 statute, which was now described as a draft for discussion, rather than a binding document. The Letter of Instructions was openly recognized as a mistake and withdrawn. The ten-man Union Council was elected, but only one new candidate was put forward to fill the vacancy left by a member who had recently died and had not yet been replaced. It was to be many years yet before delegates to Baptist congresses in the USSR were to have the opportunity to vote in elections in which there were more candidates than positions to be filled.

The process of change begun at this congress persuaded some to return to the registered churches, but the majority of the reformers and their followers were not satisfied. They were not convinced that the Union leadership had genuinely repented of its past mistakes. They found the statement that the 1959 statute had merely been a 'draft for discussion' extremely dubious in the light of the fact that many of them had been expelled from their churches for opposing it. The amendments that had been made were, of course, to be welcomed, but as far as the reformers were concerned they did not go far enough, as important aspects of their proposals had not been implemented. The failure of any of the Union leadership to stand down and make way for less discredited men was also a great discouragement for the reformers. They feared that the changes made would remain on paper only, while the day-to-day running of the Union would continue in the same way and remain in the hands of the same people.

The easing of restrictions on the Union was not accompanied, however, by any improvement in the situation of the unregistered congregations.

Indeed, the pace of arrests was not slackened, and in February 1964 a conference of the families of prisoners elected a temporary council of prisoners' relatives in order to collect information about prisoners and children taken away from their families and to channel aid to the neediest prisoners' families. That 'temporary' council was to exist for 24 years until the arrests finally came to an end in 1988 under Gorbachev. The Council of Prisoners' Relatives was to become one of the most effective ministries of the unregistered Baptist churches.

Towards the end of Khrushchev's campaign, which ended only when he was ousted from power in October 1964, the authorities realized that, unless they were prepared to return to Stalinist terror, repressive measures alone were not going to eradicate religion. Therefore, alongside the persecution, propaganda was re-emphasized as a means of re-educating believers. For most of the campaign propaganda had been directed at combating the influence of the Church by discrediting believers. Now the need was felt to train better informed propagandists who might be taken more seriously by believers themselves.

ELEVEN

Faithful Witnesses

'MY TIME OF exile was wonderfully blessed by the Lord,' wrote Nikolai Melnikov who had been sent for four years' exile to Kansk in the Krasnoyarsk region of central Siberia after serving a three-year sentence in a labour camp.

> There in Siberia, in the remote settlements of the taiga (the thick Siberian forest), in almost inaccessible places, there were many Christians whose faith had grown cold. But through contact with awakened Christians the Lord renewed their faith and fanned aflame the glimmering wick in their hearts. I remember a letter which our church received from some believers in a certain village inviting us to come and preach in their settlements, for all the people wanted to hear the Word of God.

The persecution of the Khrushchev period did not deter men like Nikolai from continuing their ministry, even while serving sentences of imprisonment and exile. Indeed, as many times before in the history of the evangelicals of Russia and the Soviet Union, the persecution served to spread revival and bring the Gospel to new places. Looking back at their own history, Christians could see that God had blessed and strengthened those who remained faithful under persecution and that the Church had always outlived its persecutors. The swift and sudden removal of Nikita

Khrushchev from power by his colleagues on the Politburo in October 1964 came earlier than anybody expected.

Khrushchev's fall and the reversal of many of his policies raised hopes that the campaign against religion would be halted. The first signs were good. The forced closure of churches ended, and there was a lull in the persecution of unregistered Christian congregations. The cases of many prisoners were reviewed: the sentences of some were reduced, some were released early before completion of their sentences, others had their period of exile cancelled and were able to return home immediately after their camp term, and in a few cases the convictions were admitted to be unjust and the prisoners were rehabilitated.

Khrushchev's removal inaugurated a period of apparent stability under the leadership of Leonid Brezhnev which was to last for almost 20 years. This period was later condemned as the 'era of stagnation' during which steadily rising industrial output and improvements in the general standard of living could not compensate for lack of new initiatives and investment. This period was to sow the seeds for the rapid economic and political collapse of the Soviet Union under Gorbachev.

In the treatment of religion what commentators have called 'a year of drift' followed Khrushchev's fall from power. It was not clear what direction future policy would take. There was a definite move away from crude attacks on religion in the form of closing churches, removing ministers and priests by adminstrative measures, physical violence, criminal trials and slanderous press articles, though all of these continued to some degree. Anti-religious propaganda continued, but became more reasoned and moderate. But apart from the release of prisoners, there was no attempt to undo the damage done to the churches in the previous five years.

This period provided a breathing space during which an Orthodox opposition emerged and the Baptist reform movement regrouped. Two Orthodox priests, Fathers Gleb Yakunin and Nikolai Eshliman, wrote an open letter to the Patriarch criticizing the church leadership for giving in to the demands of the authorities and urging him to reinstate the priest as the head of the parish. Their call was taken up by Archbishop Yermogen of Kaluga and eight other bishops who proposed convening a national church council to discuss and vote on these issues. The Orthodox Church itself suppressed these voices of protest, suspending the two priests from their parishes and removing the archbishop from his diocese and exiling him to a monastery. But neither the Church nor the Soviet authorities could silence the opposition when ordinary parishioners began petitioning for justice and protesting at persecution. Once people began to speak out, those who were shocked at what had been happening realized they were not alone and spoke out themselves. Nevertheless, Orthodox opposition remained fragmented and was not always able to give effective support to the victims of persecution.

The Baptist reform movement had built up an extensive network of contacts and was able to make use of the 'year of drift' to consolidate. The reform leaders' verdict on the ECB Union was that it was beyond redemption, and they formalized the split within the church by organizing themselves in September 1965 into a separate Baptist denomination, governed by the Council of Churches of Evangelical Christians-Baptists (known as the CCECB or 'Council of Churches' – not to be confused with ecumenical councils of churches in other countries). The two leaders of the reform movement, Gennadi Kryuchkov and Georgi Vins, became President and General Secretary of the new Council.

In spite of the beginnings of change in the ECB Union many of the old leaders were still in office and their attitude to the authorities remained the same as before. The reform movement continued to win new adherents among those who were eager to see renewal, reaching its peak in 1966. One new supporter who joined the movement at this time was Konshaubi Dzhangetov, a member of a church in Ust-Dzhegutskaya, on the northern slopes of the Caucasus mountains. He had seen this church, formed soon after the end of the Second World War and registered a few years later, gradually decline and lose its young people. At first there had been youth meetings, lively singing and enthusiastic preaching. But the authorities had banned youth meetings and then the leaders themselves excluded children from worship and refused to baptize anybody aged under 30. The members were told if they brought their children to church or encouraged young people to become Christians they would risk losing registration and bring about the closure of the church.

Early in 1966 Konshaubi was invited to a conference organized by preachers from both registered and unregistered churches. The meeting had to be kept secret both from the authorities and from the senior church leaders in the region. People spoke of their calling to work among children and young people and of the need for the Church to be independent of atheist authorities in every aspect of its spiritual life. Konshaubi went home convinced that something needed to be done in his church. He told the members that he and they needed to repent for not allowing children into church and for refusing to baptize young people. The congregation was divided: some agreed with Konshaubi, but the pastor warned that he was a candidate for prison. A week later the area superintendent expelled Konshaubi and twenty others. They decided to hold services in their homes and in a few months fifty people were attending worship, including young Christians who had been barred from membership in the registered church. Although they had no pastor they met for worship three times a week and an ordained pastor from another unregistered church visited every month to hold services of baptism and communion. Six months later Konshaubi and six other preachers from the North Caucasus were arrested and sentenced to prison.

The 'year of drift' ended with the details of a new policy beginning to take shape. The administrative assault on the churches was not to be renewed, but more subtle pressures were to continue and there would be little sympathy for those who wanted to reopen churches. The two government councils, the Council for the Affairs of the Russian Orthodox Church and the Council for the Affairs of Religious Cults, were merged into a single body, the Council for Religious Affairs, which was given greater central power to enforce policy. The development of better informed and more sophisticated propaganda was continued, with a greater emphasis on the positive promotion of atheism rather than merely attacking religion.

The strength and vitality of the unregistered churches worried the authorities and new measures were devised to combat them. In March 1966 three decrees amended Article 142 of the Criminal Code and extended the scope of its application. This article, on 'violation of the separation of Church and state', had previously provided for a fine of 50 roubles or one year's 'corrective labour' (deduction of a percentage of salary for the duration of the sentence). Now it added a sentence of up to three years' imprisonment for repeated offenders and made it quite clear that any form of organized religious instruction for children was illegal. Organizing religious activities not permitted by law (any activity of an unregistered church as well as activity other than worship by a registered church) was already an offence under Article 142, but its scope was now widened to include refusal to register and encouraging other people to engage in illegal religious activity. Although the new penalty could also be used against registered church leaders who consistently engaged in activity that was not permitted, these decrees were clearly formulated with the unregistered Baptists in mind. Almost anything they did was automatically an offence and the collection of evidence against them was extremely simple.

The new version of Article 142 indeed became a major weapon in the campaign against the unregistered Baptists, though it did not entirely replace Article 227. Later in 1966, two totally new articles were added to the Criminal Code, with a maximum penalty of three years. Article 190-1, 'the dissemination of deliberately false fabrications slandering the Soviet state and social order', could be applied to anybody who circulated information about persecution; and Article 190-3, 'organization of or active particpation in group actions violating public order', covered street evangelism and open-air baptism as well as demonstrations. Both articles were also directed against growing political dissent but were widely used against Baptists.

These new penalties facilitated a continuation of the imprisonment of unregistered religious leaders which remained an important plank in religious policy. Between 1961 and 1970 at least 500 Baptists were arrested and sentenced to various terms of imprisonment, more than half of them since Khrushchev's fall in 1964. At the same time gradual improvement in the situation of the registered churches was permitted, in an attempt to undermine support for those calling for change. This too was a continuation of the response to dissent under Khrushchev, when there had been a U-turn and the ECB Union had been allowed to hold a congress. This twin-track policy – concessions to those who were willing to work within the limitations imposed by the state and persecution of those who refused to accept restrictions – was to continue right through the Brezhnev era.

The leaders of the new Council of Churches appealed to the government for registration separately from the ECB Union and urged local congregations to do the same. In September 1965 the President of the USSR, Anastas Mikoyan, received a delegation of five, including Nikolai Baturin, Iosif Bondarenko and a representative of the Council of Prisoners' Relatives. They had prepared documentation on 30 cases, but were able to make a presentation on only ten cases. However, Mikoyan agreed to receive and examine all the documents and promised that the Baptists' complaints would be investigated. However, a month later Mikoyan was removed from office and there was no improvement. Many petitions were directed to the new Communist Party General Secretary, Leonid Brezhnev. On 16 May 1966, 500 delegates from churches all over the USSR converged on the building of the Central Committee of the Communist

Party to hand in a petition seeking permission to hold a congress of all registered and unregistered churches, and requesting recognition of the Council of Churches, an end to persecution, the freeing of prisoners, the right to teach and be taught religion and a halt to atheist interference in church affairs.

The party leaders declined to receive representatives of the Christians and the entire delegation spent the night in the open air in the yard of the building, anxious that if they dispersed they would be picked up one by one by the police. In the morning they were joined by a hundred more Christians from the Moscow area. A public protest on this scale in the centre of Moscow was unprecedented and the authorities seemed uncertain how to handle the situation. Detachments of soldiers, police and KGB arrived to disperse them. Then an official announced that ten leaders would be received and ordered everybody else to leave. Not trusting the authorities, the delegates responded that they would wait for the return of their leaders and began to pray and sing in the square in front of the building. Soon they were surrounded by auxiliary police, but not before a large crowd had gathered. Finally the members of the delegation were pushed into buses and driven off to prison. Some were released the next day after questioning, others were sentenced to 10-15 days' arrest.

Thirteen of those detained on 17 May were identified as leaders of the movement and faced criminal charges, including Nikolai Baturin and another member of the Council of Churches. On 19 May two leaders who had not been present, Georgi Vins and Mikhail Khorev, visited the Central Committee building on behalf of the Council of Churches to enquire about the fate of those arrested two days earlier. They were asked to return later in the day for a reply, and when they did so received a hostile response. They were told that the authorities would never agree to a congress under the leadership of the Council of Churches. As they emerged from the building they were arrested and taken away in separate cars. Gennadi Kryuchkov was arrested on 30 May and he and Vins, as the chief leaders of the Council of Churches, were tried together in November in Moscow and sentenced to three years' imprisonment each. They were accused of organizing illegal religious activity and masterminding the demonstration of 16-17 May. Another Council member had already been arrested on 15 May, and a sixth was detained on 20 September, leaving five members at liberty, constantly on the road, keeping one step ahead of the authorities. In August 1967 another Council member, Dmitri Minyakov, was also arrested. All the imprisoned Council members received three-year sentences.

There had already been some arrests in the period since Khrushchev's removal and after the May 1966 protest supporters of the Council of Churches were arrested all over the Soviet Union. By August 1968, 227 were known to be serving sentences and a further six had just been arrested and were under investigation. By then only seven were still serving sentences imposed under Khrushchev, though several of those now imprisoned had also been arrested in the Khrushchev campaign. More than half had been arrested in 1966. Among those arrested at this time was the popular young evangelist Iosif Bondarenko, known as the 'Billy Graham of Ukraine'. He had been speaking at a large rally in a park in Lvov, in western Ukraine. The police ordered the gathering to break up and tried to disturb it with a loud-hailer. Bondarenko told the police: 'If you don't leave us in peace here, we'll go to the market place and preach the Gospel there!' He was then arrested and sentenced to three years' strict regime camp. Not yet aged thirty, he had already been sentenced to eight years in 1962, but was released early after Khrushchev's fall from power.

These repressions directed at the unregistered churches did not, however, have the desired effect: as the continuing waves of arrests showed, the churches and their leaders were not to be deterred. Within months of Iosif Bondarenko's arrest, two leaders of his home church in Odessa were also arrested. In February 1967 seven more from the same church – five men and two women – were put on trial. They had stepped forward to fill the gaps left by those already arrested.

Although labour camp conditions were still harsh many of the prisoners found opportunities to be evangelists in their places of detention. When Iosif Bondarenko was married not long after completing his sentence, his best man was an ex-criminal converted through his ministry in imprisonment. This wedding was more like an evangelistic rally with two thousand people present. Christian prisoners were frequently mocked or worse by the camp officers and by the criminals among whom they found themselves, but with time they often won the respect of their fellow prisoners, some of whom would come to them and for the first time in their lives begin to talk seriously about the Christian faith. Sometimes even camp officials and guards behaved with kindness out of sympathy and respect for Christian prisoners. In any case it was impossible for Christians to hide their beliefs. The articles of the criminal code under which they were usually sentenced spoke of religion and soon everyone in a camp would know there was a Christian among them.

Konshaubi Dzhangetov experienced the usual 'baptism of fire' when he arrived in camp in January 1967. The officers mocked him for being a Muslim by background but having adopted the Russian faith, Christian, when they, the Russians, had already abandoned all faith. Sometimes as he prayed over his food with his eyes closed his plate of watery soup would be stolen, literally from under his nose. Often, as he prayed at night in his barrack, a dirty boot or some other missile would strike him. He was reminded of the hostility of his Muslim relatives when he had become a Christian. The Lord had not abandoned him then and he was sure that he was not forgotten now in his loneliness and discouragement. Two months later another Christian, Fyodor Makhovitsky, pastor of the CCECB congregation in Leningrad (St Petersburg), arrived in the camp. They were able to give each other mutual support and took every opportunity to have fellowship. As they prayed together openly in the barrack the missiles stopped and the prisoners even took a perverse joy in embarrassing camp officers inspecting the barrack by telling them: 'Don't make any noise! The Baptists are praying!' The whole barrack would fall silent and officer and prisoners would listen to the two Christians praying aloud together. The officer would generally not know what to do and soon walk out without disturbing them, whereupon the barrack would return to its usual hubbub of conversation and movement. Soon prisoners began to come to them to talk about God.

In April they were joined by Georgi Vins. By sharing their own food parcels with prisoners who received nothing from their families, they were able to show Christian compassion in a practical way. They were prepared to lend a listening ear to those who wanted to talk. One lonely prisoner whom they befriended had been a misfit in camp because the prisoners recognized that he was not one of their own. The night before his release he finally confided that he had been a police major. If that had been known he would probably have been murdered in camp. In tears he admitted that he had helped to break up Baptist meetings in the Moscow area and to arrest the leaders, and now the only people who had helped him were Baptists! Vins urged him to find the Christians he had persecuted and start going to their meetings. By the summer about ten prisoners were very close to faith in God and meeting regularly for discussion with the three Christians, although only one was prepared to pray with them. On her first visit Konshaubi's wife was able to smuggle in a New Testament, which was secretly lent out to those who wanted to learn more.

During his second sentence from 1974 to 1979 Georgi Vins experienced great eagerness on the part of prisoners to know what the Bible taught and to read it for themselves. His family managed to smuggle into the camp fifteen chapters of John's gospel, then a gospel of Mark and finally a complete New Testament. When he left the camp near the end of his sentence to be transported to a remote area to serve five years of exile, he gave the New Testament to the group of prisoners who were on the road to faith and took with him just the Mark's gospel, which was printed in a small format specially designed to be easily hidden by Christian prisoners and soldiers. He hid it in his soap box, but during a search on the train between prisons it was discovered by a guard, who wanted to confiscate it. Vins had already annoyed the guard by speaking up in defence of an elderly prisoner who had been too slow taking off his boots for inspection and had been struck by the guard. Now Vins clenched his fist round the little gospel and refused to give it up. He was inviting a severe beating, but for some reason the guard relented and let him keep it. By now shaking at the thought of what could have happened to him, he reflected on what had prompted him to such folly. The answer was not long coming.

In the transit prison in Novosibirsk, Vins was placed in a cell full of violent prisoners, some of them multiple murderers. The prison warders had deliberately led them to believe that he had been sent to spy on them in the hope that they would murder him. On entering the cell he was greeted by a ring of hostile faces. As he explained who he was and why he had been imprisoned, they refused to believe him. Finally the cell leader said: 'If you're a Christian, show us a Bible!' Vins produced the Mark's gospel, explaining that it was part of the Bible, and the whole atmosphere changed. That little book probably saved his life! The prisoners began to read it aloud. One of them offered Vins his bunk, and exhausted by the journey and the tensions of the day he soon fell asleep. As a ray of sunlight broke into the cell the next morning he awoke to the words of the resurrection story being read by one of the prisoners. About fifteen of the twenty prisoners housed in the cell were gathered round the table listening. Seven unforgettable days followed, during which Vins read and expounded the gospel to his cellmates and assured them that even they could know forgiveness of their sins. As he was told to get ready for the next stage of his journey, the prisoners begged him to leave them the gospel. He prayed with them and they asked him for his continued prayers.

Even a brief encounter with a Christian prisoner could have a lasting effect. Mikhail Khorev met a prisoner who told him about a Christian girl who was travelling on the same prison train. For the whole journey she sang, and for some reason the guards didn't stop her. She was the only woman prisoner on a train full of male convicts. Usually when men prisoners see a woman they make all kinds of crude and vulgar remarks. 'But,' the prisoner recalled, 'nobody said anything bad to this girl. Her singing affected all of us. "Sing some more!" "Write down the words for me!" the men called out to her . . . And when she sang, a hush fell. Even the most hardened criminals, men who had served several terms, turned their heads to hide their tears . . . I don't remember the words, but I can still feel her songs in my heart.'

Imprisoned Christians did not press their fellow-prisoners to make a Christian commitment, for they knew that intense persecution might be unleashed on new converts in prison. They preferred to let them come to faith at their own pace, and often encouraged them to look for Christians after they were released, believing that they would be better to take the step of faith in the fellowship of the Church, where they could be nurtured and grow with less risk of interference. But the love, care and counsel of Christian prisoners led some convicts to repentance and faith even in prison. When Viktor Rogalsky arrived in a labour camp in Georgia in 1985 he met a criminal called Yuri, who had had earlier contact with a Christian, and now told Viktor that he had been praying that God would send someone to help him. Later Yuri came to faith. 'I watched as the Lord helped him to grow in faith,' Viktor recalls. 'How lovingly and gently He revealed one truth after another to him. We spent a great deal of time reading, talking and praying together.' Then one day, a few months before the end of Viktor's sentence, Yuri told him: 'I want to be baptized while you're still here.' One morning in March, as Viktor prayed, he knew that he was to baptize Yuri that day. Yuri had the same conviction. They went to the 'Lenin room', which apart from political instruction lectures was nearly always empty, in order to lay the matter before the Lord. Viktor had already looked around for a place to hold a baptism, and had decided on one of two small pools near the administration block. It was a quiet corner where they were unlikely to be noticed. That evening they retired again to the 'Lenin room' to prepare and as they were talking a Georgian prisoner named Kote, with whom Viktor had also spoken about Christ, came into the room. They asked him if he would like to be a witness to Yuri's baptism. Outside there was a thunderstorm and they saw a bolt of lightning hit a power cable and all the lights blacked out. They waited till ten o'clock, then Kote went to see if any of the officials were still in their offices. Yuri was ready to go. Kote asked him if he didn't want to wait till the weather got warmer - Viktor would be released only in May, so there was still time, but Yuri was sure that he wanted to be baptized now. And so, in a little pool behind the barbed wire of a labour camp, Yuri was received by baptism into the fellowship of the Christian Church.

Sometimes the camp officials' attempts to isolate Christian prisoners backfired. Yakov Ivashchenko, senior pastor of the unregistered Baptist church in Kiev, was moved to a new camp because he had been witnessing to his fellow-prisoners. The new camp's chief of operations assembled the 150 prisoners in whose section Yakov had been placed and warned them that Yakov was an especially dangerous political prisoner and threatened to send anyone who talked with him straight to the punishment cells. 'The Lord turned human anger to His own glory,' wrote Yakov. This dire warning served to draw everyone's atttention to him, and, far from isolating him from the other prisoners, won him their immediate respect and protected him from the abuses that new inmates usually suffer at the hands of the prisoners' gangs. Many of the prisoners wanted to hear his side of the story, giving him the opportunity to share his faith.

An unusual witness in camp took place in July 1984 when imprisoned evangelist Pavel Rytikov was visited by his family just after his son Vladimir and daughter Natasha had celebrated a double wedding. The arrival of two bridal couples in their wedding clothes caused quite a stir among the women waiting to see their menfolk and left the commandant quite amazed. Pavel himself could hardly believe his eyes as they walked in. As the couples knelt before him he prayed for them and gave them a word of exhortation, then the whole family sang hymns together. Prisoners passing by the visiting rooms stopped to listen, and one of the guards even passed on a request from one of the prisoners for one of the hymns to be sung again. Of course, not all visits took place in such a relaxed atmosphere, and camp officials often tried to break the spirit of Christian prisoners by refusing, cancelling or curtailing visits on the slightest pretext.

On the other hand camp officials sometimes had a secret sympathy and respect for Christian prisoners. One night Georgi Vins was summoned from his barracks by an official, who took him to his office, tuned in his radio to a Western Christian broadcast and left Georgi there to listen to it. Once, as the prisoners gathered for a roll-call an officer started shouting at Mikhail Khorev because his boots were not clean enough, and ordered Mikhail to follow him to his office. There it turned out that the officer had been seeking a pretext to talk to Mikhail alone. He told Mikhail that ever since he was a child he had been tormented by doubts about the official atheist teaching that there was no God. After this conversation, the officer found many ways to help and support Mikhail in the difficult conditions of camp life.

On another occasion Mikhail was summoned to dig over the strip of ground between the two barbed-wire fences round the camp. He was supervised by a young man who had been sent to do his military service as a camp guard. He began talking to Mikhail, enquiring what he was in camp for. When he heard he was a Baptist he asked to look at his name tag, and said: 'Khorev? Hey, I know who you are! You're the one they write about in *Herald of Salvation*.' It turned out that his parents were neighbours of a Baptist pastor and had agreed to keep *Herald of Salvation* and other Christian magazines for him so that they wouldn't be confiscated when the pastor's house was searched. 'That's how I know your name – I've read the articles you wrote.' The guard was able to tell Mikhail a lot of news of the churches that he had read in the magazines. After three hours of conversation the guard asked Mikhail: 'When you pray, please remember to pray for me too.' 'There's no need to put it off,' Mikhail replied. 'Let's pray right now.' And so, shovel in hand, he prayed for him. Mikhail never saw that guard again, because the next day he was rearrested on new charges, as a result of which he was sentenced to a further two years' imprisonment. 'I realized that the Lord had sent me this special meeting to encourage me,' writes Mikhail. 'He arranges all our circumstances, and our God knows how to send just what we need at the right moment.'

Sometimes encouragement came from fellow-prisoners. In 1968 Jakob Esau was arrested for the fourth time and found himself in an investigation cell with forty hardened criminals who also had several previous arrests. He hoped that his case would be heard by December so that he could spend Christmas in camp where there was a little more freedom than in an overcrowded cell. However, as Christmas approached he was still there. One day, as snow gently fell during the exercise period, memories of family Christmases flooded through Jakob's mind. When he got back to the cell he began to tell his cellmates about how his family prepared for Christmas and how the children looked forward to the Christmas Eve service when they celebrated God's present to mankind – Jesus. In prison of course Christmas was not marked in any way. Christmas Eve was a normal working day and the prisoner who had the bunk next to Jakob's was taken for interrogation to the local police station where his case was being investigated. The prisoner's sister heard that he was there and quickly put together a food parcel and begged the investigating officer to let her give it to her brother. When he returned to the prison almost all was confiscated, but some bread, a piece of salami, some butter and some sugar lumps remained. Back in the cell the prisoner took out a cloth and carefully divided his food in two and offered one half to Jakob. Jakob didn't want to accept it, and said to him: 'You have your own friends.' But the prisoner replied firmly: 'This belongs to you and to nobody else.' Then Jakob said to him: 'Do you know what you have done? You have given me the greatest Christmas present I could imagine.' As Jakob put his hands together and thanked God for his Christmas dinner he was in tears.

Prisoners sent into exile to remote districts of the country on completion of camp sentences also found opportunities for ministry and witness. In the 1970s pastor Nikolai Boiko from Odessa was sent to Siberia to serve a sentence of five years' exile. His exemplary life soon won him the respect of his neighbours and people would stop him in the street and ask his advice on their problems. He was always prepared to help people in practical ways as well as offering spiritual counsel, and some of the villagers became Christians. The local atheists got very angry and got the authorities to send him home before he had served even four years there! In November 1977 Ukrainian evangelist Stepan Germanyuk arrived in his place of exile in the small town of Chumikan, on the Sea of Okhotsk in the far east of Siberia. In the spring his wife and family joined him there, and through the witness of Stepan and his family a small church came into being. 'There in the far east,' Stepan recalled, 'the Lord taught me how marvellously He can lead us if we trust Him at all times. We lacked nothing there, everyone was satisfied. We sensed God's care of us. Of course, our greatest joy was that people came to faith and that I was even able to baptize them there. How encouraging it was to hear people praying: "We praise you, Lord, for sending believers here." God had indeed sent us there, we were His envoys.'

The number of prisoners had peaked at 240 in 1968, but remained high for several years. The Council of Prisoners' Relatives, led by Georgi Vins' mother Lidia, did a great deal to inform the churches, and the outside world, of the plight of the prisoners and to ensure that prisoners' families received regular support in the absence of the breadwinner. Lists of prisoners and copies of appeals to the government were circulated among the churches. These were printed using a simple spirit duplication method. The very same method had been used by the Bolsheviks to produce underground publications and proclamations when they were an outlawed political party under the Tsarist regime. The process was actually described in the 'Great Soviet Encyclopedia', but when Christians tried it out they found it didn't work! Soviet censorship had deliberately cut out one key element in the process in order to prevent the method being used by opponents of the Soviet regime to produce subversive literature. After some further research and experimentation, however, the secret was unlocked and the duplicated sheets with their neat bluish-purple writing soon became a familiar sight. The beauty of the system was that it required no complex equipment.

One of the pioneers in this duplication ministry was Sofia Bochkarova, who lived near Moscow. She was one of the team who discovered and perfected the method and many of the early appeals were duplicated in her home. She was always so thorough in clearing up and cleaning after the work had been done that numerous police searches of her home failed to find any evidence against her and her fellow printers. It was in her apartment that a small group of Christians carried out experiments to produce offset printing plates and developed the first home-made printing press. A number of Sofia's household items ended up playing a vital role in the printing machine as the experimenters looked around for objects they needed to solve a particular problem! After the technicians had finished a night's experiments Sofia would scrub and polish to remove all traces of oil and ink before heading off for a day's work at the factory.

The Council of Prisoners' Relatives was meticulous in collecting information. In 1970 the Council produced a report summarizing the persecution that had been endured by Baptists since the formation of the Initiative Group in 1961. A total of 524 Christians had been imprisoned, some of them more than once; 44 of them were women. A further 391 people had been sentenced to periods of 10-15 days' administrative arrest, and 8,648 interrogations had taken place; in 390 instances children had been interrogated. Fines totalling 94,300 roubles had been levied, representing over 50 years' pay at the average wage of 150 roubles per month.

Regular circulation of new information about persecution enabled Christians to pray for one another and to offer practical support, and thus made an important contribution to building up solidarity among the unregistered churches and giving the reform movement cohesion. The efforts of the members of the Council of Prisoners' Relatives probably made more impact on ordinary Christians than the work of the Council of Churches. Their constant protests and circulation of appeals and information obviously irritated the authorities and in December 1969 Lidia Vins was arrested.

Spurred on by the arrest of Lidia Vins to redouble its efforts, the Council of Prisoners' Relatives continued under the leadership of its secretary Galina Rytikova, wife of an imprisoned evangelist. On her initiative a regular Bulletin was published containing information about new arrests and the situation of individual prisoners, and also about attacks on churches and individuals, blatant acts of discrimination, mistreatment of children in school and the removal of children from Christian parents. Up to 1986 over 130 issues appeared, containing thousands of pages of appeals and documentation. Sometimes as many as six bulletins with up to 100 pages appeared in the course of a year. Early in 1979 threats to place her in a psychiatric hospital and to deprive her of parental rights and send her children to an orphanage forced Galina to leave her school-age children in the care of their grandmother and go into hiding with her youngest children, while her husband was also in hiding.

The information published by the Council of Prisoners' Relatives enabled Christians within the USSR and beyond to support prisoners and their families in prayer and by writing letters of encouragement. When he was released in 1986, Pastor Yakov Skornyakov, of Dzhambul, Kazakhstan, brought home no less than 9,546 letters which he had received in camp during eight years of imprisonment – an average of over three letters per day. He used to pray for all those who had written who might be discouraged at not receiving a reply from him, since he was allowed to write only two letters and a few postcards each month. Another prisoner, Veniamin Naprienko, saw coloured postcards with Bible texts under a glass sheet on his camp commandant's desk. He guessed that these had been sent to him, even though they weren't given to him. However, he was encouraged by at least seeing them to know that unknown friends abroad had been writing to him and points out that letters are also a testimony to the camp officials who read them. 'Even when the letters are not handed over to the prisoners, they will have some effect on the dull hard hearts of the camp administration. Perhaps these people will know nothing of the love of God, but when censoring the mail, they will be forced to read about it. This is a real witness.' The volume of mail received by Christians was also a powerful testimony to their fellow prisoners of the love that Christians have for one another. The entire mail delivery – a total of 43 letters – for prisoners in one camp one day was addressed to a Christian prisoner. The other prisoners asked him to check in case maybe a letter for one of them had got mixed up with his mail, but they were indeed all for him! 'Well, you really know who your friends are when times get bad,' commented one prisoner. 'Even our wives have abandoned us, not to mention our friends, but look at him! See how they remember him!'

The membership of the Council of Prisoners' Relatives was always made up entirely of women, though there were some men involved in the background. One of the activities organized with no publicity until the authorities intervened was holding summer camps for the children of prisoners and persecuted families. The camps gave the children a holiday they would otherwise not have and often also enabled them to get away from the tensions of surveillance and harassment of their families and churches by the authorities. In August 1979 Galina Rytikova's husband Pavel, at that time working underground as an evangelist, led a camp in western Ukraine, assisted by their elder son Vladimir, Lydia Bondar, a member of the Council, Galina Vilchinskaya, daughter of another member of the Council and others. As they were waiting with the children for a train connection in Lvov they were spotted by police and the Rytikovs and Galina Vilchinskaya were arrested. Lydia Bondar, who had been living in hiding as she was wanted by the police, managed to escape in the confusion. Galina had been caught running a camp in Belorussia in July, but on that occasion nobody had been arrested and the leaders had been ordered to stop the camp and send the children home. Their trial was postponed until August 1980, as the authorities hoped to find Lydia Bondar and bring her to trial with the others, but she avoided arrest until April 1982, when she was finally discovered at a meeting of the Council of Prisoners' Relatives.

In 1982 the first camp for other Christian children was organized in the Caucasus mountains. There were considerable logistic problems in secretly getting children, camping equipment and supplies to an isolated location where the risk of detection was less. So this first camp lasted only a few days, but the following summer the Caucasus camp lasted a week and then other camps were begun near the Black Sea, the Baltic Sea and in Siberia. The leaders of these Christian camps risked imprisonment for their work, but knowing the risks that the adults took made the children all the more appreciative. Most Christian children did not belong to the communist youth movements, the Pioneers and the Komsomol (Communist Youth League), and so had no opportunity to take part in officially organized camps. In any case, their parents would not have been willing to send them because of the atheist teaching in the Communist-run camps. By 1984 two camps in the Caucasus catered for a total of 320 children. The following year one of the camps was for 300 children, including some who were not regular attenders at Sunday school: the camping movement was already beginning to be evangelistic. Grigori Bublik from Rostov-on-Don was arrested leading this camp and sentenced to one-and-a-half years' imprisonment.

TWELVE

Ministry in the Eye of the Storm

I T ALL BEGAN at a wedding in 1975. Like many other Christian weddings, the ceremony was an opportunity for a large number of Christians to meet together to celebrate, as well as to invite non-Christian neighbours and workmates to hear the Gospel. Among the guests were young Christians who were friends of Viktor Walter and his bride Maria. A group of six friends began to discuss with Viktor the idea of living together as a community in which all things were held in common and in which everybody helped everybody else according to their abilities and needs. Many people were sceptical and told them that what happened two thousand years ago was not a model for today. However, the group continued to think and pray about the plan, and a year later their vision began to become reality. Their community was established with a nucleus of young people in Viktor's home town of Akhangaran, in the Central Asian republic of Uzbekistan. As word spread couples from other cities and other churches moved to Akhangaran to join the community, whose members shared their resources to help the newcomers to settle.

Such a community could easily have become inward-looking, but one of the key aspects of their vision was that a close community could be more effective in evangelism. Members of the congregation systematically visited towns and villages up to 200 kilometres away from Akhangaran. They would seek out lone believers and help them to invite their friends and neighbours for a house meeting, or simply call on people until they found some interest. They would explain who they were, share their faith and offer to sing some Christian songs. Often they would be invited back to meet relatives and neighbours and hold a Gospel meeting for them. As a result of their evangelism and the nurture of new Christians several congregations were established. In multi-national Uzbekistan they found Germans, like Viktor and most of the founder members of the community, but there were also Russians, Armenians, Kazakhs, Kabardinians and Koreans among the new converts. Even the Muslim Uzbeks, deeply hostile to the Russians and to the atheistic Communism that they had imposed, recognized and respected the faith of these Pentecostals. There was never any friction with their Uzbek neighbours, but they were particularly closed to the Gospel.

It was not long before such an actively evangelistic congregation began to attract the attention of the authorities, and the leaders came under ever-increasing pressure to register or stop their activity. Seeing that the threat of arrest was imminent, Viktor and the other leaders decided to move elsewhere in order to make a fresh start where the authorities would not know them. The entire community voted to go with them. Before they left, the leaders helped the congregations that had been formed through their evangelism to appoint leaders of their own, so that their life and witness could continue independently. One Korean was commissioned as an evangelist to his own people in the cities of Central Asia.

In choosing a place to move to, the community deliberately looked for a town and district where there were no known churches, as well as somewhere where they would have the opportunity to find work and build themselves homes. They selected the little town of Chuguyevka, on the bank of the Ussuri river deep in the Siberian taiga in the region between the Chinese border and the Pacific Ocean. Some of their families had been deported there under Stalin, before moving to warmer climes in Uzbekistan. Gradually all the families made the long journey and the men of the community laboured to build houses for everybody on top of their regular jobs. Together the families cultivated the plots of land that they were allocated, in order to grow potatoes and other vegetables, and hay to feed their cows in winter.

To their dismay the authorities in Akhangaran sent word to the officials in Chuguyevka warning them of the Pentecostals' activity, and before long a wave of persecution began which far exceeded the pressure they had left behind. Their services were raided, so that they had to meet at different times in different homes in order to try to escape detection. Members were fined for attending meetings, and many of the men were repeatedly arrested and sentenced to 10-15 days' administrative detention. Hostile articles appeared in the local press, but this particular measure backfired: for some people the articles whetted their curiosity and they came to the services to find out for themselves. Undeterred by this persecution, members of the congregation renewed their programme of evangelization, visiting towns and villages throughout the district, using two old cars and several motorbikes as transport. Once again, as they sought out isolated Christians and encouraged them and established contacts in villages where there were no believers at all, their ministry was blessed and five new congregations came into being.

As persecution intensified the sharing and mutual support of the community became vital to its survival. Two families suffered arson attacks on their hay barns. Other families shared their hay, so that the cows would continue to give milk for the children. Gradually all the men lost their jobs, but the meagre resources were shared equally. Finally, on 10 December 1984, ironically United Nations Human Rights Day, Viktor Walter and a number of other leaders were arrested. By March, ten men, including most of the leaders but also several young Christians, were under arrest. Two received sentences of one year, but the remainder were sentenced to terms of three-and-a-half to five years. Still the spirit of the community was not broken and their care for one another in adversity was a powerful witness to the people of the town and to the officials. When all the prisoners finally arrived in their places of imprisonment and wrote home with their addresses, the congregation pinpointed the locations on a map, and discovered that they were scattered the length and breadth of the Soviet Union, from Archangel in the far north of Russia, through Siberia and Central Asia to the Far East. When they looked at the map, they concluded that their men had been sent as missionaries to the Gulag.

The unregistered Baptists' Council of Churches put particular emphasis on developing and supporting two areas of ministry: evangelism and youth work. Funds were collected and some of the most effective preachers were set apart to serve as evangelists in churches throughout the Soviet Union. Late in 1969, with Georgi Vins and Gennadi Kryuchkov and most of the members of the Council free on completion of their sentences, there was optimism that the authorities might recognize the Council. A conference was called in Tula, near Moscow, in December and permission sought from the authorities. Three days before the conference was due to start, authorization to hold it was received, although it was retrospectively withdrawn and subsequently the private house in which the conference was held, and which was also the meeting place of the unregistered church in Tula, was confiscated. Six congregations represented at the conference had been registered by their local authorities and all congregations were instructed to apply for registration. Minutes of the conference were sent to the head of the government, prime minister Kosygin, notifying him of the names of those elected to serve on the Council of Churches and requesting that they should be exempted from secular work and allowed to work full time for the Church.

However, the optimism was unfounded. Soon Gennadi Kryuchkov and Georgi Vins were instructed to find employment, and Vins was sentenced to one year's corrective labour for his activites, which meant that he could not leave his job and part of his pay was deducted each month as a fine. By the end of 1970 Gennadi and Georgi had gone into hiding to avoid arrest, as had two other members of the Council. Georgi was arrested in 1974, but despite wanted posters appearing at railway stations, some narrow escapes and constant surveillance and bugging of his home, Gennadi was never caught. The 'underground' leaders travelled constantly from place to place, visiting congregations, meeting groups of leaders, preaching, giving encouragement and helping to resolve local problems. They also formed the backbone of the nationwide organization of the Council of Churches, directing overall policy and coordinating the work of evangelists.

One of the major organizational achievements of Gennadi Kryuchkov and Georgi Vins was the establishment of clandestine Christian publishing. The Council had first requested the authorities for permission to set up a publishing house to print Bibles and hymn books, but when there was no response the formation of 'The Christian' (Khristianin) publishers was announced in 1971. This announcement was itself printed and soon Christian literature began to reach the congregations. Hitherto the Council had issued a small newsletter, Fraternal Leaflet (Bratsky listok) and an occasional magazine called Herald of Truth (Vestnik istiny). These were now printed and Herald of Truth began to appear more regularly. As the publishers had no typesetting equipment, preparation of the text was extremely laborious, involving cutting out words and letters from books and magazines and pasting them up to give the appearance of a typeset original to use as camera-ready copy. Most other items were reprints of books that had been printed abroad, or of editions of the New Testament and from 1978 the Bible, which did not require typesetting.

Organizing the printing operation was a huge logistical task. Printing supplies and large quantities of paper could not be bought openly. Ink was home-made, using bark, old tyres and scraps of metal. The residue from burning the tyres was boiled up with the other ingredients to produce the ink. A whole network of people bought paper in small packs no more than a ream at a time. Everything had to be done as unobtrusively and as secretly as possible. Teams of printers gave up their jobs, left their families and went underground to operate the presses. One of the first to join this underground ministry was Sofia Bochkarova, who had been so closely involved with pioneering many of the techniques. Even when she became ill with lung cancer, she insisted on carrying on without hospital treatment, as going to and from the hospital might reveal the secret location of the press. Johann Loewen was a pastor in Siberia. When arrest for his pastoral work seemed imminent he was approached by the Siberian leadership of the Council of Churches who invited him to go underground as leader of a printing team.

The work was very hard, often in difficult conditions, as Andrei Borinsky, who worked with a printing team in Moldavia, describes: 'The air was often full of fumes from ink, turpentine and various chemicals. Sometimes we worked for fifteen to sixteen hours a day, but the Lord strengthened us. I was amazed to see how he sustained us, especially the girls who sat at tables collating and folding pages for up to sixteen hours. I was on my feet all day at the press, and I got so tired that at night I would simply collapse into bed. But the Lord strengthened and refreshed us, and in the mornings we would wake up with new strength.'

The technical achievements of the publishing house were no less impressive than the organizational ones. The printing presses were constructed entirely out of parts borrowed from other machinery, ranging from washing machines to bicycles. Their designers paid enormous attention to small details. The presses were made as light as possible so that they could be driven by a small motor which would consume a minimal amount of electricity. In that way they hoped to avoid the risk of detection through suspiciously large consumption of electricity. Lightness was also important in moving the machines from one location to another. They could be fully dismantled and packed into suitcases, so that they could even be carried by hand and moved to new locations by public transport. The technical report of an expert witness on a press discovered in 1977 was glowing. Its designers had not only displayed amazing ingenuity, but had actually produced a machine which was technologically superior to anything of its size manufactured in the Soviet Union: the expert testified that he had never seen such a compact machine capable of printing on both sides of the paper at once.

A major police operation was launched to track down and destroy *The Christian* publishing house. But as several teams were working on separate presses in different locations it proved impossible to track them all down. When the first press was discovered and the printing team arrested the printed announcement, complete with photographs of the team members, appeared just two days later. Between 1974 and 1985 six presses were discovered; in one case the printing team had already left, but in the other five the teams were arrested and sentenced to up to four years' imprisonment each. Others involved in the operation were also arrested, including the owners of the houses where the presses had been hidden and couriers delivering shipments of books and magazines. Tens of thousands of books were lost in these raids on the presses and more were confiscated when people were discovered transporting them to the churches for distribution. But hundreds of thousands of books were successfully printed and distributed, with total output of over a million items by the late 1980s.

The literature printed by *The Christian* publishers was always distributed free, not only to churches supporting the Council of Churches, but also to registered Baptist congregations – a Bible calendar produced one year was so popular in registered churches that a special extra printing was done to meet the demand – and to Pentecostals. The cost of the operation was met by gifts of food and materials and donations of money. Some people gave sacrificially to support the work. A team of four men led by Ivan Kirilyuk were arrested in Kiev in September 1978 on suspicion of involvement with clandestine printing. They were known to have worked together on contracts from collective farms in Moldavia buying timber in the forests of the far north of Russia, felling the trees themselves and transporting the wood to the farms in Moldavia. By doing this hard and dangerous work conscientiously and efficiently they were able to deliver timber at a competitive price agreed in advance by the collective farms and still have a good income, much of which they are believed to have donated to support the underground printing operations. Between contracts they may well have been more closely involved with the work, but the investigators were unable to find any evidence linking them with the printing presses. Instead they were charged with embezzling state funds by allegedly overcharging for their work.

The case of Ivan Kirilyuk and his three friends was remarkable for the lack of sound evidence. At first when the embezzlement charges were made, the four were approached with an offer to drop the charges if they would collaborate with the KGB. The case finally came to trial a year after the defendants were arrested, and the judge, after hearing the evidence, refused to continue hearing the case, and sent it back for further investigation. It took a courageous judge in the Soviet legal system to declare someone innocent when the KGB was involved in the case, and even this action was a challenge to the power of the KGB. The second trial judge also found the evidence inadequate and the case was once more sent back for further investigation. Finally the third judge passed sentences of up to twelve years' imprisonment, even though all the collective farm chairmen called as witnesses by the prosecution spoke in defence of the four, stating that they were fully satisfied with the contracts and the work done. They had not paid more than they would expect to pay any other contractor. Passing sentence the judge strongly criticized the defence lawyers for insisting on their clients' innocence, claiming that the lawyers had 'terrorized the court'. Subsequently it was reported that two of the lawyers were expelled from the college of advocates for 'unprofessional behaviour' in their conduct of the case.

In the unregistered congregations there was a strong emphasis on the Christian upbringing of children and young people. In marked contrast to the registered churches at that time, children were not only present in church but were encouraged to participate by reciting poems or singing in children's choirs. From the very first, reform Baptist groups gave special attention to children. When he was arrested Nikolai Baturin was punched in the face by a policeman: 'That'll teach you to take children to church.' Returning home at the end of his sentence, he was delighted to find that his church now had a children's string orchestra. Later there was a youth choir as well, and before long young people formed the majority in the congregation.

Susanna Herzen began a Sunday school with her nieces and nephews and then other Christian parents asked if their children could join. When a number of children from the village got into trouble, she realized the importance of sharing the Gospel with children and was encouraged to press on with the work. Her Sunday school was later incorporated into the work of an unregistered church newly established in her village. The authorities began disrupting the church's services and one Sunday in January 1984 four officials came and disbanded Susanna's children's Bible class. She was forbidden to continue, but she could not obey such a command. In May she was fined 100 roubles, and in April 1985 she was sentenced to three years in camp for continuing her work. After nine months she was taken back to court for an appeal. Before the hearing Susanna was asked whether she was now willing to promise not to engage in children's work. 'I would rather go to prison for teaching young people,' she replied, 'than see them going to prison for committing crime.'

Training programmes were initiated for Sunday school teachers and preachers, with correspondence materials for home study and seminars for teaching and interaction with other students. Music is an important part of the life of evangelical churches. In unregistered congregations children and young people especially were encouraged to take part in musical activities, singing in choirs and playing instruments. In 1978 the Council of Churches established a department of music ministries which organized an intensive course for musical directors. Every summer young musicians gathered for three weeks' extremely intensive study, with a devotional time each morning followed by classes from 10 in the morning till 10.30 at night. One of the graduates from this course, Natalya Chervyakova, from North Ossetia in the Caucasus mountains, was arrested in 1983 and sentenced to four years' imprisonment for her music work with young people. Another girl from her church, Lydia, volunteered to continue Natalya's work. Wasn't she afraid of being arrested too? she was asked when she completed the course. 'As I see it,' she replied, 'Natalya was doing what the Lord gave her to do. She took this course and then worked with children and young people, because the church entrusted her with that ministry. Now our church chose to send me here. When I get home I will work with the youth choir. My desire is to do all I can, with the Lord's help, to serve in the church. And I trust the Lord for the consequences.'

Evangelism has been a major priority of the Council of Churches. Youth rallies often had an evangelistic character, and sometimes the action of the authorities against them turned such meetings into an occasion for public witness. In August 1977 Christian young people from the North Caucasus, from Ukraine and from as far away as the Baltic republics, the Urals and Siberia, converged on Rostov-on-Don for a youth rally. However, all the roads leading to the house where the rally was to take place were blocked by the police. The young people gathered instead in a nearby wood, but their attempts to hold a service there were frustrated by Komsomol members who drowned their words with loudhailers, played loud music and danced and finally lit a bonfire. Escaping the smoke of the bonfire, the young Christians headed towards the city centre.

Surrounded by police, but also by a large crowd of onlookers, they held their service for half an hour. Realizing that their attempts to stop the young people gathering had backfired and that they were now reaching a large number of people with the Gospel, the authorities reversed their decision to block the meeting and sent the young people back to the house where the rally had originally been planned.

Peter Siemens was brought up by Christian parents, but with no children's work in their church drifted away until he was invited to a youth rally at an unregistered church and began to attend regularly. He committed himself to God at sixteen and after returning home from military service spent all his spare time in the Lord's work, using his musical gifts both in church and at youth meetings. He felt a special burden for taking the Gospel into the villages around his home town of Shchuchinsk, Kazakhstan, and for encouraging Christian young people in the village churches. With other leaders he organized a series of rallies to bring together these scattered young Christians. Soon after he was married in 1974, he was arrested for organizing another youth rally. Halfway through his sentence he was offered conditional freedom if he would not leave Shchuchinsk for the rest of the sentence and promise to obey the laws on religion. He refused this offer and his decision caused many of his fellow prisoners to seek him out and enquire about his faith. One of the prisoners who came very close to faith under Peter's influence was a drug addict named Valera, who was half Korean. After he was released Valera became a Christian. When Peter was released too he went to visit Valera, who invited many people, mostly Koreans, to his house to hear the Gospel. Later a friend of Valera became a Christian, and then members of Valera's family, and Peter and his church began to pray for a revival among the Korean people of the Soviet Union. There are several hundred thousand Koreans living in Central Asia, mostly in and around Kzyl-Orda in Kazakhstan.

One of the most striking results of evangelism by unregistered Baptists has been the establishment of a gypsy church in a village in West Ukraine. The work began there in 1974 and the first evangelist involved, Ivan Danilyuk, was sentenced to five years' imprisonment in 1975. By 1988 their church had 83 members, of whom only ten were Ukrainians and the rest gypsies. In August 1988 32 new members were baptized (25 of them gypsies). One of the first gypsy converts, Samuel, spoke to the onlookers after the baptism: 'We are black and you are white, but the Lord doesn't look at our faces but at our hearts. When I became a Christian

I was invited by one brother in the town of Cherkassy: "Samuel, preach to us." They gave me a Bible, but I couldn't read. I didn't know what to say. "Brothers, I love you!" I repeated three times and there was nothing else I could say. Friends, now we can tell you a lot about Christ. He has shown us the true way to the New Jersualem, even illiterate gypsies can go there and not get lost . . . Friends, I used to promise people not to cheat any more, but I went away and cheated again. But when I promised Christ that I wouldn't cheat I stopped cheating. A gypsy feels more at ease if he can cheat at least a little bit. That's his job, but for the sake of Christ a gypsy renounced falsehood.'

The transformation of the Christian gypsies' village is in itself a witness to their changed lives. The houses are neat and clean, the gardens well kept and full of flowers. Many have learnt to read through hearing the Bible in church, for there are no textbooks in their own language. The Sunday services are quite unusual. Those who can read take it in turns to read a few verses each from the Bible reading that is announced, while the rest follow carefully in their Bibles learning correct pronunciation. When everybody who wants to take part has done so, everyone kneels to say the Lord's prayer together before singing a final hymn. Over a hundred hymns have been translated into the Gypsy language. Every week there is a youth Bible study. They began with just five people, then the group grew to fill two rooms. As the gypsies marry very young there are often small children present too. They love to learn 'golden verses', which are read out some twenty times, so that those who cannot read will be able to learn them by heart in order to repeat them at home. Even children from non-Christian homes love to come to the children's meetings, where they learn to read and write as well as hear the Gospel. Their parents are astounded. 'How did you bewitch them so that they come to your meetings?' they ask. 'They don't fight and they don't steal!'

If they succumb to temptation adults and children are quick to confess and to seek forgiveness of those they have wronged. One gypsy family, when they became Christians, bought a batch of chicks. They walked through a neighbouring village calling out: 'You know us! Have you ever missed a chicken?' People nodded. 'We've become new people,' the gypsies explained. 'Our hearts have been cleansed from sin and now we ask you to forgive us for causing you trouble by stealing your chickens. We want to return what we stole.' People were amazed, but nobody took a chick. 'Does this mean you forgive us?' asked the gypsies. 'Yes,' came the reply. 'Good, let's pray.' And after a prayer the gypsies began to preach the Gospel to those who had gathered and then went on to the next village to do the same.

Many unregistered Pentecostal congregations were also active in evangelism and some saw dramatic growth. Sometimes Pentecostals had a wider appeal than other evangelicals. One Moscow unregistered Pentecostal congregation was unusual in that a number of artists belonged. The nucleus of this group was three students at art college one of whom came from a Christian family. When he came to faith two of his friends also became Christians and as they witnessed to artists with whom they worked others were also attracted to the Pentecostal Church.

An important aspect of evangelism in the former USSR for Christians of all denominations was the witness of their daily lives and opportunities for individual conversation. It has often been said that evangelicals stand out from the people around them because they don't swear, smoke or get drunk. On the way to his first camp the prisoners sharing the railway waggon with Nikolai Baturin discovered he was a Christian. 'Does that mean that you don't know how to swear?' asked one of the prisoners. 'That's right.' 'You'll not survive for a day in camp!' One unusually sober and mild-mannered man, who was employed in a factory where there were a lot of Pentecostals among the workers, was assumed by management to be a secret Christian. He found himself being harassed and discriminated against, which prompted him to find out more about the reason for the Pentecostals being persecuted. Instead of being driven away from the Christian faith he was drawn to it and became a Christian.

In circumstances where large evangelistic events were virtually excluded individuals took every opportunity to engage people in conversation about the Christian faith. Anatoli Runov from Gorki region led a dissolute life until the age of 30. While living in Frunze (now Pishpek, capital of Kirgizia), he became a Christian. He worked as a cobbler and as he worked he meditated on the Lord. People liked to watch him work and then he would speak to them about God, but most people just listened politely and there was no other response. Anatoli decided to return home in order to witness to his former friends, whom he sought out in the bars. Other Christians were surprised: 'Why do you go there – is that a place for Christians?' 'Where should I tell them about Christ?' he replied. 'You can't bring drunks to church, so I have to go to them.' At the cobbler's shop where he worked he put a schedule of the times of broadcasts in Russian from Western Christian radio stations on the reception desk, which opened the way to conversations with his customers. His boss tore it up and finally sacked him for his 'agitation'. Undeterred, Anatoli began posting radio schedules on public notice-boards, handing them to passers-by and dropping them into people's mailboxes. On the back he wrote verses from the Bible or Christian poems. He would preach in markets and cafés, but the police soon stopped him. Once, handing out leaflets at a bus stop, he was detained by the police and held for questioning for three days. After that a series of enforced incarcerations in psychiatric hospitals began, first of all during the public holidays to celebrate the October Revolution. This was to prevent him from reaching the crowds on their day off work. Then he was arrested as criminally insane and spent two spells in special psychiatric prisons until he was finally released in 1987.

Valeri Barinov from Leningrad (St Petersburg) had similar experiences. At work, as a driver, he took every opportunity to share his faith and was sacked several times as a result. He commented cheerfully: 'The Lord always led me to a better job!' Working as a driver at a clinic taking doctors out on house-calls and sometimes bringing sick children back to the clinic he had many opportunities to talk to doctors and parents. Often Valeri would bring a Christian friend or someone on the way to faith along on his shift and in the sometimes long waits between calls they would sit quietly in the car deep in conversation. Off duty he was the leader of a rock band. Inspired by *Jesus Christ Superstar*, he composed and recorded secretly a Christian rock opera called *The Trumpet Call*.

Rock music opened the door for Valeri to make contact with many young people who never set foot in church and eventually to a ministry among drug addicts and prostitutes. The registered ECB church where he belonged recognized that he was one of their most effective evangelists (one of their pastors once said that half the new young people in the church had come to faith through Valeri), but could not accept the validity of Christian expression through rock music. He was censured for 'un-Christian behaviour' for his long hair and for keeping bad company. Finally, under pressure from the authorities, he was excluded from church membership and soon after was taken to a psychiatric clinic for examination. Under increasing pressure from the KGB, Valeri and a friend thought of crossing illegally to Finland to record more music, but they were caught trying to explore the border area and sent to prison (actually they were arrested at the railway station waiting for a train back to Leningrad, having concluded that the idea was not workable). After serving his sentence and following a campaign for his release he emigrated with his family to Britain.

THIRTEEN

The Carrot and the Stick

T HE UNREGISTERED Baptist Church in Izmail, near Odessa, was approached in 1969 with an offer of registration by the local representative of the Council for Religious Affairs. It was made clear to the church that they would have to obey the law and renounce adherence to the Council of Churches. If they refused to register, officials told them, they would face the full weight of the laws forbidding unregistered church activity. In 1974 they gave in to the pressure and the temptation to be able to worship in peace. As an incentive, they were even allowed to register without giving a commitment to obey the laws on religion. So they held their services without hindrance, while neighbouring unregistered congregations were undergoing intense persecution. In Odessa four leaders were sentenced to ten years' camp and exile. Leaders of the unregistered churches around them felt that the pressure on them increased: it seemed the authorities were encouraged by their success in getting the Izmail church to register and became more zealous in their persecution of other churches. Despite not agreeing to observe the regulations, the Izmail church gradually found itself restrained by fear of conflict with the authorities. The congregation remained divided between those who supported and those who opposed registration, work with children and young people was inadequate and the membership declined. Finally in January 1988 they voted on the issue again and renounced their registered status.

The policy of carrot and stick, or 'cookie and whip' as they say in Russian, became more and more clear during the Brezhnev period. This policy consisted of making concessions to those who were willing to work within the state's official legal framework and punishing those who refused. The ECB Union enjoyed continuing benefits from the authorities, while the persecution of unregistered churches went on unabated. The aim of the policy was to bring religious life under greater control. By making conditions in the registered churches look better, the authorities hoped to give an incentive to the unregistered churches to accept registration. At the same time continued persecution of those who refused registration was intended to pressure them into abandoning their stand.

There were always those within the registered churches who took their Christian work to the limit of what was legally possible and sometimes beyond. They were constantly probing to see what would be tolerated. In Odessa several young preachers at the registered Baptist church were secretly ordained as pastors and evangelists in the 1970s. They carried on an unofficial ministry until the changed circumstances of the late 1980s enabled them to come out into the open. Another preacher, in Zhdanov (Mariupol), a city where there were workers of many nationalities from different parts of the Soviet Union, worked for many years arranging secret translation work of the Scriptures and Christian literature into minority languages. Often he would have to travel to meet others engaged in this clandestine ministry or couriers from Western missions. His wife never knew when he set out on one of these trips whether she would see him again this side of prison, but she supported him completely and shared in the ministry of delivering secret supplies of Christian literature. In order not to attract any suspicion, she had to learn how to carry a heavy bag of books in such a way that nobody would guess that she was almost collapsing under the weight.

In a village near Moscow, young members of the registered central Baptist church set up a secret recording studio. They planned to record music, poetry and other material for use in programmes made by western Christian radio stations broadcasting to the Soviet Union. In 1977 the studio was discovered, the equipment confiscated and three young men were arrested. After a lengthy investigation the charges against them were dropped, apparently to avoid the embarrassment of three members of a showcase church in Moscow being put on trial. In January 1984 one of the three, Alexander Semchenko, was once more arrested for production of Christian literature and sentenced to three years' imprisonment.

However, some of the ECB Union leaders were forced into some degree of collaboration with the KGB. Investigation of KGB archives after the failed coup of August 1991 revealed that one of the members of the ECB executive had regular contact with the KGB especially in connection with his participation in international church meetings. He had the code name 'Nevsky'. Nevertheless, the concessions made by the authorities could not but have an overall beneficial effect on the churches in the Union. It seems that the younger union leadership that emerged in the 1970s were skilled in putting their case to the authorities, using the pressure of support from Baptists in the West and arguing that ever new concessions were needed to keep active members from defecting to the unregistered churches.

At the congresses of 1966 and 1969 further improvements were made to the ECB Union's constitution and most of the changes originally proposed by the reformers were incorporated. Under the new constitutional framework the independence of local congregations was more fully respected and regional superintendents became more accountable to the churches in their areas. Regional pastors' councils were elected to assist the superintendents in their work, and gradually superintendents appointed from Moscow were replaced by men elected at regional representative conferences. Selection for national congresses was made more open with congregations sending representatives to regional conferences which in turn elected delegates to conferences at republic and national level.

This democratization process reached a peak at the 1979 Union Congress. There delegates were presented with a proposal from a dissident group within the church that in the election for the Union Council there should be more candidates than places and that the Union executive should be elected directly by the Congress instead of by the Council. Although these proposals were ruled out of order, congress delegates won some significant victories. When the treasurer tried to read his report at such a speed that nobody could take notes, protest from the floor forced him to start again and proceed at a pace that enabled the figures to be scrutinized and questioned. In the election of the Council, delegates took advantage of the provision that successful candidates must receive two thirds support. When it came to the candidacy of one of the most unpopular executive members, Pyotr Shatrov, who served as Pentecostal representative in the union leadership but was widely suspected of KGB involvement, there were sufficient votes against him to remove him from the Council, thus making him ineligible for continued service on the

executive. Although the leadership argued that the vote threatened unity
with the Pentecostals, delegates insisted that they objected to him as a
person, not as a Pentecostal, and when the vote was taken again opinion
against him had hardened still further. In the end the Council co-opted
another Pentecostal from the reserve list of non-voting members elected
by the Congress, and appointed two Pentecostals to the executive, one of
them for the first time as a vice-president, so the Pentecostals emerged
from the conflict with better representation. It was only at the next
Congress in 1985 that the rules were amended to require only fifty per
cent support and Pyotr Shatrov was re-elected to the Council.

One of the first practical benefits to be conceded by the authorities was
permission to print Bibles and other Christian literature. In the
Khrushchev thaw in the mid-1950s there had been one Bible printing each
by the Orthodox Church and the ECB Union. In 1968 once again both
denominations took delivery of a new Bible printing. From this time
onwards the volume of Bibles, New Testaments and other Christian
literature printed or imported gradually increased, until in 1979 the
authorities agreed to allow the Union to print or import 30,000 books
a year. As well as the Scriptures these could also be hymn books and
concordances and gradually the pool of Christian literature available in
the churches increased.

Another important development was a Bible correspondence course
begun in 1969 – the first official opportunity for evangelical theological
training in the USSR for forty years. Although a few students had been
able since the mid-1950s to take up invitations from Baptist seminaries
in England and Germany, with others later going to Sweden, East Germany,
Switzerland and Canada, the correspondence course was less rigorously
controlled by the authorities than these few opportunities for study
abroad. Although some candidates were excluded on the insistence of the
Council for Religious Affairs, by 1985 some 500 ministers and preachers
had received some basic theological education.

At about the same time the authorities began to allow churches that
wished to join the ECB Union to be registered. From 1974 to 1984 over
450 newly registered congregations came into the Union. These were not
necessarily newly formed churches – some, like a thriving congregation
in the Bezhitsa district of Bryansk, which had been closed during the
Khrushchev anti-religious campaign, were regaining registration that had
been arbitrarily rescinded by the authorities.

However, for many in the unregistered churches joining the ECB Union was impossible. They could not accept the leadership of those who had compromised in the past, and although a younger leadership had emerged in the Union during the 1970s they were mostly regarded as being from the same stable. Pentecostals did not detect any basic change in attitude towards them in the Union, even though from 1969 there was always a Pentecostal representative in the Union's executive. In the late 1960s the authorities decided to offer an alternative to those who found the ECB Union a stumbling block preventing them from being registered. It became possible to register without joining the Union. This form of registration soon became known as 'autonomous registration', for each congregation registered in this way was autonomous, in the sense that it belonged to no denomination. At the Tula conference of the Council of Churches in 1969 six registered congregations were represented.

In the early 1970s only a handful of congregations were given autonomous registration. However, from the mid-1970s the numbers steadily increased, until by 1985 there were several hundred registered evangelical churches that did not belong to the ECB Union. In many instances the authorities put a lot of pressure on churches to register, as they saw it as an opportunity to bring them under greater control. Some Pentecostal congregations experienced particular problems, because their form of worship was regarded with much suspicion by the authorities. Sometimes it was insisted that they could not speak in tongues during their services and in one instance a local religious affairs official objected to the ceremony of foot-washing as part of the communion service. He told the church leaders: 'We agreed to register a church, not a bath house!'

In order to encourage congregations to register, the authorities sometimes even offered registration without conditions. The unregistered Baptist church in Kiev was one of the ones that took up this offer in 1975. They insisted to the authorities that they would agree to register only if they were able to continue with their full range of activities, including Sunday school and youth work, and that if they were prevented from doing so they would renounce their registered status. Despite various forms of official pressure, including fines and the arrest of some members, the congregation remained resolute in its determination to minister to its children and young people. At first its Sunday school was probably the only one in the whole of the USSR which was openly functioning in a registered church. Another congregation, in Issyk, near Alma-Ata, the capital of Kazakhstan, was offered a special registration application, 'Form B', which did not require them to agree to observe any official restrictions on church work. The leaders of the congregation, however, pointed out that their pastor Johann Steffen was serving a sentence in labour camp for violating these very same restrictions. If they were now to be permitted to do the things for which he had been arrested, they argued, he should be released, in which case they would agree to register.

Once they were registered and had enjoyed the freedom to worship without interruption and had built themselves a permanent meeting house, churches often found that the authorities had a hold over them, because it was in the power of the authorities to deprive them of these privileges. They were no longer under the physical pressure of services being broken up and leaders being locked up in prisons and labour camps, but they were under a constant psychological pressure from the authorities to conform. The unregistered church in Odessa finally succumbed to the demands of the authorities and applied for registration, but the constant interference in the internal affairs of the church, and the petty restrictions that were imposed upon them, soon disillusioned them and the members voted to become unregistered once more.

The 'carrot-and-stick' policy was seen most clearly where registered and unregistered congregations lived side by side. In the West Ukrainian town of Kivertsy there was no Baptist church until 1964. There were Baptists, but they belonged to churches in surrounding villages. This was not very satisfactory, and some began meeting in each other's homes. In 1964, 29 people signed a petition supporting the reform movement's call for a congress of all ECB churches. Ten of them were immediately expelled from their congregations and the pastor of one village church was dismissed. From that time they began holding regular services in Kivertsy. The church grew and new members were baptized. Even in the midst of the most severe persecution, the church never stopped giving priority to the Christian teaching of children and young people. In the 1970s pressure mounted with meetings being broken up, participants fined, Christians sacked from their jobs and children persecuted at school. Sometimes as many as fifteen people were fined for one service. In the 1980s the authorities offered registration. Most of the members were opposed, but one of the pastors left with twelve members to form a registered church. While this autonomous group was left in peace a new wave of persecution engulfed the unregistered church. Constant surveillance of the members' homes prevented them from holding services in anybody's house, even early in the morning or late at night. From 1983 to 1986 services were held in the forest in summer, but the police interrupted them there. From

1982 to 1987 members were fined a total of 6,000 roubles and detained for 155 days. In just sixteen months in 1983-4 six leaders were arrested and sentenced to two to three years in camp.

The improvements gained by registered churches from the mid-1960s onwards were clearly a response by the authorities to the unregistered church movements, both Baptist and Pentecostal. Officials preferred to deal with registered churches, over which they could exercise some degree of control, rather than unregistered ones, which enjoyed an inner freedom despite the persecution that was directed at them. Registered churches had a great deal to lose if they incurred the wrath of the authorities: first and foremost church buildings acquired through much sacrifice and often constructed through the efforts of the church members themselves; but also permits for the production of Christian literature, opportunities for study and other benefits.

Unregistered churches, on the other hand, had little to lose. It is true that some Christians lost their homes which had been used as churches, and some congregations saw temporary shelters that they constructed destroyed or demolished and taken away. The activities of the unregistered churches, their training courses and their production of Christian literature were all undertaken without any official permission, and although they could be disrupted by police raids and arrests, the authorities could not use the withdrawal of permission as a sanction against them. Everything that the unregistered churches did was by definition illegal, and therefore there was no reason to refrain from any particular activity for fear of reprisals. Their choice was simple: to agree to work within official restrictions and be left in peace, or to engage in whatever activity was necessary and of benefit to the life of the churches and face the consequences. Having chosen the latter course, the unregistered churches had a special kind of freedom – the freedom of the outlaw.

The determination of the unregistered churches to hold onto their freedom of action, despite the cost in arrests, imprisonment, fines and separation from loved ones, paradoxically helped to improve the situation of the registered churches. The more the unregistered held their ground, the more the authorities offered concessions in order to encourage registration. The Christians in unregistered fellowships served as a kind of shield for the whole evangelical community, bearing the brunt of the atheist attack for twenty years until the advent of *glasnost* and *perestroika*.

Developments within the evangelical community were in some ways mirrored in the Orthodox Church. Although groups calling themselves

True Orthodox had existed since Metropolitan Sergii, as acting Patriarch, had reached a *modus vivendi* with the Bolshevik regime in 1927 by declaring the Church's loyalty to the Soviet Motherland, dissidents and reformers largely remained within the Russian Orthodox Church. The Church effectively silenced Father Gleb Yakunin and Archbishop Yermogen, who had protested at the acceptance by the Patriarch and the leaders of the Orthodox Church of the closure of parishes and the loss of control by the parish priest of the surviving parishes, which were run by a committee that could be manipulated by the authorities. The clergy, deeply loyal to the unity of the Church, accepted church discipline, however much they disagreed with it, and kept silence, at least in public. Lay people, on the other hand, were not under the same discipline and began increasingly to speak out, even though they faced persecution and imprisonment as a result. However, they lacked the coordination and mutual support which made the Baptist reform movement so effective.

One of the earliest lay heroes of Orthodoxy was a maths teacher from Kirov (Vyatka), Boris Talantov. He was one of the few in 1965 to give open support to Father Gleb Yakunin in his efforts to get the Church to resist the atheist attacks on it. In 1966 Boris compiled a detailed analysis of the church closure campaign in the Kirov region and of the complicity of the local bishop in church closures by ordering the merger of parishes, which were sometimes as much as 40 kilometres apart. Boris was denounced by the local press and his report was rejected by the church leadership who claimed it was written anonymously and therefore was unreliable. In 1969 he was arrested and sentenced to two years' imprisonment for allegedly slandering the Soviet state by his revelations of the campaign against religion. Boris died in a prison hospital in January 1971, apparently a lone voice crying in the wilderness. Yet the requiem for him in the church in Kirov was attended by a large crowd of people who knew of his sacrifice and supported what he had stood for.

All across the Soviet Union lay people took the initiative in setting up parish committees to petition for the reopening of churches. In Gorki (Nizhni Novgorod), whose million-strong population was served by one small church on the outskirts, six committees formed in different districts of the city. Members of these committees and people who signed their petitions were often put under considerable pressure to withdraw their names: they were threatened with being sacked from work, or more often, as many of them were retired, with the loss of their pension. Local officials visited their homes and tried to bully them into giving up, or just to wear them down by constant pressure. Instead of defusing dissent by meeting the demands of the committees, local authorities were determined to be able to report to central government that the petitions were just the work of a few agitators without general support and could therefore be ignored.

In marked contrast to the evangelicals, who organized parallel church life in unregistered churches, these unregistered Orthodox parishes did not fully develop into viable Christian communities. The roles of the priest and of the parish church in the life of Orthodox Christians are too important to allow house churches to have any great authority or popularity. Nevertheless, the Orthodox Church does have many prayers which can be conducted by lay people and which can be used outside church, and some parish groups did hold services in private homes using these prayers and the appointed Bible readings. Such people did much to keep the Orthodox Church alive where churches were not open.

The Brezhnev era saw a growing religious awakening in the Soviet Union. It had its roots in the time of de-Stalinization under Khrushchev, when the thaw brought a degree of intellectual freedom and people began to explore alternatives to communism. Paradoxically, the Khrushchev persecution of religion fuelled this reawakening, perhaps because the crude anti-religious propaganda was so unbelievable that some were prompted to take religion more seriously. By the late 1960s, in marked contrast to the secularized West, it was no longer considered intellectually inadmissable to believe in God. The sterility of the Brezhnev years finally brought widespread disillusion with Communism. In the early years after the Bolshevik seizure of power the ideals of Communism had harnessed the enthusiasm of the younger generation, and even under Stalin many people sincerely believed that history was on the side of socialism and that even if they were suffering now they were building a better future for their children. By rejecting Stalin's terror methods and calling for a return to Lenin's principles, Khrushchev gave Communism a last chance to prove itself.

The vast majority of people, however, continued to conform in public to the official Communist and atheist ideology. Virtually all young people belonged to the Communist youth organizations, at least until they had finished their studies. They knew that ideological soundness was essential for entry to higher education and for a good career, and for some careers it was necessary not only to have been in the Communist Youth League as a young person but also to join the Communist Party. It became increasingly clear that most people in the Communist Youth Movement and in the party itself had joined because it was the done thing, because it was good for their career prospects and not because they actually understood the tenets of Marxism-Leninism or really believed in them. Of course, there were exceptions, but most people avoided discussion of ideological issues for fear of revealing that their belief in Communist principles was no more than skin deep. Yet outwardly the impression was created of great ideological uanimity.

Alexander Solzhenitsyn, in a famous phrase, once urged his fellow-countrymen to 'stop living a lie'. He was sure that if everybody came out into the open with their true beliefs, or their lack of beliefs, the Communists would prove to be a tiny minority. Increasing numbers of intellectuals began looking for new sets of beliefs and values to replace discredited Communism. For many of them the search brought them to a serious examination of Christianity. Weakened though it was by persecution and submission to the state, the Orthodox Church nevertheless remained the national Church of Russia and for many people in Ukraine and Moldavia. Georgia has its own national Orthodox Church and the Armenian Apostolic Church is also closely related to the Orthodox. It was to these churches that people naturally looked when they became interested in religion.

The Orthodox churches had a great history of spirituality, which was attractive amidst the spiritual aridity of Communism. The Russian Church in particular also had a strong intellectual tradition, and the new generation of the sixties and seventies looked back to the theologians and philosophers of the turn of the century, especially to the 'Signposts' group that had rejected Marxism and returned to the Church. The new generation felt a great affinity with their spiritual and intellectual path. The Church also had much to offer on the cultural level with its music and art having a depth that was lacking in the officially sponsored 'socialist realism'.

Many people kept secret their search for religious truth and their new-found faith. They would try to attend church where they were not known – a relatively easy task in a city like Moscow with over forty churches still open, but much more difficult in provincial cities and small towns. The majority of the population maintained at least a tenuous link with the Orthodox Church by having their children baptized, though often for fear of harassment they prevailed upon the priest not to enter the baptism in the church register which was regularly inspected by the authorities. For many people in these circumstances faith was superficial, and often mingled with superstitious beliefs, for there was virtually no opportunity for the Church to give any teaching.

Some people, however, sought to deepen their faith through fellowship with others who were pilgrims on the same road. As early as the 1950s, Christian study circles began to meet and they spread during the 1960s and 1970s. Most deliberately kept a very low profile in order to avoid conflict with the authorities and so little is known about them. One of the best known was the 'Christian Seminar' founded in 1974 by Alexander Ogorodnikov. The members of the seminar began to be harassed and persecuted by the authorities and in 1976 decided to seek protection through publicizing their plight. The members were mostly students and young people from a non-Christian background.

Alexander Ogorodnikov described their way to faith: 'My friends and I grew up in atheist families. Each of us has come along a complicated, sometimes agonizing, path of spiritual searching. From Marxist convictions, through nihilism and through the total rejection of any ideology at all, through attraction to the "hippy" lifestyle, we have come to the Church.' However, the Orthodox Church was not prepared for answering the questions of these young Christians. 'We were soon convinced,' Alexander continued, 'that our problems were not being raised in church sermons, which are the only means for the religious education of believers, nor in the pages of the church journal . . . Most important of all, in the Russian Orthodox Church the parish is not like a brotherly community where Christian love to one's neighbour becomes a reality. The state persecutes every manifestation of church life, except for the performance of a "religious cult". Our thirst for spiritual communion, religious education and missionary service runs up against all the might of the state's repressive machinery.'

Another leading member of the seminar, Vladimir Poresh, came to Moscow from Leningrad (St Petersburg) to attend meetings. He writes of the inability of Communism to give any fulfilment and of the new life that he and his friends found in Jesus Christ:

> We were born in dead and godforsaken times, we lived as Pioneers and members of the Communist Youth League, but we want to die Orthodox Christians. A longing for genuine life torments us - a life free from perversion and distortion by vulgar lies; because this vulgar life leads on not to life but to death. Acknowledging all our nothingness before our Lord God, before Russian history, we have

nevertheless decided to live at any price. This means that we die not unto death, but unto everlasting life. The godless and blasphemous world of socialist realism is running away like sand between the fingers, and its dead skeleton stands naked. By inner spiritual strength we are throwing off the fetters of a reality to which we have been shackled – the fetters of a fantastic myth which has been set up as the truth by use of force. Right and Truth, the Crucifixion and the redemptive sufferings of Our Lord Jesus Christ have revealed to us what genuine life is.

Although Alexander Ogorodnikov and his friends failed to find an adequate response to their questions in the Orthodox Church, they remained within it, conscious that it was and is the channel for Russian spirituality. Others were more fortunate in finding priests who understood their spiritual search and were able to guide them towards faith. Two such priests in particular stand out. One of them, Father Dimitri Dudko, had a high-profile ministry in several churches in and around Moscow. Under pressure from the authorities the archbishop moved Father Dimitri several times in order to disrupt his influence, but people followed him even to an inaccessible rural parish.

While in a Moscow city parish Father Dimitri began a series of public question-and-answer sessions after the Saturday evening service. Questions were submitted a week in advance and Father Dimitri would give well-thought-out answers to them. These sessions were very popular as they answered real questions while giving an opportunity for systematic teaching. Transcripts of the questions and answers circulated as underground typescripts and appeared as a book in English under the title *Our Hope*. Father Dimitri also held open house for individuals and groups of people who came for more informal discussions and counselling. When he was moved out of Moscow and banned from holding public question-and-answer sessions in church, Father Dimitri continued to receive a stream of people in the parish house, and produced an underground parish magazine in which he addressed some of the issues that were raised by his visitors. Thousands of people were helped by Father Dimitri, either through attending his public meetings or in private conversation, and were baptized by him into membership in the Orthodox Church. He was arrested in Janaury 1980 and in June renounced his work in a televised confession which was widely suspected of being induced by drugs secretly administered to him.

The other priest, Father Alexander Men, suffered no less harassment, though he avoided the high-profile approach of Father Dimitri and sought wherever possible to avoid confrontation. But he too held open house in his parish in a village a couple of hours' journey from Moscow, and also helped thousands along the road to faith and baptized them into the Church. He had a gift of being able to express the truths of the Christian faith with a simplicity which even the most poorly educated village parishioner could understand and yet with a depth that satisfied the most intellectual seeker. It was not for nothing that the KGB's code name for him was The Missionary!

Father Alexander was a prolific writer, though his books could not be published in the Soviet Union. They were printed abroad under various pseudonyms and the copies that reached Russia were avidly read. His writings, while rooted in Orthodoxy, were easy for Christians of all denominations to read and understand. He wrote a series of introductions and textual notes on the books of the Bible which were printed with the Bible in Russian by a Catholic publisher in Brussels and were popular among Orthodox and evangelicals alike. The KGB undoubtedly knew that Father Alexander had written these books and he was interrogated and threatened many times, but never arrested. He was murdered early one morning in September 1990 on the way to his church. There is speculation that his murder was vengeance from the KGB, an expression of anti-Semitism (he was of Jewish parentage) or even the result of jealousy within the Church, but the crime has never been solved.

Despite all the efforts of the KGB and the Council of Religious Affairs to control the Russian Orthodox Church, priests of the calibre of Dimitri Dudko and Alexander Men continued to be ordained. Even the hierarchy, whose selection the authorities made a special effort to influence, included bishops who annoyed the authorities by defending the parishes in their dioceses and seeking to strengthen the Church. As with many of the best priests, these bishops were frequently moved in order to prevent them having a lasting influence in any one place. One of the most severe problems of the Orthodox Church was a shortage of priests, with the surviving three seminaries not allowed to train enough to replace those who died or retired through ill-health. Some bishops began finding psalm readers and other lay people who knew the services well and had the desire and ability to serve the Church, and consecrated them as deacons and priests without any formal training. This enabled them to save parishes from closure for lack of a priest.

The 1970s also saw the strengthening of campaigning for human rights in general and religious rights in particular. The provisions for human rights and religious freedom written into the 1975 Helsinki Agreements and ratified by the USSR encouraged people to press the Soviet government to implement them. The Soviet Union had agreed to the inclusion of these provisions under pressure from Western European countries in exchange for the acceptance by the West of the post-war frontiers and the division of Europe. Groups to monitor the implementation of the Helsinki Agreements (Helsinki Monitoring Groups) were set up by dissidents in Russia, Ukraine, Georgia and Armenia with many Christians involved. Father Gleb Yakunin – who as a student had been helped to come to faith by his contemporary Alexander Men and was a neighbour of Father Dimitri Dudko – broke his ten-year silence with an appeal to the Assembly of the World Council of Churches in Nairobi in November 1975, and in December 1976 formed the Christian Committee for the Defence of Believers' Rights, which documented violations of religious freedom affecting all denominations. In less than three years the committee compiled over a thousand pages of documentation relating to the persecution of Orthodox Christians, Catholics, Baptists, Pentecostals and Jews.

The authorities reacted to these developments in a way similar to their policy towards the evangelicals. Dissidents were harassed and persecuted, especially from 1979 when leading members of the Helsinki Monitoring Groups and Father Gleb Yakunin were arrested. At the same time certain concessions were made to the Orthodox Church. Printing of Bibles and prayer books was permitted and student numbers in the seminaries increased. A new theological correpondence course was introduced which grew to an enrolment of one thousand and which provided 'in-service' training for deacons and priests who had been ordained without any theological education as well as offering more study opportunities for new priests. Whereas the Russian Orthodox Church traditionally recruited clergy from priests' families – Orthodox priests must be married unless they choose to be monks – and gave them only a minimal education, many of the new generation of priests were highly educated people who had come to faith from an atheist or non-religious background. In one respect though, the Orthodox Church did not gain ground as the evangelicals had: virtually no new churches were opened and in the twenty years after the end of Khrushchev's anti-religious campaign the number of open churches continued to fall, though much more slowly. A major reason seems to have been that unregistered Orthodox parishes that were seeking to open or reopen churches did not have the strength of a worshipping community to back their demands. Unregistered evangelical congregations led a real church life, whereas at best the unregistered Orthodox parishes had a shadowy existence involving only a small minority of Christians. It was only the advent of glasnost and perestroika which brought dramatic change for the Orthodox Church.

The last years of the Brezhnev era saw a renewal of the 'cold war' on the international arena and a fresh crackdown on all forms of dissent at home. The careful rebuilding of bridges in Europe that followed the setback of the 1968 invasion of Czechoslovakia had been crowned by the signing of the Helsinki Agreements in August 1975. The West recognized the permanence of the postwar borders in Eastern Europe, while the Soviet Union committed itself to improved observance of human rights and acknowledged that civil and political rights were a legitimate part of international relations. By the summer of 1979 the number of known Christian prisoners fell to an all-time low. Unregistered Baptist leader Georgi Vins was among a group of religious and political prisoners exchanged in April 1979 for two Soviet spies arrested in New York. A spate of early and conditional releases that brought the number of Baptist prisoners below forty led to speculation that the Soviet authorities might be planning a new initiative to end the confrontation with the unregistered churches.

The invasion of Afghanistan in December 1979 abruptly sent the Soviet Union into a new period of isolation, with many Western nations boycotting the Moscow Olympic Games the following summer. A new crackdown on religious and political dissent had, however, already begun, linked to the name of Yuri Andropov, head of the KGB, who was to succeed Leonid Brezhnev as head of the Communist Party in 1983. The 'Andropov purge' put behind the barbed wire of the Gulag members of the Helsinki monitoring groups who had sought to put the USSR's new commitments to human rights to the test, campaigners for the rights of national minorities, defenders of religious freedom and many leaders and active members of unregistered churches. Father Gleb Yakunin was arrested in November 1979 and the other members of his Christian Committee for the Defence of Believers' Rights either intimidated or forced to emigrate. Alexander Ogorodnikov, who had been arrested in November 1978 on accusations of 'parasitism' (being without employment) and sentenced to one year's imprisonment, was rearrested in camp in September 1979 and charged with 'anti-Soviet agitation and propaganda' for organizing the Christian Seminar. Vladimir Poresh had already been arrested on the same charges in August. Other members of the Seminar were arrested on various other charges and its activities were halted.

Optimism about a new policy towards the unregistered Baptists rapidly dissolved as the leaders in the Council of Churches were systematically tracked down and arrested. By the beginning of 1981 Council members Nikolai Baturin (secretary), Mikhail Khorev, Pyotr Rumachik (vice-president), Ivan Antonov (imprisoned June 1979-June 1981, rearrested May 1982) and Dmitri Minyakov and evangelist Alexei Kozorezov were all serving new terms of imprisonment. In October 1983 a vicious new article was added to the Criminal Code of the Russian republic (and shortly thereafter to the codes of all the other Soviet republics), punishing 'malicious disobedience to the requirements of the administration of a corrective labour institution' by imprisonment of one to five years. In order to secure a conviction the prosecution needed to demonstrate three violations of labour camp discipline in a period of a year. The only evidence required was the camp administration's record of punishments, which were often quite arbitrary acts of victimization against religious and political prisoners. From 1983 to 1985 this article was used to extend the sentences of several leading Baptists, including Mikhail Khorev. Nikolai Baturin, Yakov Skornyakov and Rudolf Klassen were each sentenced to an additional three years for telling prisoners about the persecution of Christians. Others were arrested shortly after completion of a sentence, like Pastor Ivan Danilyuk who had baptized the first gypsy Christians. He was rearrested in 1982 only three weeks after completing a two-and-a-half year sentence. The authorities began to threaten imprisoned Baptist leaders that they would never be released unless they cooperated with the authorities: they would simply be rearrested on new charges. And indeed, it seemed as if there was a deliberate policy of keeping as many of the members of the Council of Churches behind bars as possible.

PART III

Perestroika
and After

FOURTEEN

Gorbachev
and Glasnost

ON SUNDAY 19 JUNE 1988, 13,000 people gathered in a clearing in the woods close to the river Dnieper in Kiev. All over the forest groups of people made their way along the paths and tracks converging on the spot where a special baptismal service was to be held to mark the thousandth anniversary of the baptism of the citizens of Kiev in 988. Most of those who gathered were Christians, but many participants had invited neighbours and workmates with whom they had shared their faith. As the preachers explained the message of salvation and the meaning of the commitment that those being baptized were making, here and there in the congregation individuals dropped to their knees and committed their lives to Christ while those around them supported them in prayer. Then the crowd proceeded to the bank of the river to watch 75 new Christians walk into the water. A team of pastors baptized them, dipping each one of them right under in a symbol of the washing away of sins and rising to a new life in Christ. Although no official permission for the event had been granted, the police merely observed and the celebration passed off without incident.

The baptism was preceded on the previous day by a packed-out evangelistic service at the church of the autonomous Baptist congregation, for which thousands of invitations had been printed. Such was the throng that Christians were asked to leave the hall and wait outside to make room for the non-Christians. In the evening an open-air service was held at the statue of Saint Vladimir, the prince of Kiev who adopted the Christian faith. Booklets outlining how to become a Christian that had been produced on the secret printing presses were distributed free of charge to enquirers. When the police asked for the service to stop, the preachers turned the challenge over to the crowd: should they stop or continue? When the crowd urged them to continue the police quietly withdrew.

These events, which only a couple of years earlier would have resulted in police interference, arrests and widescale interrogations, symbolized a new era of religious freedom in the Soviet Union. The new freedom was a fruit of the changes that swept over the USSR under the leadership of Mikhail Gorbachev. The improvement for Christians was striking.

When Gorbachev came to power in March 1985 he took over the running of an economy that had run out of steam, a political system in which corruption and nepotism were rife and a society in which initiative was stifled. In the previous six years, under three leaders who were most of the time too ill to govern, growing political dissent had been ruthlessly suppressed. The number of known religious prisoners, mostly from unregistered churches, had doubled after reaching a low point in 1979. For many people the succession of sick and dying leaders – Brezhnev, Andropov and Chernenko – destroyed the last vestiges of confidence in the Communist Party that they might still have had.

Mikhail Gorbachev saw clearly the need for new initiatives and launched a three-pronged policy of renewal: glasnost (openness), perestroika (restructuring) and democratization. These themes caught the imagination of many people within the Soviet Union and especially outside, both in the Eastern European 'satellite' countries and in the West. However, he encountered widespread opposition from conservatives within the party. Religion was one of the most ideologically sensitive areas and it seems that at first any reform in religious policy was sacrificed as a sign to the hard-liners that Gorbachev's reforms were intended to revitalize the USSR while preserving ideological purity. The only perceptible change was a slight reduction in the number of arrests on religious and political grounds. In fact the number of known religious prisoners reached a new high in November 1985 and only then began to fall as a result of new arrests no longer outnumbering releases.

Curiously, the head of the government's Council for Religious Affairs, Vladimir Kuroyedov, was replaced a few months before Gorbachev came to power. Kuroyedov symbolized the repressive policy against religion. He had been appointed head of the Council for Russian Orthodox Church

Affairs in 1960, because his predecessor, who had served since the creation of the Council in 1943, was considered to have too cosy a relationship with the church leaders and was not vigorous enough in the campaign to close churches. When the two Councils – for Russian Orthodox Church Affairs and for the Affairs of Religious Cults – were merged to form the Council for Religious Affairs, Kuroyedov became the chairman. He was the epitome of the faceless bureaucrat and rarely made public appearances or pronouncements, though he was the author of several booklets claiming that there was religious freedom in the USSR.

The new chairman of the Council was a totally different person. Konstantin Kharchev's previous appointment had been as ambassador to Guyana. He had an outgoing and flamboyant, if rather short-tempered, personality. However, he brought with him no specialist knowledge of religious affairs and there was no obvious immediate change in policy. In any case the Council was not a policy-making institution: it largely carried out instructions from the government and Communist Party, and had close links with the KGB. Some of the staff were seconded from the KGB and the Council and its local officials were expected to work in close cooperation with their KGB opposite numbers responsible for religious affairs in the fourth department of the Fifth Directorate.

For the unregistered churches it looked as if glasnost was all words and no actions and that one obedient bureaucrat had replaced another in the Council for Religious Affairs. Arrests continued right through 1985 and 1986 and Christians continued to be fined for leading or taking part in services. The legislation passed in 1983 making a criminal offence of persistent violations of labour camp regulations threatened to create a category of permanent prisoners. Among those resentenced under this article was evangelist Nikolai Boiko from Odessa, sentenced in July 1985 to an additional two-and-a-half years' strict regime camp shortly before the end of a five-year sentence. Pyotr Rumachik, a vice-president of the Council of Churches, was arrested in August 1985, just two weeks before completing a five-year sentence in Chita near the Chinese border and in February 1986 sentenced to an additional five years on charges of 'anti-Soviet agitation and propaganda' for speaking to fellow prisoners about the persecution of Christians. However, these were the last two Baptist victims of the practice of resentencing, and although new arrests continued to the beginning of 1987 those who completed their sentences during 1986 were released on time.

In 1985-6 there was a renewed campaign against the members of the unregistered Baptists' Council of Prisoners' Relatives. Serafima Yudintseva was tried and given a two-year suspended sentence in March 1985 and in May simultaneous house searches in members' and supporters' homes led to the confiscation of the CPR archive. In June, facing threats of arrest, Alexandra Kozorezova, the CPR president, went into hiding. In July Ulyana Germanyuk, whose evangelist husband Stepan was already in prison, was herself arrested; she was subsequently sentenced to three years' imprisonment. In April and May 1986 three CPR workers and another member of the Council were also arrested. They all received sentences of eighteen months to two years, because the information compiled by the CPR was alleged to be slanderous of the Soviet state and social system.

In the town of Kulebaki, near Gorky (now Nizhni Novogorod), local officials and police came to every single service of the unregistered Baptist church from the end of 1985 to August 1987. Every time they ordered the Christians to stop their service and go home. When the church insisted on finishing the service the members were accused of not obeying police orders, and leaders, ordinary members and visitors were taken away to the police station. The next day they would be fined or sentenced to 7-15 days' imprisonment. Sometimes someone would be released on Saturday, charged for being at the service on Sunday and sentenced again on Monday! One member was arrested 19 times, the pastor 30 times and two of the pastor's sons between them spent over 200 days in prison in the course of 1986. Friends and family brought them food parcels, which they shared with their fellow prisoners. Many knelt to pray with them in the cells and asked them to sing them Christian songs and hymns. Some people the Christians met in prison came to services when they were released. Kulebaki is a small town and word of the persecution and the faithfulness of the Christians soon spread. Even their persecutors began to soften: 'If it was up to us,' they told their prisoners, 'we wouldn't keep arresting you.'

In April 1986 the local council demolished the building which the Odessa unregistered Baptist church had been meeting in for ten years. For part of this time the church had agreed to be registered, so the building had been in legal use, but the congregation's renunciation of registration because of interference by the local authorities in the life of the church meant that they were no longer entitled to the use of a place of worship, even though they had built it themselves! The following month their Easter service in a member's home was brutally dispersed by a special police detachment, which arrived towards the end of the service and began forcing the Christians out of the house and pushing them into buses. In the midst of the confusion a KGB officer climbed into the house through a window and began rummaging through the owners' possessions.

However, as glasnost gathered momentum in the press, journalists began to write in a more friendly way about religion. Hitherto the media had been almost entirely hostile to religion in general and particularly vicious in attacking unregistered churches. The only neutral reporting consisted of occasional brief announcements of major events in the official life of the churches and some reporting of church-sponsored peace conferences. Now some articles appeared that were informative and sympathetic. One of the first articles hinting at a new attitude to religion was a major feature in the government newspaper *Izvestiya* in January 1986. It was published in order to counter continuing allegations of violations of religious freedom in the Soviet Union. But for the first time, instead of quoting rebuttals from state officials or statements from prominent foreign visitors praising the degree of religious liberty they found in the USSR, the *Izvestiya* reporters visited four religious communities - Catholic, Orthodox, Baptist and Muslim - and talked to ordinary members and clergy. None of them said anything about persecution (or if they did it was not quoted), though the Orthodox priest certainly could have done, as he had earlier been imprisoned. Before glasnost if he was going to be quoted in the press at all, he would have been forced to admit that he had been rightfully imprisoned. The Baptist superintendent did mention that problems occurred, though none that could not be solved by talking to the Council for Religious Affairs. What was significant was that the article was a first sign of acceptance of religion as a part of everyday life, enjoying normal relations with society and the state.

The year 1986 was a turning point for glasnost. On 26 April there was an explosion at the Chernobyl nuclear reactor near Kiev. The inability of the Soviet leadership to admit the truth to the world until presented with incontrovertible evidence, and the failure to warn and protect people affected by fall-out from the accident showed how hollow 'openness' had been hitherto and spurred people to press for greater accountability from government and the media. In writing about religion some journalists began to reveal past and present injustices.

The Soviet leadership under Gorbachev showed a willingness to gain goodwill with the West by making concessions in the cases of well-known dissidents. Since the invasion of Afganistan in December 1979 and the resulting Western boycott of the 1980 Olympic Games in Moscow, the Kremlin had shown little indication of wanting to end the Cold War and therefore made few concessions to Western opinion. In February 1986 one of the most prominent political prisoners, Anatoli Shcharansky (Nathan Sharansky), was exchanged for a Soviet spy. As a member of the Moscow Helsinki Monitoring Group and a prominent Jewish 'refusenik', he had received enormous support from Western human rights groups and Jewish campaigners. In October, on the eve of a summit meeting in Reykjavik between Mikhail Gorbachev and US President Ronald Reagan, another political prisoner was pardoned: Irina Ratushinskaya, a Christian poetess, had been sentenced to the maximum of seven years' imprisonment in camp followed by five years of exile for writing allegedly subversive poetry. She too had become a cause célèbre because of her harsh treatment.

In a highly unusual case which heralded the intention to make the legal system more just, Vladimir Poresh, the leader in Leningrad (St Petersburg) of Alexander Ogorodnikov's Christian Seminar, was released from prison after a judicial review found that his conviction for violating labour camp regulations was illegal. Not only was he released from imprisonment (having already completed his original sentence), but his term of exile was cancelled and he was offered compensation for wrongful imprisonment.

In December 1986 Mikhail Gorbachev took a bolder step by personally phoning Dr Andrei Sakharov to inform him that his exile to the city of Gorky (Nizhni Novgorod) was being lifted and that he was free to return to Moscow. Sakharov, perhaps the most highly-respected of all the human rights campaigners, had been sent to live in Gorky without any kind of trial in an attempt to silence him without the publicity that a court hearing would have attracted. One by one the people whose cases were most often raised by western diplomats, statesmen and pressure groups were being released. It seemed as though every time there was an important international meeting another prisoner would be released as a sweetener to increase goodwill towards the Soviet Union.

In February 1987 there was a more dramatic move when a hundred political prisoners were pardoned under a special decree of the Supreme Soviet (the Soviet parliament). Among those released were several well-known Christians, including Father Gleb Yakunin, who was freed from exile and Alexander Ogorodnikov, who had been first arrested in 1978 and resentenced twice without ever having been released. Some were invited to write pleas for clemency, others were required to sign statements that they would not engage in criminal activity in future and others were just released. Some refused to sign any statements, but were released anyway, because the continued existence of political prisoners was now an embarrassment to the government. The vice-president of the unregistered Baptists' Council of Churches, Pyotr Rumachik, who had also been rearrested during his sentence and given a supplementary term on charges of anti-Soviet agitation and propaganda, was one of the first to be released. His release was a wonderful example of the evil intent of the Church's enemies being turned to good. By charging Pyotr with a serious political offence, the authorities had been able to sentence him to an additional five years' imprisonment, but the political prisoners were the first to be pardoned, and so Pyotr was released before any of his fellow-Baptists!

Baptist pastor Nikolai Danilchenko was one of those approached by a state prosecutor and invited to apply for a pardon. 'Have you ever thought of an early release?' asked the prosecutor. 'No.' 'Why not?' 'Christians are not criminals,' explained Nikolai. 'We are tried illegally. For an early release you have to confess your guilt, but how could I do that since I was sentenced for faith in God?' The prosecutor produced from his briefcase a model statement requesting release and promising to stop committing crimes. 'I can't write a statement like that,' insisted Nikolai. 'Well, write whatever you want!' replied the prosecutor. So Nikolai carefully wrote: 'I consider my release to be more useful for society, and also for my family and children (I have eight children). I do not intend to commit crimes since I believe in God and my faith does not permit doing evil to people.' Less than two months later Nikolai was ordered to pack his things and was informed that he was pardoned and free to go home.

At the same time Baptists were still being arrested and put on trial. Vasili Berezovsky, from West Ukraine, was arrested on 6 January (Russian Christmas Eve) and three Christians were sentenced to terms of 3-5 years in Tashkent on 13 February, even as the first of the special releases were taking place. Three other trials took place in Ukraine in January-February 1987 and in Khabarovsk (in the Far East) Vladimir Vyushkov was sentenced to one year of exile on 10 March. Disruption of services continued in 1987, especially at Easter, and many were fined for leading and taking part in worship.

June brought an amnesty to celebrate the coming 70th anniversary of the Bolshevik revolution, under which more religious prisoners were released, including all the women. Other prisoners had their sentences reduced under the amnesty, or were released on parole for good behaviour. In July one Baptist, Jacob Steinle, was tried, sentenced and amnestied – all on the one day. Prisoner numbers dropped steadily until at the end of 1988 the last few Baptists serving sentences of exile were allowed home.

There were at last no Christians imprisoned directly for their religious activity, though some remained in detention for refusing military service on grounds of conscience.

The year 1988, however, was much more important for the churches in the Soviet Union than simply as the year in which the last Christian prisoner came home. It was the year that officially marked the millennium of Russian Christianity. The Christian faith was brought to Kiev, now the capital of Ukraine but then the capital of the princes of Rus, in 988 from the centre of Eastern Orthodox Christianity in Byzantium. The millennium celebrations were therefore of special importance for the Russian Orthodox Church, which was directly descended from the first church in Kiev.

The approaching anniversary had been the subject of theological and historical conferences organized by the Russian Orthodox Church and also of a lively debate in the Soviet media on the significance of the introduction of the Christian faith. Some of the old-guard atheist writers disputed the date and the traditional account of events and insisted that the Church had never brought any benefit to Russia. They accused the Church of trying to use the anniversary to portray itself in a favourable light by claiming that the introduction of Christianity was a watershed in Russian history and that the Christian faith was at the very heart of Russian culture. Others, however, wrote of the contribution of Christianity to the development of Russia, arguing that at certain points in history the Church had made a positive contribution.

Amidst all this controversy it remained unclear even at the beginning of the anniversary year what form of celebrations the Soviet government would permit. The Church had been planning a programme of events since 1980, and in 1986 announced the dates and places in which celebratory events would take place. But would these events be private, limited to conferences for theologians and church historians and special liturgies in the cathedrals, or public celebrations in which the millions of ordinary believers would have a chance to take part?

In April, Mikhail Gorbachev broke new ground by meeting the Patriarch of the Russian Orthodox Church and its leading bishops. This was the first such meeting since Stalin had invited Metropolitan Sergii to the Kremlin in 1943 to reward him for the Church's loyalty during the war by re-establishing the Patriarchate. Despite the widely differing circumstances, there are nevertheless certain interesting parallels. In the crisis of the Second World War, Stalin needed the active support of the Church and of the millions of Christians in the Soviet Union, and of the United States, where there was much concern about religious liberty. Any concession that could unite people in the war effort and convince the western allies to give greater support to the Soviet Union was worthwhile. Although there was no external enemy, Mikhail Gorbachev faced a crisis of equal proportions: the viability of the Soviet Union was at stake, and he too needed every ounce of support for his programme of reform, both at home and abroad. The time had come when he needed to rally the Church behind him and show the Western world real progress towards freedom of religion. And what better moment than this great anniversary of Russia's official adoption of Christianity?

Officially the meeting took place at the request of the Patriarch and the Holy Synod of the Russian Orthodox Church, but it seems very likely that they were invited to request a meeting. Certainly Mikhail Gorbachev set the agenda. In his speech he admitted that the Church had been wronged under Stalin and his successors. He claimed that believers supported perestroika and welcomed their contribution.

> Believers are Soviet people . . . and they have the full right to express their convictions with dignity. Perestroika, democratization and glasnost concern them as well, fully and without restriction. This is especially true in the area of ethics and morals, where universal norms and customs are so helpful for our common cause.

He went on to make a statement that contradicted the message of decades of atheist propaganda that had portrayed the Church as something alien in Soviet society and without a future:

> We have a common history, a common Motherland and a common future.

From this moment on it became increasingly clear that the millennium celebrations would take place with the full cooperation of the state authorities and in a blaze of publicity. Extensive media coverage allowed the entire Soviet population to share in the church celebrations on television. One of the major events, a concert in the Bolshoi Theatre, symbolized the cooperation between Church and state in marking the millenium. State orchestras and church choirs combined in a musical celebration of Russian Christianity before an audience of church and public dignitaries including Gorbachev's wife Raisa.

An important exclusively church event which opened the five weeks of celebrations was a Church Council at the beginning of June. For the first time in Soviet history it was called not to elect a new Patriarch but to discuss the life and work of the Church. When the Council was first announced in 1986 nobody had any idea how quickly events would move or of the atmosphere of openness in which it would take place. There was a mood of optimism and even of joy. A major piece of church legislation was a new constitution which overturned many of the restrictive provisions imposed in the past by the authorities, at last restoring the priest as head of the parish. It even claimed rights for the Church which it did not yet have in law, including the right to own property and act as a legal entity. Reports on the activity of the Church were upbeat and largely in accordance with the spirit of glasnost, for the first time offering detailed and comprehensive statistics relating to many areas of church life. Sixty new churches had been opened in the past year, more than in any other previous year since Khrushchev's closure campaign, and hopes were expressed that this was just a beginning. Since the previous council in 1971 there had been about 30 million baptisms.

The public celebrations were attended by many thousands of people and shown nationwide on prime-time television. The other churches were in danger of being left out in the cold. Representatives of non-Orthodox churches in the Soviet Union had been invited to take part in the various conferences and seminars, and the foreign guest list was truly ecumenical, ranging from Catholic cardinals to Baptist evangelist Dr Billy Graham. But the beneficiary of the nationwide and international media publicity was undoubtedly the Orthodox Church.

There were, however, also unofficial events. Alexander Ogorodnikov's revived Christian Seminar held an ecumenical conference which was attended by foreign guests and representatives of non-Orthodox denominations from within the USSR, notably two bishops of the underground Ukrainian Catholic Church. Attempts to hire a hall for the conference, for which 300 people had registered, were thwarted by the authorities. The Red October House of Culture, which was billed as the venue, was closed on orders of fire inspectors as allegedly being a fire risk, and a small amateur theatre in which the conference opened was closed without explanation by the local council. The conference continued in private apartments.

In Western Ukraine, where the Ukrainian Catholic Church has its roots and is strongest, two large celebrations were held. On 10 July, 8,000 worshippers came to Hrushiv, despite the recent reopening of the village chapel as an Orthodox church and police attempts to turn them back. The pilgrims were attacked with bottles and stones by drunken youths and adults and many pilgrims went home. However, 5,000 remained for a mass which was held in the open air some distance from the village. The following week 15,000 Catholics from all over Western Ukraine gathered in Zarvanytsa. Once again there was harassment by the police, who stopped buses five kilometres from the village, but the pilgrims walked the remaining distance. This was the largest gathering of the still-illegal Ukrainian Catholic Church since it had been forcibly merged with the Russian Orthodox Church in 1946.

Baptists took note of one aspect of the millennium which linked the events of 1000 years ago with their own tradition. The celebrations were officially of the 'baptism of Rus', when the citizens of Kiev were baptized in the river Dnieper on whose banks the city stands. Although the circumstances were vastly different – in 988 conversion to Christianity was by decree of the prince – the original baptism in the river was very much like their own practice. Few of their churches have an indoor baptistry, and most hold open-air baptisms in lakes and rivers. The 'millennium baptism' in the river Dnieper in Kiev, organized by an imaginative group of leaders, mostly from autonomous Baptist churches, in cooperation with some Pentecostal and ECB Union pastors, became an example for other churches.

Many churches had been planning baptisms over the summer, and some were emboldened by the experience of the Christians in Kiev to ask the authorities for permission to turn their baptisms into public celebrations of the millennium. Seeing the prominent media coverage that the Orthodox celebrations had received, some local councils were more than cooperative. For example in the city of Saran in Kazakhstan, the 500-strong Baptist church was not only given permission to hold an open-air baptism but offered a site in one of the city parks and the council even proposed to arrange for ice-cream and soft drink stands. On the day, the city council laid on special buses to the park with destination boards reading 'Baptism', with the result that 3000 people gathered on the grass by the riverbank to witness the baptism and hear the Gospel preached.

Other churches organized special lectures and concerts on the theme of the millennium. The first such meetings were arranged in August 1988, but the millennium continued to be used as a pretext for holding public meetings until well into 1989. It was the first time since the 1920s that evangelicals had been allowed the use of public buildings, even though religious meetings in state or public premises were still technically illegal. These events were not billed as evangelistic, for evangelism was still a taboo word, an activity that was strictly and specifically against the law. However, in actual fact they were clearly planned and conducted as evangelistic, New Testaments and other Christian books were available to enquirers and the audiences were invited to find out more by coming to church.

FIFTEEN

The Collapse of Communism

O N A WARM summer evening the tanks rolled towards the White
House in Moscow, home of the Russian parliament. As the
news broke, Bible Society staff and volunteers gathered up all the
New Testaments they could find and headed off in the same direction.
The coup on the night of Sunday 18 August 1991 that ousted Mikhail
Gorbachev threatened to reverse all the progress towards freedom that had
been made in the USSR during the six amazing years of perestroika.
Religious liberty was one of the many areas in which there had been
subtantial improvements and Christians were perhaps more aware than
many people of what opportunities might be lost if the coup succeeded.

Russian president Boris Yeltsin, in a public appeal to Patriarch Alexi of
the Russian Orthodox Church issued on the Monday of the coup, urged
the Patriarch and all believers in Russia 'not to be passive observers of
deeds of inexpressible lawlessness' and warned that 'the Church, which
suffered in the years of totalitarianism, could again experience the burden
of tyranny and lawlessness'. Among Christians who responded to the
appeal to defend democracy were Alexander Ogorodnikov and a group
of Christian Democrat supporters who worked round the clock to provide
four tons of sandwiches to sustain the human chain that encircled the
White House and manned the barricades.

The Bible Society workers were led in prayer at the barricades by
Moscow priest Fr Alexander Borisov, one of the founder members of the

Society's board, and then began distributing New Testaments to the tank crews. 'It was a glorious sight to watch the soldiers who had come with orders to shoot at the people if necessary, sitting on their tanks, reading the Word of God,' commented Mikhail Seleznev of the Bible Society staff. 'The officers allowed us access to the soldiers, even in the areas closed off to traffic. On Monday night we heard rumours of an impending gas attack, and that KGB troops would be coming to replace the soldiers who had defected to the people. But strangely enough, our fear was gone. We prepared ourselves for the gas with wet towels and tablecloths, but the mood was actually good, even happy. When the KGB soldiers arrived on Tuesday night, they too were given New Testaments. Sadly, we did not have enough for everybody and could not reach those who shot the three youths. On that night no soldier could hold a New Testament in one hand and fire on the people with the other.'

Paradoxically the failed coup hastened what it was trying to prevent – the collapse of Communism and the break-up of the Soviet Union. The process of change begun by Mikhail Gorbachev with his policies of glasnost and perestroika and the decay of the Communist economic and political structure had reached a point where they could no longer be reversed. As in the countries of Eastern Europe over the previous two years the change in the USSR was dramatic and sudden, once more confounding the experts and taking by surprise even the most optimistic supporters of reform.

The three years since the celebrations of the millennium of Russian Christianity in 1988 had seen growing religious freedom for Christians of all denominations. Members of unregistered churches, young people especially, were encouraged by the slow-down in arrests to be more open in their evangelism, although in many places there was at first still resistance from the local authorities and the police. Young people from Novosibirsk found that police were turning people away from a meeting they had arranged in one village, and when they began to sing Christian songs the police switched on the sirens on their cars. However, elsewhere there was no interference and the young Christians from Novosibirsk planned a programme of visits to surrounding towns and villages where there was no church. In Bryansk, on Russian Christmas Eve in January 1988 the young people from the unregistered Baptist church went out in groups of twenty to sing carols and wish people a happy Christmas. They took with them tracts and gospels of John printed on the clandestine presses. As they sang on the streets people came out of their houses and took the tracts with interest. In blocks of flats people came out onto their balconies to listen and then the young people went into the blocks and went door-to-door distributing the tracts. To those who were most interested they gave gospels. In the course of three hours only five people refused to take a tract and the group was heartened to find that younger people were especially eager to read them.

Young people at one church in Ukraine began visiting nearby villages where there were no churches or groups of believers. In one village a young man called on all the houses and found that most people were keen to listen to the Gospel. Finally he came to a house where an old Christian lady lived, whom everybody had forgotten. She was delighted to see the young preacher and offered to host a service for all the villagers in her home. In another village a group of young people arrived by bus on Saturday evening. As they stood at the bus stop wondering how and where to begin, a man approached them and asked them what they wanted. They explained that they were looking for people who wanted to hear the Gospel and listen to Christian songs, but knew nobody in the village. 'Then come to my house,' said the stranger. After they had sung, read the Bible and talked with him, their host suggested that they have a service in his house on Sunday, to which many of his neighbours came. Two people became Christians.

In the spring and summer of 1988 hundreds of young people gathered at special meetings to meet recently released Baptist prisoners. In Kursk in May 600 young Christians and their friends gathered from nearby cities and even from Moscow and as far away as Leningrad (800 miles). They were addressed by Nikolai Baturin and Dmitri Minyakov. In Sumy 600 young people shared in an evangelistic rally with Dmitri Minyakov and in a forest clearing in Moldavia about 1000 came to hear Pavel Rytikov. At all of these meetings many young Christians made a fresh commitment and scores of other young people, some of them at a Christian meeting for the first time, invited Christ into their lives.

The years of imprisonment, however, had their effect. Forty years after his first arrest as a young man, Nikolai Baturin died in October 1988. Since his release in 1987 he had visited 111 churches from Siberia in the east to Belorussia in the west. Just two weeks before his death he had been preaching in Central Asia. His funeral was attended by Christians from all over the Soviet Union and was a celebration of his life and ministry and of Christ's triumph over death. A three-hour service in the yard of his house was followed by a two-hour procession to the cemetery, accompanied by three church brass bands. Ten times on the way they stopped so that the curious crowds could be addressed, and many non-Christians joined the procession. Nikolai was an indefatigable evangelist and it was fully in keeping that his funeral should be a testimony to the new life in Jesus. The familiar words of the gospel were read out: 'He that believeth in me, though he were dead, yet shall he live . . . Do you believe this?' 'We believe,' replied Nikolai's wife and children.

During 1988 it became much easier to supply Bibles and other Christian literature to the Soviet Union. Import permits were granted for larger consignments of Bibles than ever before as gifts to the Russian Orthodox Church in honour of the millennium. Official permission to deliver Bibles was now secured by missions that had previously engaged in smuggling Bibles, including Open Doors with Brother Andrew in Holland and a consortium of missions in Scandinavia who reprinted a pre-revolutionary three-volume edition of the Bible with commentaries. Other consignments came from the Bible Societies and from the Taizé community in France. However, unregistered churches were not able to receive shipments: churches in Leningrad and Makinsk were told they would have to register in order to get them. In Makinsk, the Bibles were handed over to a registered church instead.

With increased supplies of Bibles there was increasing controversy over the practice of selling them. The Orthodox Church and the Baptist Union had always sold Bibles and New Testaments, but as there was such a severe shortage Christians gladly paid to have their own copy, and the price was usually less than half the cost on the black market. But when large consignments were donated by western churches and Bible Societies, people began to complain about the sale of what was intended as a gift for Russian Christians. The unregistered churches did not usually sell Bibles and other books, and the Baptists' secret publishers *Khristianin* had a strict policy of not charging for its books. The work was supported by gifts from the churches in order to provide books where they were most needed. They even supplied the registered churches. For example, in 1988 a Bible calendar was published with passages for every day and a list of related verses for Bible study. Two hundred were given to the young people of the Moscow registered Baptist church and then another thousand for general distribution to the members. The Moscow registered church leadership offered representatives of the unregistered churches part of a shipment of Bibles they had recently received from the West. However, the offer was refused when it became clear that they would be expected to pay for them. In response to the widespread sale of donated Bibles three Christian ex-prisoners, two Orthodox and one Catholic, founded a society for the free distribution of Bibles, guaranteeing to supply Bibles they received to people who needed them without making any charge.

In March the government newspaper *Izvestiya* announced that customs regulations had been changed and that Bibles and other items of religious literature could be received by post and many individuals and churches were able to express their love and solidarity with Russian Christians by sending in parcels. New friendships were built as letters of thanks came back to the senders, often with requests for more Bibles. One Christian family received a letter from the West informing them that a Bible had been posted to them. When after some time there was no sign of the Bible, they made enquiries at the post office, and were told it had been delivered. A little while later their postwoman came to them in tears begging their forgiveness. She had been searching for a Bible and when she realized that the packet she was delivering contained a Bible she had taken it for herself. She begged to be allowed to keep it and offered to pay any price the family named. When they heard the story, the Christian family were glad to give her the Bible meant for themselves.

On another occasion a postwoman was pursued by local people who begged her to let them have a Bible from the parcels they knew the Christians in the village were receiving. 'Give them to us,' they said. 'We have never seen or read the Bible. They know what's written in it already!' The postwoman refused, but asked the Christians to request enough Bibles so that she could deliver one to every home in the village! Even prisoners were allowed to receive Bibles by post. Ivan Plett, imprisoned for his involvement with the secret printing of Christian literature by the Baptist *Khristianin* press, was called to the camp censor's office shortly before his release in September 1988. 'A Bible's come for you and I am obliged to pass it on!' said the censor, handing him a Schofield study Bible.

The spirit of glasnost began to be reflected by the Council for Religious Affairs. Detailed statistics on religious life were made available to the media – though there were inconsistencies when compared with figures issued by the churches – and some of the Council's files relating to the closure of churches under Khrushchev were transferred to a public archive where they were accessible to researchers. Konstantin Kharchev made himself available to the press, most notably in a series of interviews with the independent journalist Alexander Nezhny, in which he spoke frankly of the need to establish a new relationship between Church and state and to extend religious liberty.

In autumn 1988 Kharchev visited the World Council of Churches in Geneva and then Britain, where he stood on the balcony with the Queen at the Remembrance Day ceremony at the Cenotaph in London and was received by the Archbishop of Canterbury at Lambeth Palace. He also spoke in public at Coventry Guildhall and paid private visits to Keston College and the Quakers. On these occasions he was angrily defensive when the question of religious prisoners was raised and totally rejected the idea of allowing objection to military service on grounds of conscience. However, in exchange for Keston College's list of religious prisoners he presented Keston researchers with his own official list, consisting only of those convicted under the two articles of the criminal code directly relating to religious activity. Despite Kharchev's hostile attitude on the issue, the provision of his list was more than a symbol of glasnost, for it actually contained details of several Jehovah's Witness prisoners who were unknown to Keston, as well as supplementing and confirming information on other cases!

Kharchev claimed in an interview early in 1989 that during 1988 the Council for Religious Affairs had approved the reopening of over 500 Orthodox churches; in 83 cases the Council had overturned decisions by local authorities to refuse applications to open churches. In a gesture that indicated his intention of extending religious liberty beyond concessions to officially recognized church groups, Kharchev in January 1989 received a group of unofficial Orthodox activists including Father Gleb Yakunin. Kharchev spoke frequently of the need to revise legislation governing religious affairs and promised a new law, but no draft appeared. Nevertheless, it was obvious from the behaviour of the authorities that many of the legal restrictions were no longer being enforced and Kharchev himself admitted that the old law was in large part de facto suspended.

Kharchev's implementation of religious policy was undoubtedly largely in the spirit of glasnost and as a result he made himself enemies among opponents of glasnost in high places. In the spring of 1989 there were widespread rumours about his future, including the possibility of his return to the diplomatic service and dispatch to a minor African country. Council for Religious Affairs spokesmen insisted that he was on sick leave. According to some analysts Kharchev antagonized the top hierarchy of the Russian Orthodox Church by demanding greater financial accountability. The Orthodox church leaders evidently had influential friends, and may well have pointed to their past loyalty to the official Soviet line on religious liberty and their efforts to get the World Council of Churches and other international church bodies to support Soviet peace propaganda. On the other hand, Kharchev himself later claimed that it was members of the ideological commission of the Communist Party Central Committee who were opposed to him.

Whatever the circumstances, the rumours that he was out of favour proved to be true, and Kharchev was replaced in May by Yuri Khristoradnov, a long-serving party bureaucrat who had briefly been chairman of one of the chambers of the USSR's parliament, the Supreme Soviet. He had become redundant when he failed to be re-elected in the Supreme Soviet's first contested elections in March 1989. Curiously the two parts of Khristoradnov's surname are made up of the words 'Christ' and 'joy'. Nevertheless, he had an inauspicious background: as party secretary in Gorky he had been responsible for ensuring the isolation of Andrei Sakharov and for implementing a very tight local religious policy in which a vigorous campaign for opening churches had been totally ignored. However, as a faithful bureaucrat Khristoradnov continued the existing policy of allowing the churches greater freedom. He also travelled abroad to defend the Soviet record on religious liberty: in April 1990 he attended a human rights symposium in Oslo with two of his colleagues, even agreeing to debate with two dissident Orthodox Christians, Viktor Popkov and Father Georgi Edelstein, and with myself representing Keston College. Father Edelstein was greatly amused at the official dinner on the eve of the symposium to be seated next to the chairman of the Council for Religious Affairs of the Russian Republic, who had not long ago expelled him from the CRA office with the words 'Get out of here – I don't want ever to see you again!'

Political change accelerated in 1990. The pace of glasnost was such that the March elections to the Russian parliament and to parliaments in the other republics and to local regional and city councils throughout the USSR were conducted in a much freer atmosphere than those to the USSR Supreme Soviet only a year earlier. Hundreds of independent candidates were elected. The Russian parliament included a strong block that had stood on a democratic ticket and in the Baltic republics the new parliaments had majorities in favour of re-establishing their independent statehood. The Popular Front movements in Latvia and Estonia embarked on policies designed to increase their independence within the Soviet Union with the long-term aim of secession as sovereign states, while the Lithuanian parliament, in which the movement for national renewal, *Sajudis*, had an overwhelming majority, declared immediate independence and elected Vytautas Landsbergis as President. In July the Ukrainian parliament passed a declaration of national sovereignty within the Soviet Union and other republics representing both large and small nations followed the Ukrainians' example.

In the midst of all this political turmoil the ageing head of the Russian Orthodox Church, Patriarch Pimen, died. Pimen in many ways symbolized the old relationship between the Church and the Soviet state and he had been much criticized by dissidents within the Church for passivity and submissiveness. A council was called early in June 1990 to elect a successor. Curiously, all three leading candidates were not Russians. Metropolitan Alexi of Leningrad and Tallinn, who was elected Patriarch, is of German and Estonian background, while his two main rivals, Metropolitans Filaret of Kiev and Vladimir of Rostov are both Ukrainians.

It was during Khristoradnov's period in office that drafts of a new law on freedom of conscience were published and discussed, although it was clear that the Council for Religious Affairs had only a secondary role in finalizing the draft that went before the Supreme Soviet. The new law was finally passed in October 1990, but was immediately upstaged by a much more democratic and radical law on religion passed by the Russian parliament. Among the independent deputies were Father Gleb Yakunin, who became a leading member of the Democratic Russia bloc in parliament, and another priest Father Vyacheslav Polosin, who became chairman of the parliamentary committee on religious affairs and who steered the Russian law on religion through parliament. Among other things it declared as illegal any kind of government agency for the control of religion and ordered the abolition of the Council for Religious Affairs in Russia by the end of the year. Since the USSR law on religion actually recognized the supremacy of the laws of the republics it was at once superseded in Russia itself by the new Russian law.

To mark the passing of the Russian law unregistered Baptist leaders in Moscow were asked to provide a copy of the New Testament for all the deputies of the Russian parliament, to be presented on the day that the new law came into force. It is interesting that the independent non-Communist deputies made this request not to any of the officially recognized, registered denominations, but to the persecuted Church that had made the greatest contribution to religious liberty through its vigorous defence of its prisoners and campaigning for the rights of the churches and for true separation of Church and state. The Baptist leaders readily agreed to the request and decided to present Bibles rather than New

Testaments. On the appointed day a steady stream of deputies queued up to receive their copies. The supply ran out, however, and so 5000 gift-wrapped parcels containing a Bible, a children's Bible, and a book entitled *Biblical Principles of Family Life* were brought from Germany. This time the Russian Congress of People's Deputies was meeting in the Kremlin, where the gifts were distributed in one of the reception halls. Soon after, a similar request was received from the Moscow city council, which also now had a non-Communist majority. The council had supported the Moscow unregistered Baptists in their petitions to Soviet customs to release to them a shipment of 500,000 New Testaments. Customs officials finally relented and the Baptists were once again happy to make a presentation to all the city councillors.

In 1991 still more dramatic political change was to rock the Soviet Union and finally lead to its disintegration with complex implications for the churches. Gorbachev's attempt to hold the USSR together by negotiating a new 'Treaty of the Union' brought ambiguous results. He was out of touch with the democratic and nationalistic aspirations of the peoples of the republics, including Russia. His referendum in March 1991 on the desirability of a new union treaty was worded sufficiently vaguely that it secured a majority, but he was unable to prevent certain republics from adding their own questions to the referendum. Thus, Ukraine simulataneously voted in favour of a new treaty of union and for Ukrainian sovereignty and independence, while Russian voters agreed to the election of a president for Russia. When Boris Yeltsin in June secured an overwhelming majority against an official Communist Party candidate and other independent candidates to become Russia's first president, he immediately became a challenge to the entire old power structure. As a directly elected president, he could claim a mandate from the people which all the other Soviet leaders lacked. Mikhail Gorbachev had not even faced the electors in a constituency vote when he became a member of the USSR Supreme Soviet as a Communist Party nominee, and his appointment as president had been by an undemocratically elected parliament and not by universal suffrage.

The August 1991 coup which threatened to reverse all the reforms and reimpose the dictatorship of the Communist Party caused widespread alarm among the Churches. When Boris Yeltsin emerged as champion of democratic reform he received cautious support from the leaders of the Orthodox Church, who condemned the use of violence and urged the armed forces to avoid bloodshed. Patriarch Alexi is believed to have insisted on issuing this statement against the advice of some of his senior colleagues who wanted to sit on the fence and wait to see how the power struggle ended. One Metropolitan is reported to have gone as far in the opposite direction as to visit the leaders of the coup. Other Christian activists were unequivocal in their support for Yeltsin against the coup. Father Gleb Yakunin became the unofficial chaplain to the Russian parliament besieged in Moscow's White House and was everywhere to be seen hurrying about in his flowing priest's robes. A bearded monk was a striking figure rallying support on the barricades and conducting prayers for those who were risking their lives in support of Russia's fledgling democracy.

In the three Baltic republics all the Churches united in support of independence. Lithuania had declared independence following the victory of the national renewal movement *Sajudis* in the 1990 elections. The Catholic Church fully supported independence and, to the dismay of some of his flock, the Russian Orthodox Archbishop of Vilnius, Khrizostom, also expressed his solidarity with the Lithuanians. Christian opinion in all three republics was outraged at the violence perpetrated by the Soviet army in the Baltic republics which culminated in civilian deaths on 13 January 1991 at the television tower in the Lithuanian capital Vilnius, followed a week later by more deaths at the Latvian parliament building in Riga. Church support at this time was not just moral but practical too: in Riga the Lutheran cathedral was opened as a shelter for demonstrators, with food and medical assistance made available. In August, the Latvian and Estonian governments, fearing the reversal of progress towards independence if the Moscow coup succeeded, immediately declared full independence with solid support from church leaders. Even Russian Christians, who overnight became minorities in Lithuania, Latvia and Estonia, and as such feared future discrimination from the majority, welcomed the final sweeping away of Communism that independence brought.

In contrast, evangelical Christians in Russia tended to steer clear of political involvement. Even so, they welcomed the changes under Gorbachev as positive, and some went further in active support. Baptist Viktor Rott was the leader of one of the first Christian Democrat groups in Moscow and in Oryol a Baptist congregation participated in a public demonstration on 31 August 1991 against the city council, whose leaders had supported the coup. The church lent its public address system, enabling the demonstration's organizers to speak to a far larger crowd, and evangelist N. Novikov organized the collection of signatures on a petition calling for the resignation of the council and its chairman, a former Communist official. Such active involvement by evangelicals, however, seems to have been rare.

For the Churches the major consequence of the failed coup was the resulting outlawing of the Communist Party and, with the demise of Communism, an end to discrimination against the Christian faith. As the Soviet Union broke up into independent states the leaders of the republics renounced their communist past and, if not actually embracing the Christian faith, declared their commitment to religious tolerance. President Yeltsin has cultivated church leaders, especially the Orthodox Patriarch, and attends church, though his personal position remains ambiguous. The President of Armenia, Levon Ter-Petrossian, a noted scholar, is an active member of the Armenian Apostolic Church and part of the team translating the Bible into modern Armenian. In neighbouring Georgia President Zviad Gamsakhurdia was a long-standing campaigner for the rights and renewal of the Georgian Orthodox Church; his successor, former Soviet foreign minister Eduard Shevardnadze, was baptized into the Church in 1993. Even in Ukraine, President Leonid Kravchuk, who before independence was ideology secretary of the Ukrainian Communist Party, and therefore the party's chief atheist, has tried to build friendly relationships with church leaders, though there has also been political interference in church affairs, with ham-fisted attempts to get the churches to come together to form a Ukrainian national church.

SIXTEEN

Renewal of the Churches

ONCE PERESTROIKA began to affect the churches, whole areas of Christian life and activity opened up which had previously been heavily restricted or forbidden altogether. At first those bold individuals who had been in the forefront in exploring what was possible, and who sometimes had suffered because they had gone too far, were often the pioneers when it came to taking new initiatives. Generally the church leadership was still cautious and many people in registered evangelical churches were still very conservative about adopting new methods and branching out into new areas of ministry. The attitude which had condemned Valeri Barinov and Anatoli Runov for working with prostitutes and drunks was deeply embedded. But those with vision were undeterred and their small beginnings in Christian publishing, charitable work, evangelism and prison ministry have taken root and grown and often been taken up by the churches on a wider scale.

Growth into new ministries was a return to the wholeness of the Church. Soviet church leaders had often justified the passivity of the Christian life of their congregations by referring to the story of Martha and Mary, the two sisters who received Jesus into their home. While Martha was busy with all the things that had to be done, Mary sat at Jesus's feet. Jesus gently chided Martha for being so busy and for wanting Mary to come and help her. 'Mary has chosen the right thing,' said Jesus, 'and it will not be taken away from her.' 'We are Mary Christians,' the church leaders claimed. It is true that the devotion and love of Russian Christians for their Lord is very great, yet often it was those with the greatest love and devotion who felt themselves compelled to engage in outlawed activity despite the consequences. Soviet restrictions, in preventing children's work in many congregations and depriving the Church of practical expressions of Christian care through charity, succeeded in some ways in diminishing the churches, making them less than complete in their corporate witness. More often than not it was individual Christians working in unofficial groups who lived the Gospel in all its fulness.

A return to the whole message of Christ for the society in which they lived brought a perestroika within the churches also. One of the first new reform movements was the Latvian Lutheran Movement for Rebirth and Renewal begun by a group of ministers and theology teachers in 1987, initially to defend Pastor Modris Plate who had been dismissed from his parish on the insistence of the authorities. Modris Plate, who graduated in nuclear physics before studying theology, had had a successful ministry in the town of Kuldiga, establishing an active parish life with Bible studies, classes in New Testament Greek, literary evenings and Christian concerts. Regular Sunday services were revitalized and many services for special occasions were added to the parish's calendar: in 1986 more services were held than in any other Latvian parish. Young people and intellectuals were attracted to the Christian faith and the membership of the parish increased by 50 per cent, while the number of worshippers attending services trebled. For five years a group of mainly young pastors had maintained an informal fellowship as they worked in their parishes for renewal and revival. Early in 1987 Modris Plate had himself spoken out in defence of another young pastor, Maris Ludviks, who had become a Christian in his parish, and who was blocked from taking up a parish by the Latvian Council for Religious Affairs and then vilified in the press.

The Lutheran Church leadership, afraid of the consequences of rocking the boat, reacted with alarm and dismissed several of the leaders of the group. The group's intention was to bring about a spiritual revival in the Latvian Church and to persuade the church leadership to cooperate with them in renewing the church and equipping it for bringing the Christian message to the Latvian people, for example by publishing Christian literature for children. Conflict with the authorities and their own church hierarchy forced the group to become a campaigning movement, but the spiritual goal was never forgotten.

In 1989 the Synod of the Latvian Lutheran Church voted to replace the entire church leadership. All the pastors on the newly elected consistory were members of Rebirth and Renewal. Archbishop Eriks Mesters, who had lost the confidence of the Church for giving in to the authorities and trying to crush Rebirth and Renewal from within the Church, was voted out of office. His replacement, Karlis Gailitis, was a member of the Latvian National Independence Movement and a strong believer in the importance of a Christian renewal of Latvian society. When Archbishop Gailitis was killed in a car crash in 1993, a founder member of Rebirth and Renewal, Pastor Janis Vanags, was elected to succeed him.

Relaxation of religious policy also enabled the German Lutherans to re-establish themselves as a denomination. Since the pioneering work of Eugen Bachmann, who founded the first registered German Lutheran parish in Tselinograd (Akmolinsk), other congregations had been founded in Siberia and the republics of Central Asia, and after 1975 many of them had achieved registration. By the era of perestroika there were 500 congregations spread across thousands of miles, but with no organized structures and few pastors. Almost half of these congregations had been registered by 1985, and many of these registered congregations had large memberships, sometimes over one thousand. Those remaining unregistered were generally much smaller house churches. An elderly German-speaking Latvian pastor, Harald Kalnins, had been appointed as superintendent to have pastoral oversight over this scattered flock. He travelled widely, preaching, giving encouragement and conducting the sacraments. In November 1988 he was consecrated as bishop and was thus enabled to begin to ordain pastors. With a growing band of pastors the German Lutherans were able to re-establish the German Evangelical Lutheran Church of the Soviet Union and began to reclaim churches in their old home areas along the Volga and in Ukraine. In Odessa the parish claimed back its city centre church which was just a shell without a roof. This did not deter them from worshipping together under the open sky but once again within their own four walls. With the break-up of the Soviet Union, independent Lutheran churches were established in each republic where there were parishes. In 1993 the Lutheran Church of Kazakhstan was recognized by the Kazakh government.

The Baptists, at their congress in February 1990, reflected the growing centrifugal forces in the USSR by reorganizing themselves as a union of national Baptist associations. At this point only the Estonian and Latvian Baptists went so far as to declare independent national unions while continuing to be affiliated to the union in Moscow. However, after the collapse of the Soviet Union the Baptist associations in the other republics soon proclaimed themselves national unions also. For the first time since the formation of the Baptist Union, the president and three vice-presidents were directly elected by delegates without any interference from the Council of Religious Affairs. The retiring Union president Vasili Logvinenko admitted that previously the CRA had influenced elections. Officials had always monitored the elections of the Union council, even though all other non-delegates were excluded from the congress session at which the voting took place; and the indirect election procedure, under which the Union council elected the president and executive, had facilitated CRA control.

The new constitution for the Union agreed by the congress could have been designed with the collapse of the USSR in mind. It emphasized local and regional autonomy and built organizational structures from the bottom upwards. The Union was stated to consist of associations and unions of churches coming together voluntarily for fellowship and cooperation, with a board consisting of the president and three vice-presidents and the presidents from all the republic assocations. The new Union council included vice-presidents from the republics and all the regional superintendents, all of whom were to be elected by regional association conferences. The Baptists had applied Gorbachev's policy of democratization, taking it to its logical conclusion, and thereby bringing themselves firmly back to the European Baptist tradition of autonomy and voluntary association. At the same time the abolition of the post of General Secretary gave the new Baptist Union President greater executive power, curiously just a few weeks before the parliament of the USSR voted to make Mikhail Gorbachev Soviet President with greatly increased executive powers.

The disintegration of the Soviet Union after the failed coup led to further transformation of the Baptist structure within its more flexible framework. In November 1992 the Union became a federation, in the hope of creating a body to which all Baptist groups could affiliate without sacrificing their independence. The new federation aimed to restore the democratic structure which had existed in the 1920s but had been crushed by Stalin. The central leadership was reduced by removing the three vice-presidents, leaving the president as head of the 'Federation of Baptist Unions of Eastern Europe and Northern Asia'.

The progress of perestroika had other effects on the Baptist Union. Many congregations were weakened as more and more Germans received permission to move to Germany. Almost 400 congregations were either entirely German-speaking or held German services alongside Russian ones. By the time of the 1990 Congress one thousand German Baptist families had left from Kazakhstan alone. Then Russians and Ukrainians took opportunities to emigrate especially to the United States and Canada. Some previously large and flourishing congregations declined drastically in numbers and were left without experienced leaders. In May 1989 the Pentecostal leaders in the ECB Union combined with leaders of autonomous Pentecostal churches to secure permission from the government to re-establish a separate Pentecostal Union. Virtually all Pentecostals transferred their membership from the Baptist Union, causing a further reduction in overall membership in the Union. However, their departure removed a long-standing cause of friction, especially within mixed congregations, ending decades of faltering attempts to maintain a unity which had been imposed by the state authorities.

Autonomous Baptist churches held discussions with the Baptist Union, but they could agree only to cooperate as much as possible, especially on the local level. Nationally, the autonomous churches proposed dissolving the Baptist Union and the unregistered Council of Churches and calling a congress to establish a union that would be acceptable to all. The Council of Churches ignored this proposal and the Baptist Union leadership turned it down. In March 1989 the autonomous churches began to form their own union with a conference in Donetsk region of representatives from churches in eastern Ukraine and the northern Caucasus area of Russia. They agreed to come together in the Fraternal Council of ECB Independent Churches of the Southern Region and immediately applied for registration, which was granted by the Council for Religious Affairs in Moscow.

The unregistered Baptists had a mixed experience with perestroika. With the release from exile of the last of their prisoners their churches did not experience total relief from all forms of harassment and persecution. Some local authorities continued to impose fines on congregations for holding illegal meetings, and Christians were threatened with much higher fines under new laws passed in 1988 designed to combat a growing wave of political street demonstrations. In several places tents and other temporary structures used for worship were torn down and destroyed. One of the worst cases was in Tashkent, where a disabled woman, Nadezhda Matyukhina, allowed the church to worship in her home. For this she had been sentenced to three years imprisonment in 1966, and she had been threatened with new charges in 1986. In February 1988 she was evicted and the house demolished. The excuse was redevelopment of the area, though the city council had not yet passed the plans. None of the neighbouring houses was demolished for a year and she was offered no compensation. A year later a letter from the city council conceded that the reason for the demolition of Nadezhda's house was because it was being used for worship by the unregistered church. Another lady, Mrs Lyapunova, offered to allow the church to put up a shelter in the yard of her home. She died soon after and her daughter, although willing to allow the church to continue to meet there, faced obstruction from the local authorities, who prevented her from registering her ownership of the house, and there were constant threats to demolish the shelter. In Minsk P. Yanush was ordered by the local council in October 1989 to demolish the shelter at the back of his house in which the church met for worship. In Rostov-on-Don a light building constructed for worship was bulldozed in April 1989, and in September police brought in a squad of workers who began to demolish the replacement shelter. However, when some Christian families nearby came and started to sing and pray inside, the workers refused to continue with the demolition and the police decided not to remove the members of the congregation. The structure was left in a dangerous state and the timbers had to be reinforced.

However, in July 1989, for the first time since 1969, the Council of Churches was able to call a national conference which was held openly and without interference in a large tent in Rostov-on-Don. The 700 delegates present on the first day to approve the work of the Council and to vote in new members were joined by over a thousand guests on the second day. The chairman of the Council, Gennadi Kryuchkov, who had been living in hiding since 1970 under threat of arrest, appeared in person to speak to the conference. His review of the past twenty years showed that he had remained closely in touch with the Church through regular meetings with leaders. Others spoke of the joy of being able to meet old friends for the first time in so many years. Mikhail Khorev reminded the conference that although everyone who had been sentenced to imprisonment was now free there were still voluntary prisoners:

Our printers continue their ministry in the 'solitary confinement' to which they have sentenced themselves out of love for the Lord and His work. We pray that the Lord will renew their ranks with new workers. We still need Christian literature, magazines, gospels. For some people it is easier to be locked up than in freedom to shut the door behind them and give up everything for the sake of the gospel. Let us remember these 'prisoners' from our brotherhood.

Though the authorities made no attempt to detain Gennadi Kryuchkov at the conference, they did put up road blocks and institute identity checks at stations and the airport; but Gennadi had anticipated this and had already made arrangements to slip out of the city in secret. He had earlier been notified that all charges against him had been dropped, but the leaders elected to the Council feared that the authorities would use a meeting with Gennadi to mislead the churches into thinking that relations between the unregistered Baptists and the state were becoming normal. At this stage, however, they felt it important to wait for new legislation before deciding any change in their approach to the authorities. Harassment of Gennadi's family continued into 1990 and he was vilified in a series of press articles. Since then, however, all threats of arrest have been lifted and in August 1990 he finally returned home, exactly twenty years after first going into hiding.

Even after the conference several churches reported that members had been fined for allowing services to be held in their homes, for example P. Soroka of the church in Slavuta, West Ukraine, was fined for a harvest festival service held in his home without permission. In Brest, Boris Barmin was fined in June 1989 for reading the Bible to a crowd of people at a market, and again in October for praying and reading from the Bible at the vegetable market. And in Stry, near Lviv in West Ukraine, Pastor Zakhar Tseikhner was fined for conducting an open-air baptism in a river. A group from the church in Bezhitsa visited a nearby village to hold an evangelistic meeting in February 1990. A friendly crowd gathered and listened to the music and the preaching, but local officials called out the police who did everything they could to disrupt the gathering. On another occasion the police tried to disperse the crowd by force and detained three Christians for three hours. However, the last known criminal trial for specifically Christian work ended with the release of the defendant. Susanna Herzen was put on trial in February 1990 in Karaganda, accused of repeatedly breaking the laws on religion and especially for leading a Sunday school of the unregistered Baptist church. Susanna had originally been charged in 1982, but the charges were dropped. The following year the case was reopened and her passport (identity card) was confiscated. She went into hiding, and only in 1989, when no more Christians were being arrested, did she appear at the prosecutor's office to claim her passport. She was not formally declared innocent, but the court ruled that the case should not be continued 'due to changed circumstances and her actions no longer presenting any danger to the public'. This ruling was official recognition that legal restrictions on Christian work were de facto suspended.

The Russian Orthodox Church began to respond to the desire for national autonomy, but more cautiously than the Baptist Union. The dioceses in Belorussia and Ukraine were already grouped together as church provinces (Exarchates), but early in 1990 these provinces were granted autonomous status with the titles of Belorussian Orthodox Church and Ukrainian Orthodox Church. This autonomy did not, however, satisfy the desire of many Ukrainian Orthodox for full independence from Moscow. In the summer of 1989 a committee had been formed to re-establish the Ukrainian Autocephalous Orthodox Church. This church had been founded in Ukraine during its brief independence after the Bolshevik revolution, dissolved by Stalin, revived during the German occupation of Ukraine during the Second World War and then once more promptly suppressed by Stalin. A retired archbishop defected from the Russian Orthodox Church to become leader of the newly emerging Church and several hundred parishes followed him. In June 1990 the Church held its first council and elected an exiled bishop, Metropolitan Mstyslav, head of the Ukrainian Autocepahalous Church in the USA, as Patriarch.

An even greater threat to the position of the Russian Orthodox Church in Ukraine came from the campaign by Ukrainian Catholics to re-establish their church – finally granted by the Soviet state when Mikhail Gorbachev visited Pope John Paul II in December 1989. Mass demonstrations and huge open-air services in West Ukraine in the autumn of 1989 were accompanied by the defection of some parishes from Orthodoxy. When the relegalization of the Ukrainian Catholic Church was announced, a flood of transfers transformed the religious map of Western Ukraine almost overnight. The previously banned Ukrainian Catholics became the largest denomination in most districts, with the Orthodox divided between those still under the jurisdiction of Moscow and those who had gone over to the Autocephalous Church.

After the proclamation of Ukraine's independence in August 1991 the head of the Ukrainian Orthodox Church (under Moscow's jurisdiction), Metropolitan Filaret of Kiev, made a sudden U-turn and became an ardent Ukrainian nationalist. Previously he had attacked any suggestion of independence for the Orthodox Church in Ukraine and had even sacked

priests for preaching in Ukrainian. Now he began to press for full
ecclesiastical independence from Moscow to match Ukraine's state
independence, with enthusiastic backing from Ukrainian President Leonid
Kravchuk, who had undergone a similarly rapid conversion to the national
cause. Cynics trace Filaret's sudden change of heart to his ambition to
become Patriarch. Having failed to be elected as Patriarch of Moscow he
was seen as putting his energies into becoming Patriarch of Kiev. When
Filaret took his demand for independence to the synod of bishops in
Moscow in spring 1992, Patriarch Alexi insisted that independence could
not be granted overnight, his bishops confirmed the status quo and Filaret
was forced to resign. Returning to Kiev, Filaret withdrew his resignation
and proclaimed the independence of the Ukrainian Orthodox Church. The
Patriarch stripped Filaret of office and a synod of Ukrainian bishops elected
Metropolitan Vladimir of Rostov, the third main contender for Patriarch,
as his successor. However, some parishes followed Filaret and he retained
control of St Vladimir's Cathedral in Kiev and of his official residence.

Thus there was a three-way split in Orthodoxy in Ukraine, although
Filaret soon joined forces with the Autocephalous Church to form the
Ukrainian Orthodox Church-Kiev Patriarchate, which elected him as
deputy Patriarch. When Mstyslav died in June 1993, however, Filaret's
ambitions to become Patriarch were thwarted, as Metropolitan Volodymyr
of Sumy and Chernihiv was appointed by the Synod as acting Patriarch.
Union with Filaret had never been accepted by Mstyslav, and his supporters
held a rival Synod of the Ukrainian Autocephalous Orthodox Church
which elected Metropolitan Petro of Lviv and Halych as acting Patriarch.

SEVENTEEN

Evangelical Explosion

*I*T LOOKED AS though the conference would be overshadowed by the death of a young Christian in an accident in a local mine: his funeral was on the opening day. Instead the youth conference in the town of Nikolsk, near Dzhezkazgan, in May 1988, encouraged young Christians in Kazakhstan to go out in evangelism. The young people who had arrived joined the local church and the entire staff of the mine to make the biggest funeral that the town had ever seen. As is customary at Christian funerals the Gospel was preached. Non-Christians listened reverently and gladly accepted John's gospel - printed on the secret printing presses - distributed by the young people. After the church service following the burial about 100 of the young people felt led to continue witnessing and went out onto the neighbouring streets in small groups to call at each house. Some groups visited a lot of houses, while one got no further than the first house because the people were so eager to listen and ask them questions. Especially in streets where Muslim Kazakhs lived, the initial reception was hostile, but then many agreed to hear them out after all. The next day at the conference the young people recognized many of the people they had called on who had accepted the invitation to come to the meeting.

Waiting for their train at Dzhezkazgan station the group from Karaganda began to pray and sing on the platform. They distributed John's gospel to about half the people on the station while the police went for reinforcements who demanded that they stop singing and disperse. Then the station public address system was used to drown out their singing. On the train someone was reading a John's gospel in almost every compartment, and as the young people continued singing they were drawn into conversations. Then they were invited by two of the women who worked in the restaurant car to come later and talk to them there. When the young people went along they found that the attendants from each carriage had been invited. At 11.30 P.M. some uniformed and plain-clothes police came to the restaurant car and ordered them to stop. The train crew protested: 'At last we have heard the truth. These are good people. They fear God. This is no time to stop them. When all sorts of vulgarity is shown on television, when people are torn apart morally, especially young people, you don't say anything. We are going to complain, we are going to write to Gorbachev.' As the young Christians went back to their carriages they found others from their group engaged in conversations – everywhere they found that people felt oppressed by their unbelief.

In June the young people from Karaganda decided to hold a brief service in the city park on a Sunday afternoon. They met on the Thursday before to plan the service and on Friday prayed and fasted during the day and held a prayer vigil through the night. On Sunday too they committed their service in prayer before leaving the church and before entering the park. On the main avenue the 35 young Christians began to sing 'O Lord my God, when I in awesome wonder . . .' People stopped to listen, somebody read a poem and songs and poems alternated followed by a brief sermon. Then they noticed two policemen reporting what was happening over their radio and began distributing John's gospels. Before police reinforcements arrived, they had handed out 600 gospels. The police presence attracted still more people and the crowd protested at the police order to the Christians to stop their meeting. To calm the crowd, officials said that if permission was sought in advance the Christians could use one of the stages and that they would even supply a public address system. Meanwhile another 400 John's gospels were distributed as well as some Luke's gospels in Kazakh and New Testaments in Russian and German – many Germans exiled during the Second World War from Ukraine and the Volga region live in Kazakhstan.

Word of these events spread to all the churches in the city, and young people from the Mennonite Brethren church asked to join them if such a service was organized again. So the next Sunday eighty young people went to the town of Temirtau to hold a similar service in the market place.

By the time the police came to stop them they had already fisnished their short service and were distributing gospels and New Testaments in Russian, German, Kazakh and Uzbek. The following Sunday, back in the city park in Karaganda, the group of young people had grown to 140, but officials and hostile groups of Communist Youth League members were all over the park to prevent them holding a service. Loud music was played over loudspeakers to drown out their singing. The following Sunday every band and orchestra that could be mustered was in the park, occupying every place where people could gather and providing a continuous programme of entertainment, making any further outreach in the park impossible. But the young Christians had learnt how to witness to their faith and the whole city had heard of their outreach. With the city park closed to them the young people began visiting outlying villages instead. The Karaganda prosecutor called in Pastor Andrei Wiens and asked him: 'How is it that the whole city and region is talking about you? You have got all the authorities and the public on the move and the papers are writing about you.'

The length and breadth of the Soviet Union evangelism, previously totally outlawed, began to come into the open. Registered churches became less cautious and the unregistered congregations found that they could now often work openly in public. For many churches it was a totally new experience. A church in Abakan reported: 'We had never gone to people openly preaching the Gospel. We felt it was quite beyond our strength – our congregation is just 50 people. We didn't know how to begin, how to make contact with people, where to preach.' An unregistered church in Anzhero-Sudzhensk, Siberia, held special meetings for non-Christians for the first time early in 1989. They put up posters around the town and handed invitations to people they met. At Easter 120 people came to the meeting. 'We owe you a big apology,' began the first speaker, 'because we were very bad at preaching to you about Christ, who loves every sinner and gave His life for your salvation. Our congregation has existed for such a long time and yet we never publicly invited you to our services! Please forgive us!' Then he and others went on to talk about the meaning of Easter. There was total silence in the room, the preachers were amazed at people's thirst to hear them and the total attention they gave.

Sports stadiums and public halls could be made available for evangelistic events, and now it made little difference whether the churches involved in outreach were registered or unregistered. In 1990 unregistered Pentecostals in Saratov on the Volga were able to hold a Gospel service in a sports stadium seating 10,000. At first the city authorities had been unwilling to allow the meeting unless the church agreed to register, but eventually gave permission for the use of the stadium. The stadium management, unconcerned by the distinction between registered and unregistered, decided that the service was a worthwhile cause and allowed use of the stadium free of charge.

Unregistered Baptists in Magnitogorsk were invited to use the town's theatre free of charge. One of their members was a piano tuner who always took every opportunity to share his faith. When he was talking to some of the performers at the theatre they asked him if he would come to talk to the whole company. The meeting was a success, and then the church approached the theatre director with the suggestion of holding a public meeting there on a day when there was no performance and the theatre was unused. 'I don't mind,' said the director, 'it's good to let people get to know the Bible. I hope you're registered!' 'No,' replied the church representatives. 'Oh well, I don't think it makes any difference!' concluded the director. There were no further problems, the meeting was advertised through posters and there was standing room only in the theatre.

Everywhere churches found a new openness to the Gospel and an enormous interest in reading the Bible and Christian literature. Indeed such was the eagerness to get Christian books that when they were distributed at meetings there was often an undignified scramble to get them! When the Odessa unregistered Baptist church offered gospels at the end of an evangelistic meeting in 1989 people began to push and shove and they had to be reassured that there were enough for everybody. Moscow unregistered Pentecostals who hired a village club outside the city in 1990 for a Gospel meeting were unprepared for the demand for books. When they announced that New Testaments were available they lost control of the crowd: those who pushed hardest managed to get a copy, but some people were left without. There was a growing awareness among people that they had been deprived of the spiritual dimension of life. Most people had never heard a straightforward presentation of the Christian Gospel, but were ready to listen. Preachers found a spiritual openness which led people from non-Christian backgrounds to accept Christ in increasing numbers.

Often there was an atmosphere of revival at meetings. Even at events not planned as evangelistic, people were converted, as at a choir festival organized by German Baptist churches in the Omsk region of Siberia in June 1988. Fifteen choirs with altogether 400 singers sang to over 2000 people. Many people came forward to repent of their sins and seek forgiveness and many Christians rededicated their lives. In Brest an evangelistic meeting was organized in January 1989 in a tent seating 600. Before the scheduled start all the seats were filled and there were still more and more people arriving. To accommodate everybody the benches had to be taken out so that there was room for everybody to stand. The third speaker was supposed to conclude with a call to repentance, but well before he had finished speaking people's hearts were moved and they began confessing their sins. At the front, where people were on their knees praying for forgiveness, a young boy was wandering about. Finally he too fell to his knees seeking forgiveness for sin. The preacher turned to the audience: 'Dear friends, I was going to ask this boy to leave, I thought he was getting in the way. But God saved his soul too. Are you adults really less guilty before God, so that you are in no hurry to be at peace with Him?' And more people pressed forward to find forgiveness. As they confessed their sins, parents prayed for the salvation of their children, and children for their parents. That day 105 people accepted Christ into their lives.

Evangelization reached out also to the minority peoples of Russia. In Ordzhonikidze (Vladikavkaz) in the Caucasus mountains there were already many Christian Ossetians in the churches. The unregistered Baptist congregation organized an evangelistic meeting in March 1989 for which members gave personal invitations to friends and neighbours. About 400 people came and over 60 opened their hearts to Christ. One girl just stood there with tears streaming from her sad eyes. She was invited to pray, but just made signs with her hands. They realized she was deaf and dumb and found someone who could understand sign language. The interpreter translated: 'From now on I want to be only with Jesus!' Three young Ossetians were so moved by her conversion that they too knelt to give their lives to God. The church especially remembers from this meeting the spiritual struggle of a girl from the Kabardinian people. Her mother had recently become a Christian, the first from this small Muslim nation. The girl read a poem about a Muslim father beating his Christian daughter. Sighing, she said: 'This is what awaits me, but I cannot resist Jesus any longer and I give Him my heart.'

Sergei Bogdanov, a Russian Baptist living in the Fergana valley in Uzbekistan, was imprisoned for two years for his church work. Since his release in 1988, he has become aware of the need to share the gospel with his Uzbek Muslim neighbours. 'We Russians have lived among the Uzbeks for many decades,' he explained, 'yet we never wanted to learn their customs or language. We were concerned only about maintaining our own faith, but now our churches are trying to reach the Uzbeks for Christ . . . The Uzbeks are very hospitable, but you must pay careful attention to their customs. To gain access to their home, first you go to the front gate, but you never enter the yard. You stand by the gate and shout: "Anybody home?" . . . You don't enter until the man hears you, makes his way to the gate and invites you in. To enter any other way shows great disrespect. The Uzbek asks: "What business do you have?" And I answer: "Oh, very important business!" This conversation takes place, of course, in the Uzbek language, which really warms his heart. All Uzbeks speak Russian, but it is very special for them when a European Russian speaks in their native language.'

The Uzbek then invites his visitor in for tea. Even though there is plenty of tea, he serves a little in one cup, which he drinks from first. This shows that the tea is safe to drink and he also wants to see if his guest will drink from the same cup. After tea sweets are served, and only then can serious conversation begin. The Uzbeks regard Russians as atheists, so it is interesting for them to meet a Russian who believes in God. Sergei admits that the Russians have much to learn from the Uzbeks, who have a great respect for the elderly, which Sergei sees as being thoroughly biblical. They also have a reverent attitude towards bread. Russians are often careless with bread, explains Sergei, throwing stale bread in the dustbin, while an Uzbek will always find somewhere to put the bread so that the birds can eat it.

In Alma-Ata, the capital of Kazakhstan, a Kazakh mission church was established by the 'Renewal' mission. The *Kutkaru zholy* (Way of Salvation) congregation consists of Kazakh Christians and Russians who have learnt or are learning Kazakh. The Kazakhs teach the Russians their language, translate hymns and teach them to sing in Kazakh. They share a church building with a Korean congregation and rent a conference room for Sunday evangelistic meetings conducted in Kazakh and Russian. One of the Russians had learnt enough Kazakh by the end of 1992 to preach in the language.

Many churches and groups were able to make wide use of the 'Jesus film', made for Campus Crusade for Christ on the basis of Luke's gospel and translated and dubbed into Russian. In 1990 it was shown extensively in cinemas in many places and copies were available for evangelistic meetings. Groups of Christians took film and projector to village clubs and schools. In the Black Sea resort of Anapa the local Baptist church in a short period of time showed the film in six cinemas and 'palaces of culture' and in three schools. In one school a meeting was held for the teaching staff before the film was shown in order to explain the meaning and content of the Bible. In another school over 300 senior pupils and staff watched the film. Afterwards a group of Christian young people sang and the meeting concluded with a short address.

Equipped with a copy of the 'Jesus film' and a small library, Andrei Lapin arrived with his family as a missionary in 1990 in the Arctic town of Kogalym. In two weeks he and his wife showed the film in all the town's cinemas with the library set up in the foyer. But what could they do next? How could they afford to continue to live in the town's hotel? Where would they put up the book table with the library during the Arctic winter? The prayers of Andrei and his wife were wonderfully answered: the hotel management let them stay free in the hotel in order that they could continue with their work, and the oil and gas company gave them a basement for the library – also rent-free. Young people began to visit Andrei, and as he prayed for them they began to come to Christ. In the summer of 1991 a church was established with the first baptism in the still chilly river Ult-Yagun. That summer Andrei was summoned to the town council. Far from telling him his missionary endeavours were not welcome, as might have been the case a few years earlier, the official offered him a three-room council flat. When it came to filling in Andrei's place of employment the official simply wrote 'missionary'.

An unusual missionary expedition in the summer of 1991 reached towns and villages along the Siberian rivers Ob and Irtysh by hiring a river steamer for a month. In four weeks the international team organized by Iosif Bondarenko's Church of the Cross in Riga held evangelistic meetings in fifteen places. Some of the towns had been visited earlier by teams preparing for the steamer's arrival, and venues for meetings had been arranged and publicized. In the town of Khanty-Mansiisk a mission team had come the previous autumn, and a Christian group had been formed. The new Christians' first request when the steamer docked was to be baptized.

The mission's goal was to reach in particular the native Siberian peoples as well as Russian settlers. In several places the mission team was welcomed at the jetty with the traditional gifts of salt and bread and by local people dressed in national costume. The further north the team sailed the warmer was the response to the Gospel. In the south one quarter or one third of audiences came forward in repentance to pray for forgiveness, further north the majority did, while in the most northerly port, Kharp, beyond the Arctic Circle, not a single person remained in their seat. Two members of the mission team volunteered to stay and teach the new converts and help them to form a church. Some villages away from the rivers had to be visited by helicopter, for example on the Yamal peninsula which borders the Arctic Ocean. In the local language Yamal means 'end of the earth'; as one member of the mission team commented, this lent new meaning to Jesus's words: ' . . . you will be witnesses to me . . . to the ends of the earth.' (Acts 1:8).

Many Christians exiled to remote regions had been able to be missionaries in the areas where they were forced to live. Now that there were no more exiles these remote areas might have been abandoned, but 'voluntary exiles' heard the call to go as missionaries to the unreached peoples and regions of Siberia and Central Asia. Yakov Ivashchenko, pastor of an unregistered Baptist church in Kiev, serving a sentence of exile in northern Siberia, wrote in 1988 to his home church: 'Please do not pray that I will be released early. I am needed here. I was brought here by God and it is necessary that I remain until the end of my term.'

Vasili Yudsintsev from the Donetsk region of Ukraine was imprisoned in 1986 in a labour camp in Mukhorshibir in Buryatia, in eastern Siberia near the Mongolian border. After a year his sentence was commuted to compulsory labour in the same place. His wife and some of his children came to join him and when Vasili was pardoned they decided to stay. Vasili's son Andrei, himself a former prisoner, explains:

The Lord brought my parents here when my father was sent on a forced labour project. No one ever thought that we would stay here, not even my father. But the Lord surrounded us with so many blessings and the local residents are so warm and helpful that this place has become like home to us. Right now my parents are not even thinking of leaving. Actually they want all their sons to come and help start a church . . . In our village there is not even one believer. Many of the inhabitants are Russian, but there are also quite a few Buryats. When you talk to the Buryats about the Bible, they listen rather cautiously, because they profess to be Buddhists. But when they see the Christian life style they are favourably impressed and consider you a brother. The Buryats are very affectionate people and don't like meanness or roughness . . . When my parents go from house to house they are received like angels from heaven, because they remind people of something holy which they have forgotten. The people are very sorry that they have fallen so far spiritually, especially the Russians, who have lost all religion. They listen to what my parents say and keep inviting them to come back.

Another ex-prisoner, Stepan Germanyuk, left his native Ukraine in June 1990 to settle in the Khabarovsk region of the far east of Siberia, returning to the place where he had been exiled in 1977. One Christian family moved from Novosibirsk to Yakutsk and in 1988 Valeri Sidorenko and his family moved from Ukraine to the Yakut village of Mokhsogollokh to build on the work begun by three pastors who had earlier been exiled there at different times.

Work with young people and children also grew as Christians discovered that the authorities were beginning to tolerate it. The unregistered churches had always placed great emphasis on this side of the Church's work, and subsequently many registered churches had resumed it, usually quietly and informally. In Tallinn, Estonia, the Methodist pastor's wife invited children to their home rather than openly organize a Sunday school in the church building. Many had used the cover of birthday parties to gather children together. Young people had been encouraged to sing in the choir, so that choir practices were often simultaneously a youth meeting. Some churches chose to hand over one of their weekday services to the younger preachers, who would invite young people to read poetry and sing in the service. It was not publicly announced as being specially for young people, and it was open to all, but in practice it was a youth service.

Without any official announcement that work with children and young people was now possible (and according to the law, until 1990 it was still illegal), churches realized that the old restrictions were no longer being enforced and began to organize Sunday schools and youth groups. Within a few years Sunday schools were catering not just for children from church families: in many of them a high proportion of the children attending had no Christian background at all.

Children's camps could now be openly organized, although in July 1988 two camps held by unregistered Baptists in Rostov region were broken up by police and the children sent home. However, by summer 1990, registered and unregistered churches all over the Soviet Union were organizing camps. Unregistered Baptists in Belorussia arranged a camp in Moldavia for children from regions affected by fallout from Chernobyl.

It was very much a venture of faith, and the needs of the camp were wonderfully met, from a gift that exactly covered the budget that had been worked out only the night before, to Christians visiting the camp with supplies of fresh fruit just when it was needed and the local church lending a piano and other musical instruments for the children to play. The camp was an opportunity to give the children a holiday in an uncontaminated area, but also a chance to enable the children to draw closer to God, whether they were from Christian or non-Christian families.

EIGHTEEN

Reaching Out in Word and Deed

'*H*AD I BEEN TOLD a few years ago, that I, the head doctor of a major hospital, a Communist, would stand here before you in a Baptist church, I would never have believed it . . . The word charity itself was in oblivion for a long time, but it has emerged now.' Dr Valentin Kozyrev was speaking at a thanksgiving service at the central Baptist church in Moscow to celebrate the work of fifty church volunteers helping on the wards at the nearby Kashchenko psychiatric hospital – ironically a place where in the past Christians had been interned for their faith. Since April 1988 a team of volunteers had been giving daily help in the form of cleaning, making beds, washing patients etc. Most important of all, they were able to offer the patients a degree of personal attention that the hard-pressed staff had either no time or no inclination to give. They were there to show love and companionship in the name of the Church and in the name of Christ. Despite initial doubts from some of the staff, Dr Kozyrev had welcomed the Baptist volunteers. He continued his address by speaking of the volunteers' contribution: 'Pierre Dusson, a famous psychotherapist, in his book *Fighting Insanity*, drew up a formula for curing these unfortunate persons: "Chemistry plus love". And if we as doctors are able to fulfil the first part of this formula to some extent, we are virtually incapable of fulfilling the second part, which is love . . . Our patients' gratitude and impatient waiting for your sisters are the best testimony to the fact that we have chosen the right road. We feel that we ourselves are participating in the good work simply by granting you this opportunity.'

Charitable activity of any kind, especially by churches, had been banned for sixty years. While evangelicals worldwide had been moving towards a greater awareness of social concerns, Soviet evangelicals had been able to express this awareness only on international issues – some of which, like peace and disarmament, were considered quite 'safe' topics by the Soviet authorities. Of course, the personal testimony of individual Christians could never be completely suppressed, and similarly acts of Christian love for neighbours and the needy both within and outside the churches had continued despite the legal ban on any organized charitable enterprise.

Early in glasnost the Soviet press had begun to express disquiet at the harshness and selfishness of Soviet society. A concept that had previously been considered weak and redundant in the socialist state came back into fashion, expressed by the word 'mercy'. In theory the state would care for the needy, and there was no need for individual citizens to divert themselves from building the bright future of Communism. As for the churches, it was totally unacceptable for them to back up their words about a God of love with practical acts of charity that might persuade people that Christianity was relevant in the twentieth century after all. This attitude was expressed remarkably pithily by Konstantin Kharchev, whose public pronouncements were usually in favour of new attitudes to the churches, when he spoke privately to the Communist Party Higher School in March 1988 (even such an elite institution had somebody prepared to leak his speech!). Was it right, he asked, in socialist society to allow a man's dying vision to be a believer bringing him a bedpan? Should he go to the grave in the realization that the socialist state is incapable of organizing someone to bring him this relief? On the other hand, even to this audience, he had to admit that the state needed the help of the churches – in Moscow region alone there was a shortage of 20,000 staff in the caring professions.

Public donations had long been made by the churches to officially sponsored good causes, notably the Soviet Peace Fund, which received a substantial annual income from individuals and organizations who were forced to make 'voluntary' contributions. The workforce of entire factories would be invited to give a day's wages, taxi drivers would donate a day's takings and nobody dared to refuse. The churches were in the same position – they didn't want to be accused of being opposed to peace, even though everybody knew that the Peace Fund was a Communist front organization and little was known about what its money was actually spent on. With the advent of glasnost other opportunities for giving emerged, notably the Lenin Children's Fund, and money was collected to help the victims of the Chernobyl disaster. While keen to respond in Christian love, church leaders still felt it necessary to assure the state that they were not seeking to undermine its monopoly of care from the cradle to the grave. In offering support for the Chernobyl disaster fund the head of the Armenian Church, Catholicos Vazgen I, was almost apologetic: 'Our state has taken all measures to provide housing, food and medicine for the evacuated population', he said in a telegram to president Gromyko, but the Church felt a moral obligation to contribute. Churches of all denominations responded quickly and generously to the Armenian earthquake in December 1988.

Some Christians, however, longed to be able to do more than just give money. They wanted the opportunity to show Christian love in practice. A new national charity organization, the 'Mercy and Health Fund' (*Miloserdie*), was formed in September 1988 on the basis of secular charitable groups that had formed spontaneously in the major cities on the model of the *Miloserdie* Society established in Leningrad (St Petersburg) in April. Unlike previous state-sponsored funds, *Miloserdie* was a genuinely public organization that encouraged people to get actively involved in showing compassion for their neighbours. It welcomed the participation of individual Christians and church groups and it provided a context in which Christians could begin to explore new areas of ministry.

Churches were often able to serve as channels for humanitarian aid sent by Western Christians and, as economic collapse cut deeper into the social welfare system, the help offered by Christians was more and more welcome. They brought enthusiasm and joy into institutions that had often long been neglected: the Soviet state had always given low priority to the 'unproductive' elements in society, the sick, the elderly and the handicapped. This was an area of Christian service where it no longer mattered whether helpers came from registered or unregistered churches. Two women from the unregistered Baptist church in Brest began visiting a women's ward in the local cancer hospital, taking food with them for lonely patients. They asked if they could read from the Bible and ended up taking a small service and being invited back. On their next visit word had obviously spread and all the patients who were not confined to bed gathered to hear them. Since then some of the men have begun visiting the male wards. Unregistered churches were also able to receive and distribute aid for victims of the Armenian earthquake and in April 1991 the charity work of unregistered churches received official commendation when the state news agency TASS reported on an aid consignment to Baptists in Dushanbe, the capital of the Central Asian Republic of Tadzhikistan. A cargo plane with 35 tons of aid from Germany was met at Dushanbe airport by former prisoner Peter Peters, who explained to TASS that the shipment would be divided into 2000 parcels which Christians would distribute to the most needy, especially orphans, the disabled and the elderly, while medical equipment would be presented to health centres in the city.

Christians also discovered new opportunities in areas that in the past had been considered ideologically sensitive: schools, colleges and universities, the media and prisons. Even before the collapse of Communism there was a growing awareness that atheistic Communism had been a moral failure. It had not created the 'new man' capable of building a society based on the principle 'from each according to his ability and to each according to his need'. Instead it had left a moral vacuum and educated new generations that had no moral standards except 'survival of the fittest' and 'every man for himself'. Could Christianity provide a moral foundation that would save Soviet socialism? Of course, opening up these areas from which Christians had previously been barred was part of the process of glasnost, and was a sign of the lack of belief in Communist principles of those who were still party members and even senior party members. But was there not also a degree of hypocrisy, like parents in Western societies who send their children to Sunday school but never darken the doors of the church themselves? Undoubtedly there was in some quarters, but there was also a sense of urgency and of desperation. There was the feeling that anything that might work should be tried. And as far as Christian education in schools was concerned, many adults felt that for themselves it was already too late, but could the children be given a fresh chance?

Christians found themselves being invited into schools to teach the Bible either in regular class time or in voluntary groups outside lessons. The new law on religion of 1990 specifically permitted the teaching of religion on school premises, but some schools had already begun classes teaching the Christian faith. In this climate of looking for something - anything - to fill the moral vacuum, there was a danger that Christianity would become seen as the new official line, replacing the Communist youth organizations as what was required of the children. The rigid methods of

Soviet education, learning everything by rote and not encouraging a questioning mind, contributed to this. In one of the first Moscow schools to introduce a religious education class on an experimental basis one little girl from an Orthodox Christian family reported a conversation she overheard between two classmates. The first girl asked her friend: 'Do you believe in God?' 'I'm not sure,' replied the second. 'Well, you've got to!' insisted the first.

For Christians it was a strange experience to be given opportunities to teach in school, as the Soviet government had rigorously excluded them from the teaching profession. Access to any form of higher education had been difficult for active Christians, and the 'ideological purity' of applicants for teacher training institutes was particularly carefully monitored. Those who somehow slipped through the net were expelled if it subsequently became known that they were Christians, and teachers who became Christians were usually dismissed from their jobs. Valentina C., from the Donetsk region of Ukraine, had begun training as a primary school teacher when she was expelled from the institute for her Christian convictions. For years she worked at menial jobs, but was able to make some use of her training when she had the opportunity to lead a Sunday school. Then she was invited to teach the Bible in school and was delighted to point out God's plan and sense of humour – for she was now teaching the very thing that she was expelled from college for.

Invitations to schools tend to be at the discretion of school directors. Christian teaching is permitted in schools, but is not required by the curriculum, though many schools are now trying to find a syllabus to replace the previously compulsory ideological programmes and there is great interest in promoting moral and religious education in their place. Teachers are generally unaware of the distinction between registered and unregistered churches and welcome any Christians who are willing and able to teach the children from the Bible. In a school in Kishinev, the capital of Moldavia, Veniamin Khorev, son of former Baptist prisoner Mikhail Khorev, in 1991 began a voluntary Bible class which met after the end of regular lessons. Visitors from Germany found the children were eager to be tested on their homework, actively took part and asked questions and listened attentively. At the end of the class they asked Veniamin if another boy could join them. At first this boy hadn't wanted to come, but when he heard from the others what they had been learning he changed his mind, but he didn't want to come without asking first! Unregistered Baptists received so many invitations to take classes in schools that the

Council of Churches arranged a series of training courses for school workers.

An independent mission in Kiev, *Dobra volya* (Good will), organized a programme of study over a whole school year covering the Bible, Christian morality and the history of the Christian Church. In the 1992-3 school year twenty volunteer teachers taught 12,000 children for one lesson a week, with the number of pupils increasing to 18,000 from September 1993. There would be still more opportunities if teachers could be paid to do the work full time or more volunteers could be found and trained. At the same time the mission is aware that programmes covering the material in greater depth need to be prepared for senior classes who have already completed the one-year course, and that out-of-school activities need to be organized for children who want to explore further and grow in the Christian faith.

For Christians barred from further education it was strange now to be invited to colleges and universities to debate with students and lecturers. If the debates of the 1920s had been organized with the intention of demonstrating the intellectual superiority of atheism, these debates were usually a forum for honest questioning, for those present to receive an objective account of Christian faith, something which the Soviet educational system had denied them. Such debates took place in institutions as diverse as Novosibirsk University and the Siberian branch of the Academy of Sciences in nearby Akademgorodok (Academy City) and the teacher-training institute in Brest. In Akademgorodok young people from the Novosibirsk unregistered Baptist church were invited to a debate. A visiting Christian preacher spoke first and a woman lecturer then made a counter-presentation on 'scientific atheism'. Next the audience had the opportunity to ask questions and it was evident that they were not interested in theoretical questions of science and religion, but in what Christians believe and how it affects their lives. Afterwards John's gospels and some New Testaments were distributed. Even the atheist lecturer gladly accepted a New Testament and immediately began to look through it. Although her job was to argue against religion, she had probably never had the opportunity to read God's Word to find out what she was arguing against. Even village clubs invited believers and villagers to debates, which gave the Christians an opportunity to present their faith in an atmosphere in which they were accepted as normal members of society.

An even stranger experience was going to prisons. Christian men and women who had served prison sentences for preaching and living the

Gospel and who had been persecuted even during their imprisonment for their Christian faith, began to be allowed into prisons and labour camps to preach to the prisoners. Sometimes they were even welcomed back like old friends to the prisons and camps where they had served sentences themselves. Orthodox priests and bishops also visited prisons to address the prisoners. In October 1989 the Ministry of Internal Affairs issued a document that noted the positive results of visits by religious groups to prisons and labour camps. Recommendations were outlined on procedures for admitting believers to take services and speak to individual prisoners. It was not always easy to persuade prison and camp directors that such visits would be beneficial. It took four months of petitioning for the independent Baptist church in Rostov to get permission to visit Camp no. 2 in the city, and the director changed his mind only after the church appealed to the Ministry in Moscow.

For many Christians embarking on this ministry it was very much a step into the unknown. One describes his first visit:

I experienced a deep anxiety for myself and my brothers in the faith. What will I say? What will the others say? Will we be understood? And now, after completion of all the formalities, accompanied by an officer, we are inside the camp. We look at the barbed wire and the high fences and feel a shiver inside: not long ago our brethren were here, but not as free visitors . . . 'Which section will we go to?' asks the officer. 'Where we're most needed,' someone replies. We head for the nearest hostel. People pass us on the way. Some look at us with a blank expression of hopelessness, others with puzzlement, interest, indifference and some with open hostility. The section head talks to us briefly, announces names that mean nothing to us. A few minutes later a man is sitting opposite me, to whom I as yet mean nothing. I want to guess his age, but my anxiety prevents me, I am concentrating on what I can ask. Maybe he'll ask the first question, but he is silent too, lost in thought. I recall some encouraging Scripture verses. I look at the others: they are already talking. Glancing at my prisoner's clothing I see his name tag, so I address him by name and ask my first question: 'You know we're Christians?' 'Yes, they told us,' he says slowly. 'We've come to obey Jesus's commission,' I explain, 'and tell you He loves you. Have you heard of Him?' A few minutes later we are sitting side by side at the table, our heads bowed over' the open Bible between us and talking, and feel God's blessing on us. The two hours pass in a flash. We conclude our meeting: 'What do you think, are meetings like this a good idea?' 'Yes!' We exchange addresses and agree to meet again. When the literature we have brought has been distributed we suggest: 'If you want, we'll pray for you.' After receiving a positive response, we prayed to Jesus, bowing our heads and committing our new friends to him. As we said goodbye we saw tears of joy . . . They accompanied us as far as they could. We warmly shook their hands, which they had hesitantly extended to us.

Three Baptist ex-prisoners, Alexei Kalyashin, Alexei Kurkin and Vladimir Filippov decided to try to visit a criminal prisoner whom Alexei Kalyashin had got to know during his imprisonment. Early on a cold January morning in 1990 they approached the camp, situated north of the Arctic Circle, and asked for the camp commandant. They explained that they wanted to visit Alexei's friend and tell the other prisoners about Jesus Christ and give them gospels. The commandant asked for documentation showing they were Christian leaders. Alexei Kurkin produced the certificate showing he had completed the unregistered Baptists' Bible course, Alexei Kalyashin showed the court verdict that showed that he had been imprisoned as a Christian worker, but Vladimir had nothing to show. After further questioning the commandant gave the order for all the prisoners to assemble in the camp meeting room. As the three addressed over 200 prisoners, telling them in simple terms about God's love and His salvation, the men listened attentively. After answering questions, the three evangelists closed with a prayer of thanksgiving and distributed gospels and tracts which the prisoners eagerly accepted. As they left the room, the officer in charge of political education commented: 'Well, if you moved my heart, you must have moved theirs even more!' Then they were allowed to meet privately the prisoner that Alexei knew and another who wanted to talk more with them about becoming a Christian.

Prisoners responded warmly to visits from Christians. Prisoner V. N. wrote: 'I am hearing for the first time about Christ, salvation, hell and eternal life. For the first time I have seen a service of worship to God – and in a place of imprisonment! Isn't all this a dream? What force motivates these pure young people? I can't absorb all that I hear . . .' Alexei Buldakov describes the results of visits by Christians to his camp in Lokot, near Bryansk: 'I am writing to you from a strict regime camp. Early in 1990 a choir from the Bryansk Baptist church came to our camp to give a charity concert. Then they came several times more: they held meetings and discussions, preached and brought us Bibles and New Testaments, but there were not enough for everybody who wanted to know about God. Every time they came was a celebration for us. We await the day of their arrival as an encounter with something exalted and fine, probably this day in the life of a prisoner could be compared in importance only with the day when a long sentence is behind him and he is standing by the last door that leads to freedom. Thanks to the Lord, the administration has given us a room to meet with the Christians. We have renovated it ourselves. Please help us with literature and advice on how we should decorate our room. They are promising to let us open a bank account, so that we can send you our offerings.'

Soon groups of Christian prisoners were meeting together for worship, as Viktor Mural-Sikorsky reports from a camp in Kiev region: 'If only the commandant would permit us believers to meet in some little room. As it is we meet wherever we can – most often people come to me because I am on crutches . . . Almost all the booklets you sent arrived and are being read. How amazing it is: people are coming to know the Lord and are drawn to His light. We received your present on 2 June and 3 June was Pentecost and ten of us prisoners gathered together. I told them what I know about the day of Pentecost and we read the Bible, and discussed it. I had some blackcurrant jam and we boiled some water and thinned the jam with it to make juice and had communion together. We prayed for our families and friends, for Christians and for good people . . .' In Klekotki camp, Ryazan region, a Baptist church was formed in 1990, whose members hold evangelistic events, speak to fellow-prisoners about the life of Christ and distribute Christian literature within the camp. 'In all the years of existence of the camp,' they wrote, 'the prisoners for the first time have the chance to pray and have fellowship with the Lord. Praise Him for everything!'

Pastors received permission to come into camp to baptize Christian prisoners who wished to be received into the Church through baptism. Water tanks served as baptistries. Later, as trust for the churches grew and as camp directors saw the changes in the lives of Christian prisoners, converts were allowed out of camp to be baptized. On a sunny Sunday afternoon in August 1993 a church minibus brought three women from the strict regime camp in Mariupol, Ukraine, to a quiet beach on the Sea of Azov. Strings of flowers floating on the water marked the 'baptistry'. A group of Christians quickly put up a tent in which the three changed out of their prison uniforms into white baptismal robes. They were joined by six 'free' women who had also been liberated from their sins and made their covenant with Jesus by burying their old selves in the water of baptism and rising to a new life. One by one they went into the water to make public profession of their faith in answer to the pastor's questions before he baptized them in the clear water.

The Orthodox Church also took up a pastoral ministry to prisoners and in 1991 the first Orthodox prison chapel was constructed by prisoners themselves in a labour camp in Leningrad. In 1992 evangelical prisoners built themselves a 'house of prayer' in a camp in Bukhara in Uzbekistan. It was dedicated by the pastor of Tashkent Baptist church and an evangelist of the Central Asian Christian Charity Mission.

Christians who began to take up the new opportunities under perestroika and glasnost did not, however, always find the support they needed from church leaders. Past repressions and the efforts of officials of the Council for Religious Affairs to impose compliant leaders on the churches meant that there was a deep-rooted caution and conservatism about new initiatives and new methods. This applied equally to the Orthodox and the evangelical churches, though there were many individual exceptions, notably Metropolitan Alexi of Leningrad – the future Patriarch – who accepted a nomination to the Supreme Soviet from *Miloserdie*, and Mikhail Zhidkov, in the past a vice-president of the Baptist Union and a senior pastor of Moscow Baptist Church, who has devoted himself in retirement to the development of 'Compassion Ministries'.

In the evangelical churches many of those who were pioneers in charity work banded together to form independent missions in order to give one another the support that was not forthcoming from church leaders. A new liberal law on associations permitted citizens to form political organizations (though not yet political parties) and all kinds of clubs, including charities like the local branches of *Miloserdie*. Although churches were specifically excluded from registration as associations, charitable groups based on Christian principles could register under this law.

In a country where there had been no missions and no charity work for sixty years, these new missionary groups saw enormous needs all around them. It was hard to know where to begin and so they tended to do something of everything: evangelistic meetings, prison visiting, Sunday schools, distribution of Christian literature, church planting, talks in schools, hospital visiting, distribution of relief. There were increasing opportunities to offer practical support to staff in hospitals, orphanages and homes for the elderly and, most important of all, to give personal attention to the children, patients and old people themselves.

The very first of the new missions broke through not only the conservatism over new ideas but also the barriers of isolation between denominations and nationalities. The Latvian Christian Mission, founded early in 1989 by Vadim Kovalyov, a young Baptist minister, drew together Russian and Latvian Christians from Baptist, Pentecostal, Lutheran and Catholic backgrounds and struck a balance between service and evangelism. One of the mission's earliest new opportunities was to visit a labour camp for women on the edge of the Latvian capital Riga. The visits were not only evangelistic, but also contributed to the rehabilitation of prisoners by giving them individual attention and counselling and contact with the outside world. A simple gesture of compassion often meant much more to the prisoners than the unfamiliar religious language of the evangelists. On the first visit, during which a Baptist choir sang Christian songs, a Catholic gardener presented each of the women who came to the service with a daffodil. These rough women were not used to receiving flowers and this gift broke the barriers and left a deeper feeling of warmth and love than any other aspect of this first meeting.

Anatoli Teslenko, a secretly ordained evangelist, who was soon to found the South-West Christian Mission in Odessa, was among many mission-oriented Christians who came to learn from the experience of the Latvian Christian Mission. Visiting the women's camp with workers from the mission, Anatoli was told by two of the prisoners of their reaction to the first visit. They had been very suspicious, thinking that bringing in Christians was just a new tactic on the part of the camp administration to 're-educate them'. Indeed, here and in other prisons that opened their doors to Christians, the camp directors were quite pragmatic in their assessment of the value of the visits: they noticed a distinct calming of the atmosphere after the meetings with the Christians. But the sincerity of the visitors won through, and cautiously at first the prisoners began to listen to the message that they could come to God in prayer, confess their sins and receive forgiveness and begin a new life in Christ. The two women told Anatoli of their first faltering steps in prayer. Then one of them, Inessa, asked Anatoli if prayer should just be about themselves. He explained that they could pray for each other and for their new Christian friends, asking for God to give them strength and wisdom in their visits to the camp.

Later Anatoli received a letter from Inessa. She told him how she had had a vision of Jesus and how Jesus had urged her to pray for Anatoli. She prayed to God to help him in his situation and to give him strength in adversity, and then she had a feeling of peace. At this time Anatoli was engaged in an uphill struggle with the authorities in Odessa persuading them to register the South-West Christian Mission. Finally, after adding the words 'Mercy and Charity' to the name of the mission, he convinced the officials that it fell under the provisions of the new law and there were no grounds for refusing his application for registration. At last the 'South-West Christian Mission of Mercy and Charity' officially existed! Reading Inessa's letter, Anatoli realized that she had been praying for him during this crucial meeting and that the mission had been born with the help of the faith and prayers of a convict.

Since 1989 the South-West Christian Mission has held over 60 evangelistic events attended by some 100,000 people and charity concerts to raise money for the needs of the disabled, the poor and single elderly people. Christian literature is made available to all enquirers and of 30,000 who have made a Christian commitment many have gone on to become members of local churches of various denominations. In the winter of 1991-2 the mission planted a church in a large postwar housing district on the edge of Odessa where there was no place of worship of any denomination. Services are held in a large tent which gives shelter from the wind but little protection from the cold. The congregation wears fur hats, thick coats and scarves and warm boots in winter, but has grown to over 200 members. Gradually they are building a church next to the tent. Once the basement is finished and roofed over it will be possible to provide some heating.

All of the mission's staff, including the four pastors, support themselves and their families by working in secular jobs. They look for jobs that give them the flexibility to be available at the mission during the day. Others in the congregation help out when they are able, for example visiting housebound disabled people in the area on foot or by bus and taking them hot meals from the mission's kitchen – originally a garage that also doubles up as a Sunday school room. They cannot provide many hot meals, but there is a constantly growing list of disabled people for whom volunteers are needed to do shopping, washing and housework.

While I was there Yura, a homeless man recently released from prison, came for help. He said he would like to go straight and was trying to work as a porter at the station, but he was sleeping rough in a basement. He tried to get a room in a hostel, but they wouldn't take him because he and his clothes were too dirty. A couple of the mission workers took him into the shed where charity clothing sent from Germany is stored. They found him some clothes the right size and sent him away with some money to the public baths. After a while Yura was back, washed and shaved and looking slightly uncomfortable in his new clothes. He was upset, because while his back was turned somebody stole the carrier bag with his old clothes which he had put down for a moment! He didn't want to ruin his new clothes portering at the station. At least he'd already put his papers in the pocket of his new coat, but he'd lost a fur-lined jacket, which though splitting at the seams and dirty was at least warm. Despite this setback he still wanted to go straight. We prayed with him, blessed him by the laying on of hands and sent him back to the hostel with money to pay the rent for a room in advance.

Oleg, who was a drug addict before he became a Christian, is the mission's youth leader. He visits local schools to give introductory talks on the Bible and the Christian faith. I went with him to the school just along the main road from the mission, where he was going to talk to two classes for the first time. The teachers were more than happy to leave us in charge and the children were open and receptive. Oleg spent time finding out what the children believed in and their ideas of God before developing the themes of God the creator and conscience as a pointer to God. In conclusion he invited the children to come to young people's meetings at the tent if they were interested in learning more, or to attend services there or at any of the city's other churches.

Oleg's first love, though, is the children's detention centre, where he and a couple of the Sunday school teachers go every week to teach the juvenile criminals held there. Having been in trouble himself, his heart goes out to these children, many of them runaways or abandoned to fend for themselves on the streets. About 25 sit down in two rows in the recreation room. With their shaven heads and drab clothes it's hard to tell which are boys and which girls, except that a couple of the girls have skirts. Oleg reminds them that last week they learnt to pray. Would they like to pray again? 'Yes,' they answer in unison. Slowly Oleg takes them through the Lord's prayer and then asks if any have tried to pray during the week. A few shy hands go up and he encourages them to bring their daily needs to Jesus. The two Sunday school teachers take over with a Bible story. On the way out the police captain shows us the punishment cell – empty today. The fresh paint does not disguise the fact that the walls are bare roughcast concrete – there's no warmth in them or in the smooth cement floor. One of Oleg's dreams is to have a refuge where the homeless children can live when they are released from the centre to try to keep them off the streets

and from going back to crime. The city council has given the mission the
field next to the tent so that the refuge can be built there.

Another of the earliest Christian missions was founded in Armenia by
members of an evangelical movement within the Armenian Apostolic
(Orthodox) Church, the Brotherhood, which traces its roots back to the
fifth century. During Soviet rule the Brotherhood existed underground,
working alongside the Church, which was restricted to formal worship in
the small number of churches that remained open. Members of the
Brotherhood preached and taught and explained the Gospel in everyday
language that people could understand in meetings held in private homes.
In 1988 it became possible for this work to begin openly, at first continuing
to meet in people's houses and later using public halls. The meetings are
more informal than church services, but are intended to complement
worship in church by deepening people's faith, encouraging them to make
a personal commitment and helping them to understand the meaning of
the church's liturgy. Brotherhood meetings are timed so that they do not
clash with church services and people are encouraged to go to church as
well.

One of the Brotherhood's leaders, Khachik Stamboltsyan, founded the
charity mission *Gtutiun* (Compassion) in response to the twin disasters of
the Armenian earthquake in December 1988 and the increasing flood of
refugees from neighbouring Azerbaijan following pogroms against
Armenians in February 1989. As well as wanting to help to meet the needs
of the homeless and the refugees, Khachik was spurred to greater
evangelistic effort, as he saw these disasters as signs of God's judgement
against the Armenian people, who had been the first Christian nation but
had drifted far away from God. Alongside an extensive social welfare
programme – including home helps for the elderly and disabled, medical
care and a free dispensary for the needy, a home for the elderly and a
house for young people who leave orphanages at the age of eighteen with
nowhere to go, sheltered workshops for the handicapped and retraining
programmes for refugees – there is an active mission department with full-
time evangelists and children's workers. The mission's 'Sunday schools',
held not just on Sundays but for different groups on every day of the week,
now reach 15,000 children. Some of the children who have come to faith
through this work have themselves been trained by *Gtutiun* to teach others.

The mission opened a bookshop in Yerevan in 1991, selling Bibles and
books published by *Gtutiun* itself and by other publishers, including Billy
Graham's *Peace with God* (the second most popular book after the Bible)

and classic Armenian religious works translated into modern Armenian. Three branch bookshops have opened in other cities. The bookshop staff do more than sell books – they are available to answer questions about the Christian faith or to discuss Bible passages which readers have had difficulty understanding. A priest comes twice a week to help people with their questions about Christianity and the Armenian Church. The shop is also popular with Christians from other Churches because the books are about the basics of the Christian faith and the staff point visitors towards the universal truths of Christianity in a way that does not exclude other denominations.

Publishing is another area of Christian work which has grown enormously since 1988. During the 1930s there had been no Christian publications of any kind, and since the Second World War each main denomination had just one magazine and from time to time received permission to print or import Bibles, New Testaments, hymn books and service books and occasionally to publish a collection of sermons or theological essays. In November 1988 the first issue of a new Christian newspaper, named *Protestant*, appeared in Moscow. Its editor was Alexander Semchenko, recently released from a three-year term of imprisonment for unofficial Christian publishing. *Protestant* was unofficial too, but unlike previous publications came completely out into the open, naming its editorial board and giving contact addresses and phone numbers. It was produced by hand, using a mixture of typewritten text and text that was 'typeset' by assembling words and letters from printed magazines etc., and then photocopied. It had no official permission and had not been submitted to a state censor. It was also unofficial in the sense that, although Alexander and his fellow editors all came from registered Baptist churches, *Protestant* had no backing from the official Baptist Union leaders; indeed it was quite critical of them and their style of leadership, in particular their lack of initiative. Alexander accused them of having been infected with the 'stagnation' of the Brezhnev era during which they had risen to positions of leadership. The paper was thus a challenge both to state control over religious affairs and to the religious establishment.

Protestant was not the only unofficial publication at this time. Alexander Ogorodnikov was producing a journal called *Bulletin of Christian Opinion*, two other Moscow Orthodox intellectuals began publishing a magazine called *Choice*, and countless human rights groups and political discussion clubs were producing newsletters and other publications, most notably the magazine *Glasnost*. And the publications of the unregistered Baptist

Council of Churches also continued. But *Protestant* was the first to achieve a wider circulation: as well as being distributed in churches in the main cities it was mailed to every congregation in the Baptist Union. Perestroika and glasnost were sufficiently advanced that no serious measures were taken against these unofficial publications and their editors. Soon after, the Baptist Union launched its own new publication *Information Bulletin*. It appeared with official permission granted by the Council for Religious Affairs, because technically it wasn't considered a newspaper but an internal church bulletin, though in format it was a newspaper. Later it was registered as a newspaper which could be distributed to the public and the name was changed to *Christian Word*. *Protestant* was also registered as a newspaper and went on sale on newsstands in Moscow.

Soon dozens of local, regional and national Christian newspapers and magazines followed. Getting official permission was not always easy, especially at the beginning. The editors of an independent Baptist magazine, *Revival*, had to make 17 visits from Rostov-on-Don to Moscow before they finally secured authorization in 1989. Three issues had already appeared while they were negotiating with the authorities! In January 1991 *Protestant* hosted in Moscow a conference attended by over fifty Christian editors, publishers and writers, representing fifteen Baptist publishing houses. As well as continuing with its newspaper, *Protestant* also revived the old titles of the Evangelical Christian and Baptist Unions that had been terminated by Stalin's persecution at the end of the 1920s. *The Christian* reappeared in 1990 and *The Baptist* in 1992.

Meanwhile, *Protestant* had also begun to publish brochures and books, including New Testaments and Bibles, translations of Western Christian literature and work by Russian Christian writers. By 1992 it had grown into a substantial publishing house: it was not only the largest Christian publisher but its output rivalled that of major secular publishers. Independent commercial publishers also made a contribution to the spread of Christian books. Phoenix Publishing, run by an Armenian Christian, produced a Russian edition of Ernest Gordon's *Miracle on the River Kwai* and reprinted a pre-revolutionary Armenian Bible dictionary. In 1991, after the failed coup, Phoenix was offered the opportunity to turn the journal *History of the Communist Party of the Soviet Union* into an independent political science journal. Phoenix inherited not only the Communist journal's mailing list, but also its offices, complete with a phone with a direct line to the Kremlin on the old editor's desk!

Perestroika also enabled the re-establishment of Bible Society work. The first new Bible Society was founded in Latvia at the end of 1989. It was soon followed by the Bible Society of the Soviet Union, which held its inaugural meeting in Moscow in January 1990. The Bible Society saw itself as successor to the Russian Bible Society of the early nineteenth century and like its predecessor aimed to be a truly national society transcending denominational and ethnic differences. One of the main initiators of the Bible Society was Father Alexander Men and the inaugural meeting was held in the lecture theatre of Moscow's Library of Foreign Languages, whose staff had under Communism quietly built up a strong collection of Western religious and theological literature. Since 1988 Father Alexander had frequently given public lectures at the library. The meeting was attended by Christians of many denominations, and also by Konstantin Kharchev, the ousted chairman of the government Council for Religious Affairs - still on the Foreign Ministry staff as an 'ambassador without appointment'. He became a founder member and was willing to stand for election to the Bible Society's board, but was considered ineligible because he was not a member of any church. He still professed to be an atheist, but said he believed that it was important that everybody should have the opportunity to read the Bible - an opportunity that he had only when he became CRA chairman! Anatoli Rudenko, a Baptist and a founder member of the editorial board of *Protestant*, was appointed as Bible Society director.

National Bible Societies were subsequently established in all the European republics of the USSR, and with the collapse of the Soviet Union at the end of 1991 the Bible Society in Moscow was renamed the Russian Bible Society. At the same time the Russian Orthodox Church began to place greater emphasis on Bible work. Building on scholarly work carried on in the theological academy in Leningrad (St Petersburg), the North West Bible Commission had been founded there just a few weeks before the Bible Society in Moscow. Under Orthodox leadership the commission welcomed participation from other denominations. Orthodox Bible commissions followed in Moscow, Belorussia and in the Chuvash republic, on the river Volga, whose people had accepted Christianity as a result of pre-revolutionary Russian Orthodox missionary efforts. Later, the Society for the Distribution of Holy Scripture, which had done so much to take the new Bible translation to the Russian people in the 1860s and 1870s, was revived in Moscow. The Society declared itself open to membership from all denominations, but was also under Russian Orthodox leadership, as its founders felt it was important that it should be based within the national Church of the majority of Russians.

All of these Bible organizations found an enormous demand for the Scriptures and also for children's Bibles, which many adults unfamiliar with the Bible also found easier to read. Much of this demand could be met only with help from churches, missions and Bible Societies in the West. The economic collapse in Russia and the other ex-Soviet republics makes it very difficult for the work of the Bible Societies and other Christian publishers to be self-financing.

Many churches and missions responded to the demand for scarce Christian literature by setting up lending libraries. The first Christian libraries were boxes of books that were unpacked onto a folding table on a street corner or in a market. The 'librarians' required anybody who wanted to borrow a book to produce their internal passport (identity card) and leave their name and address. Sometimes people who did not have their passports with them reserved a book and rushed home in order to get back with their passport before the stall was dismantled. The libraries also served as focal points for evangelism, as passers-by enquired who the Christians were and asked about their churches and their beliefs. Readers brought books back eager to discuss what they had read. People were amazed that Christians should offer such a service. The unregistered Baptist church in Krasnodar set up a book table outside the city library. Passers-by looked at the books and searched for a price. 'How much does it cost?' people asked. 'It's free!' 'Free?!' 'Yes, take the book, just leave us your address. Read the book and come back next Saturday and you can exchange it for another book.' Most people were honest and even came back to ask if they wanted to keep their book for an extra week.

Christians in Voronezh who set up a portable library had similar experiences. One woman was sceptical when the library was suggested:

> At first I didn't have any confidence in the success of our library ministry . . . But the Lord obviously blessed this work from the very beginning. The first time I went, I arrived at the place where we set up the library and found that a crowd had already gathered. I looked at their faces: they were waiting and watching for somebody to come, someone to talk to. As soon as we came, they saw from our faces that we were believers. They quickly gathered around and started asking questions. When the men appeared with the table the crowd quickly formed a queue and even started to shove each other. Our men calmed them down: 'There's enough for everybody; everyone will receive something.' Then everyone settled down and queued up.

News of the library spread quickly and soon their record book showed that people from all over the city were coming to borrow books. Sometimes they give booklets or gospels away, even New Testaments to those who are really interested. One military cadet who had been given a New Testament came back for more because all of his comrades wanted to read it. Some people don't have identification with them, but when the 'librarians' see that they have a real thirst to read the Bible they trust them to give their real name and address. Sometimes people like that say when they bring back the book: 'I felt like a real person because you believed in me.' If people are late returning a book somebody goes to find them at home. One such visit resulted in an invitation to come and talk to the staff of a kindergarten. At first the local authorities were hostile and sent the police who told the Christians to pack up the bookstall as they had no right to engage in commerce where they had set up their table. They explained to the police that the library wasn't commercial - everything was free. The sergeant insisted that the order had been given to get them to go home. Otherwise he would have to take them to the police station. The group agreed to come to the station when it was time to pack up the library and the policemen went away. The police came back, but saw that people were very happy with the library and beginning to get angry with the police: 'Why are you coming here? We want to hear about God, and you're interfering.' After that the police left them in peace.

Soon churches everywhere followed the example of these pioneers and set up their own libraries. Books from the secret presses and received in parcels from abroad made up the stock. Many libraries were portable like these first ones, set up in city-centre parks, or in pedestrian subways, markets or other places where there were many passers-by. Others were set up in people's homes, as well as in churches and missions. Although it is not easy to stand outside in the cold in winter for three hours - with temperatures as low as minus 20 or 30 - the outdoor libraries are preferred by many, because they enable Christians to take the Gospel to the people. And later, when people have met the Christians and talked to them, some begin to come to services.

An important Western contribution to the development of new Christian ministries in Russia was the Congress for World Evangelization held in Moscow in October 1990. The inspiration for the congress came from the Lausanne Committee's second Conference on World Evangelization in Manila, Philippines, in July 1989. For the first time at such an international Christian gathering the organizers did not invite official church delegations to Manila, as they realized that church leaders could send only those with a 'seal of approval' from the KGB and Council for Religious Affairs. Instead they invited personally Christians from different denominations who were actively involved in evangelism and related ministries in their local situation. Some were well known to the world as former Christian prisoners, like Iosif Bondarenko, while others were recommended because they were actively involved in key ministries behind the scenes in registered churches.

Not all those invited were issued visas by the Soviet authorities, and there was a last-minute delay in securing visas from the Philippines Embassy in Moscow as a result of which the 70 Soviet participants missed the opening day. Their entry to the conference hall was all the more dramatic as the announcement of their arrival was greeted with tumultuous applause. The group felt that a similar conference staged in Moscow could play a vital role in stimulating the evangelization of the Soviet Union by enabling a large number of Soviet Christians to take part. The conference organizers, used to making plans for such events years in advance, very much doubted whether it could be arranged for the following year, as requested by the Soviet group. But they agreed to try, and a Soviet organizing committee was formed to make arrangements in Moscow and invite participants from across the USSR.

The Moscow congress came at a strategic moment for those engaged in all kinds of new initiatives to share their experience and their vision. As well as 900 Soviet participants there were over 100 western guests representing many missions and international Christian organizations. Some of them were there to lead workshops on various forms of ministry, but many workshops were organized or jointly led by Soviet Christian workers. For most people the congress provided an opportunity to make new contacts and to lay the foundations of new friendships and partnerships in mission, with the workshops providing valuable focal points for those interested in particular areas of ministry.

Over the previous two years since the millennium celebrations the churches had continued to hold evangelistic events, and the word evangelism itself was no longer taboo, even though it remained a technically illegal activity. Visits by Billy Graham, Luis Palau and other western preachers were openly advertised as evangelistic. On the eve of the congress Christians in Leningrad (St Petersburg) held their first city-wide evangelization. A special newspaper inviting people to a series of meetings addressed by Finnish Lutheran evangelist Kalevi Lehtinen and giving details of all the participating churches - Baptist, Pentecostal, Adventist, Lutheran and Orthodox (though many Orthodox parishes were not involved) - was distributed by volunteers from the churches to every home. For many Christians it was the first time that they had engaged in door-to-door visiting and they were nervous about the reception they might get. They were amazed at the friendly welcome they received in most homes and at people's openness and interest. The event was covered by local television and the numbers at the evening meetings increased every day until on the last evening the city's largest sports stadium was filled with a capacity audience.

The interdenominational cooperation seen in Mission Leningrad and the Moscow Congress on Evangelization was the model for a new project in the summer of 1992 - Mission Volga. An international team of 300 travelled by ship from St Petersburg on the Baltic Sea, reaching the Volga via northern Russia's inland waterways, stopping at ten cities along the Volga and ending up at Rostov-on-Don. In each city, mission teams worked with local Christians preparing for the visit of the ship and distributing special editions of a Mission Volga newspaper. The main meetings were addressed by Kalevi Lehtinen and follow-up meetings were organized by the local teams. Orthodox Christians took part alongside evangelicals and until the last minute the mission had the official backing of the Russian Orthodox Church. Shortly before the start of the mission, under pressure from conservative groups within the Russian Church, Patriarch Alexi withdrew the Church's official support but extended his personal blessing to all Orthodox who wished to take part. In the cities along the Volga the extent of Orthodox participation depended on the attitude of the local bishops. Some condemned the mission as a venture alien to Orthodoxy and Russian tradition and banned their flock from taking part, while others gave their enthusiastic support and contributed articles to their local edition of the Mission Volga newspaper.

NINETEEN

The Challenge of the Gospel

GROWING PUBLIC interest in any and all aspects of religion and the spiritual and transcendental side of life helped the meteoric rise to television stardom in 1989 of a hypnotist and faith healer named Anatoli Kashpirovsky. He conducted live weekly seances with a studio audience, and thousands of people claimed to have been helped by the psychic force he generated while watching his programme on their own televisions. Others, however, got a strong sensation of evil.

Do-it-yourself religious cults have proliferated, with leaders who claimed to have new teachings through direct divine revelation or via astral beings who visited them in UFOs. The decades of anti-religious propaganda diminished people's knowledge of the teachings of the Christian faith. Now that religion is back in fashion many people are totally uncritical when confronted with the claims of psychics and prophets.

In the spiritual vacuum left by Communism, the Soviet Union was like the man in the parable: 'When an evil spirit goes out of a person, it travels over dry country looking for a place to rest. If it can't find one, it says to itself, "I will go back to my house." So it goes back and finds the house empty, clean and all tidy. Then it goes out and brings along seven other spirits even worse than itself, and they come and live there. So, when it is all over, that person is in a worse state than he was at the beginning.'

In this new free market for religion, the Russian Orthodox Church is particularly vulnerable. It feels under growing pressure not only from evangelical missions, but also from the Catholic Church and a whole host of other religious groups from Mormons and Jehovah's Witnesses to Hare Krishnas and Oriental mystics, not to mention practitioners of black magic and faith healing through hypnosis or extrasensory perception. Many of these groups existed underground during the Communist era, but others emerged or came in from abroad as Communism began to weaken its grip.

All of the churches are aware of the challenge from occult forces and new religions, and have responded to it by trying to fill the spiritual vacuum themselves. However, the Russian Orthodox Church is deeply divided over the approach it should take in the evangelization of Russia. During the Communist era the Church had clung to the traditions and practices that had reigned before the Bolshevik revolution. It was not the right time for the Church to reconsider these when it was under fierce attack from its enemies. For many Orthodox the pre-revolutionary Church was the ideal that had to be emulated and restored. They failed to note the mounting pressure for reform in the Church at the beginning of the twentieth century or to take into account that Russia had been changed irreversibly by 70 years of Communist rule. The Russians of the late twentieth century were not the same as they had been before Communism. On the other hand, those Orthodox, like Father Alexander Men, who had been actively involved in bringing people to the faith under Communism, understood that the Christian faith had to be expressed in a way that was relevant to people today, that took into account their experience under Communism. Others, while adhering closely to traditional Orthodoxy, see the need to use up-to-date teaching methods and to modernize the image of the Church. However, the majority of the hierarchy and clergy tend towards the conservative wing of the Church, so much so that in some dioceses Father Alexander's books are even banned from sale on church bookstalls.

Many Orthodox feel that their position as the national Church of Russia is under threat from the other Churches and the cults, which are often backed by their Western counterparts. Thus American tele-evangelists can buy time on Russian television at what are to them knock-down prices, but which are beyond the reach of those without foreign subsidies. There has therefore been a strong backlash by the conservative majority in the Orthodox Church against foreign Churches and religious organizations. Orthodox hierarchs from Patriarch Alexi down have complained at efforts by the Catholic Church and western evangelical missions to convert the Orthodox population. However, the true challenge to the Orthodox Church is to put over the messsage of the Gospel in a way that is relevant to the Russians, Ukrainians and other historically Orthodox peoples as they look forward to the twenty-first century.

Under pressure from conservatives and nationalists, in July 1993 the Russian parliament amended the liberal law on religion of 1990 to require all foreign religious organizations to obtain an official authorization before engaging in any religious activity in Russia. The move received the support of Patriarch Alexi, but was vigorously opposed by evangelicals, who were afraid that Western Christians working in partnership with them would be excluded from Russia. Leaders of Russian Baptists, Pentecostals and Adventists signed an appeal to Russian President Boris Yeltsin, pointing out that liberty was indivisible and that to limit religious freedom in this way could lead to the erosion of other civil liberties. Catholics expressed concern that they might be considered a foreign Church. Yeltsin refused to sign the amended law and sent it back to parliament for further consideration, insisting that it should be brought into line with international agreements on human rights. Parliament's response was to tone down some of the amendments to which Yeltsin had objected, but introducing new restrictions elsewhere and pledging state support for 'religious organizations whose activities preserve and develop historical traditions and customs, national-cultural identity, art and other cultural heritage of the peoples of the Russian Federation'. This new wording was widely interpreted as meaning the Russian Orthodox Church and the non-Christian religions of some of the ethnic minorities of Russia. These amendments were also rejected by President Yeltsin. However, in October, even while they were under siege in the White House, the opposition Communist and nationalist deputies voted on further amendments to the law on religion. The bill was finally pushed aside altogether when the Russian parliament was forcibly dissolved. Nevertheless, Father Gleb Yakunin, who was almost a lone voice in parliament opposing the amendments, fears that the opposition will try to force through restrictions on religious liberty in the next parliament.

Evangelicals everywhere in the former Soviet Union are afraid of similar attempts to limit their work at the instigation of national Churches or Islam. At the very least they note a tendency for the dominant Church to seek an exclusive or privileged position for itself at the expense of religious minorities. Especially in the republics of Central Asia, with their predominantly Muslim populations, Christians are already under pressure, with a ban on evangelism in Uzbekistan and death threats against Christians producing Christian literature in local languages. Even in

Ukraine, where evangelicals are strongest and where the Orthodox majority has been reduced by defections to the Ukrainian Catholics and been split into warring camps, there is concern among evangelicals that government attempts to create a Ukrainian national church could be accompanied by new restrictions on the activity of religious minorities.

In their own way evangelicals are often as conservative as the majority of Orthodox. Many evangelicals adhere to a rigid puritanism that focuses on externals and find it difficult to accept new Christians who do not conform to their traditions. Participation in the wider life of society and in politics is often regarded as 'worldly', and this attitude has been reinforced by decades of Soviet promotion of atheism through education, culture, youth organizations, trade unions and political life. The result is that some Christians have been forced into an 'evangelical ghetto' and have lost the ability to relate to ordinary people outside their churches. Atheist propaganda has instilled in some a definite prejudice against evangelicals and this is fuelled by Christians who consciously or subconsciously emphasize the ways in which they are different from other people.

Evangelicals are challenged today to rethink their theology in relation to society, now that society is not overtly hostile to all forms of religion, and to examine their traditions to see whether they are a stumbling block to non-Christians. In order to minister better in the new situation, some of the missions that have been formed over the past few years have found themselves starting new congregations because new Christians did not feel welcomed by traditionalist evangelicals.

For all of the Churches in Russia, Ukraine and the other nations of the former Soviet Union, the challenge is to reach people with the Gospel of Jesus Christ while they are still open. Economic instability and massive inflation make the task of churches and Christian organizations more difficult. As Christians face political uncertainty, which may lead to new restrictions on religious liberty, they need our prayers and support. They appreciate help offered in a spirit of partnership and welcome those who come to share their own experience of Christian ministry and to work alongside them. Although Western Christians have much to offer by way of resources and methods, we need to respect and affirm the ministries of our Russian sisters and brothers. If we are willing to share in their Christian life and work in a spirit of humility we have much to gain and learn from their spirituality, their faithfulness and their experience of God's grace and blessing.

Bibliography

Amburger, Erik, *Geschichte des Protestantismus in Russland*, Evangelisches Verlagswerk, Stuttgart, 1961.

Beeson, Trevor, *Discretion and Valour*, 2nd edn, Fount, London, 1982.

Bourdeaux, Michael, *Faith on Trial in Russia*, Hodder and Stoughton, London 1971; *Religious Ferment in Russia*, Macmillan, London, 1968; *Gorbachev, Glasnost and the Gospel*, London, Hodder and Stoughton, 1990.

Bourdeaux, Lorna & Michael, *Ten Growing Soviet Churches*, MARC Europe, London, 1987.

Brandenburg, Hans, *The Meek and the Mighty*, Mowbrays, London, 1976.

Byford, C. T., *Peasants and Prophets*, 2nd edn, London, James Clarke & Co. and Kingsgate Press, London, 1912.

Christian Appeals from Russia, eds. Rosemary Harris and Xenia Howard-Johnston, Hodder and Stoughton, London, 1969.

Christian Prisoners in the USSR, Keston College, 1977, 1979, 1981, 1983, 1985.

Ciszek, Walter, *With God in Russia*, Peter Davies, London, 1965.

Die Kirchen und das religiöse Leben der Russlanddeutschen: Evangelischer Teil, Verlag Landmannschaft der Deutschen aus Russland, Stuttgart, 1978.

Durasoff, Steve, *The Russian Protestants. Evangelicals in the Soviet Union, 1944-64*, Dickinson University Press, Fairleigh, 1969.

Fountain, David, *Lord Radstock of Mayfield*, Mayflower Christian Books, 1984.

Hebly, J. A., *Protestants in Russia*, Christian Journals Ltd, Belfast, 1976.

Heier, Edmund, *Religious Schism in the Russian Aristocracy 1860-1900*, The Hague, Martinus Nijhoff, 1970.

House, Francis, *The Russian Phoenix*, London, SPCK, 1988.

Istoriya Yevangelskikh Khristian-Baptistov v SSSR [History of the Evangelical Christians-Baptists in the USSR], Moscow, USSR Evangelical Christian-Baptist Union, 1989.

Kahle, Wilhelm, *Evangelische Christen in Russland und der Sovetunion*, Oncken Verlag, Wuppertal and Kassel, 1978.

Latimer, R. S., *Dr Baedeker and his Apostolic Work in Russia*, London, Morgan & Scott, 1907.

Latimer, R.S., *Under Three Tsars*, London, Morgan & Scott, 1909.

McCaig, A., *The Wonders of Grace in Russia*, Riga, The Revival Press, 1926.

McCaig, A., *Grace Astounding in Bolshevik Russia*, London, The Russian Missionary Society, 1929.

Martsinkovsky, V.F., *Zapiski veruyushchego* [Notes of a believer], Prague, 1929. English abridged edition: *With Christ in Soviet Russia*, Prague, no date.

Poysti, N.J., *With Christ in Russia and Siberia*, 2nd edition, Russian and East European Mission, Chicago, 1938.

Rasskaz byvshego katorzhnika [The story of a former convict], reprinted COV, Seligenstadt, 1990.

Religious Prisoners in the USSR, Greenfire Books and Keston College, London, 1987.

Remember the Prisoners, ed. Peter Masters, Moody Press, Chicago, 1986.

Sawatsky, Walter, *Soviet Evangelicals Since World War II*, Herald Press, Kitchener, Ontario and Scottdale, Pennsylvania, 1981.

Simon, Gerhard, *Church, State and Opposition in the USSR*, London, C. Hurst & Co., 1974.

The Story of Jacob Vagar, CSSM, 1946.

Vins, Georgi, *Three Generations of Suffering*, Hodder and Stoughton, London 1976.

Vins, Georgi, *Wie Schäfe unter Wölfen: Erfahrungen eines Christen in sowjetischen Straflagern*, Friedensstimme, Gummersbach and Hänsler-Verlag, Neuhausen-Stuttgart, 1987; *Konshaubi: A True Story of Persecuted Christians in the Soviet Union*, Baker Book House, Grand Rapids, Michigan, 1988.

Voronaeff, Paul, *My life in Soviet Russia*, Christian Crusade Publications, Tulsa, Oklahoma, 1969.

World Christianity: Eastern Europe, ed. Philip Walters, MARC, Eastbourne, 1988.

PERIODICALS

Article 227, Friedensstimme (UK), 1985-89, continued as Partners, Radstock Ministries, 1990-

Frontier, Keston College, 1987-

Keston News Service, Keston College, 1974-91.

Nachrichten von den Feldern der Verfolgung, Friedensstimme, Gummersbach, 1974-1989, continued as *Nachrichten von Missionsfeldern im Osten*, 1990-

Prisoner Bulletin, International Representation for the Council of Evangelical Christian Baptist Churches of the Soviet Union, Inc., (since 1989 Russian Gospel Ministries) Elkhart, Indiana, 1980-

Religion in Communist Lands, Keston College, 1973-1991, continued as *Religion, State and Society*, Carfax Publishing, 1992-